IN THE EYE OF THE STORM

IN THE EYE
OF THE STORM

Commanding the Desert Rats
in the Gulf War

Major General Patrick Cordingley

Hodder & Stoughton

First published in 1996
by Hodder and Stoughton
A division of Hodder Headline PLC

10 9 8 7 6 5 4 3 2 1

A CIP catalogue record for this book is available
from the British Library.

ISBN 0 340 68245 0

Typeset by Hewer Text Composition Services, Edinburgh
Printed and bound in Great Britain by
Mackays of Chatham PLC, Chatham, Kent.

Hodder and Stoughton
A division of Hodder Headline PLC
338 Euston Road
London NW1 3BH

In memory of those soldiers in the 7th Armoured Brigade Group
who gave their lives for the liberation of Kuwait during
the Gulf War October 1990 – March 1991:

Corporal C. A. E. Bolam, Royal Corps of Transport
Corporal R. H. Going, Royal Army Medical Corps
Gunner P. P. Keegan, Royal Artillery
Private C. Moult, The Staffordshire Regiment
Sapper R. A. Royle, Royal Engineers
Private S. P. Taylor, The Staffordshire Regiment

Contents

List of Maps and Diagrams

List of Illustrations

A press conference in November 1990.

Headlines from the *Evening Standard* of Thursday 30th November 1990.

The leader heading from the *Sunday Express* of 2nd December 1990.

An Iraqi propaganda leaflet.

Captions from articles in the *Sun* newspaper, February 1991.

The press corps waiting to join an exercise.

Bazoft's Revenge being commanded by HRH The Prince of Wales. (Author's collection)

Mr Tom King and Lieutenant General Sir Peter de la Billière on the commander's tank.

An explanation of the name of *Bazoft's Revenge*. (Richard Kemp)

The 1942 Desert Rat pennant.

The crew of *Bazoft's Revenge*.

A Challenger tank manoeuvring in the desert.

The reconnaissance vehicle, Scorpion.

The infantry armoured personnel carrier, Warrior.

Infantrymen debussing from a Warrior.

The Multiple Launch Rocket System.

M109 guns firing into Iraq. (Richard Kemp)

Chieftain bridgelayers manoeuvring in the desert.

A Challenger tank crossing an oil pipeline.

A Giant Viper being fired into an 'Iraqi' minefield.

Martin Bell of the BBC with Major James Myles. (Richard Kemp)

Lieutenant Colonel Charles Goodson-Wickes MP, our medical officer.

Kate Adie discussing tactics with the brigade commander.

Philip Jacobson of *The Times*. Colin Wills of the *Sunday Mirror*. (Author's collection)

The brigade commander and Richard Kemp playing chess. (Author's collection)

Lance Corporal Boardman and Lance Corporal Dye.

Officers of 7th Armoured Brigade receive their final briefing. (Author's collection)

Major General Rupert Smith, the general commanding the 1st British Armoured Division.

Colour section

Bazoft's Revenge advancing into Iraq on 25th February 1991.
The Staffords' battlegroup attack into Objective Platinum. (The Staffordshire Regiment)
The Scots Dragoon Guards' battlegroup assault an Iraqi communications centre.
Crossing the border from Iraq into Kuwait. (Richard Kemp)
The commanders meet on 27th February in Objective Varsity.
The brigade headquarters advance towards the Kuwait City to Basra highway. (7th Armoured Brigade)
The Irish Hussars at the moment the cease-fire was announced. (The Queen's Royal Irish Hussars)
The carnage of the Muttla Pass.
The true horror of warfare. (Richard Kemp)
Preparing to go home. (Author's collection)
The burning of unwanted kit. (Author's collection)
The Prime Minister visits the brigade on 6th March 1991.
Our wives in Fallingbostel celebrate the victory. (Tim Ockenden/PA News)
The reception committee at Hanover Airport when the brigade returned to Germany. (*Sixth Sense*)
An investiture at Buckingham Palace on 5th November 1991. (Stephen Lock/*Daily Telegraph*)
General Mike Myatt, commander of the 1st Marine Division. (Chris Barker)

I am most grateful to *Soldier* Magazine for their permission to reproduce the photograph of Lieutenant Colonel Rogers.

All unattributed photographs were taken by servicemen, mostly by Lieutenant Commander Nigel Huxtable RN and Staff Sergeant Andy Mason, and are Crown Copyright/MOD. These are reproduced with the permission of the Controller of HMSO.

Foreword

During the Gulf War I kept a diary. At the end of each day, without fail, from 11th September 1990 until 17th March 1991, I recorded the events as I saw them and more often than not my thoughts. As the diary is the basis of this book some facts may be wrong, however I have made no attempt to correct what I thought was true at the time or how it affected me and the soldiers under my command. To begin with this command was the 7th Armoured Brigade Group of twelve thousand soldiers. My own brigade of five thousand was swollen by the additions needed to bring the regiments and battalions to a war establishment and by thousands of extra logisticians. And then in January 1991, when the 1st Armoured Division and 4th Brigade joined us in Saudi Arabia, we reverted to a more manageable size; we became once more the 7th Armoured Brigade, the Desert Rats.

The story is incomplete because the logisticians do not get the mentions they deserve. Their extraordinary tale would make the book too long and it has already been told by Martin White, then the commander of the Force Maintenance Area, in his book *Blackadder's War*. I hope they will forgive me.

I found that converting the voluminous diary into a book much more difficult than I had expected; every small detail seemed to me vitally important. So I sought advice and no-one was more helpful than my wife Melissa, and a regimental friend, Ben Rooney. Towards the end of the project Michael Bilton injected further enthusiasm and along the way others also helped with criticism, facts, photographs or by typing or drawing maps: Pam Carpendale, Michael Cordingley, Joe Couchman, Gerardine Goddard, Richard Kemp, Sue Limb, Euan Loudon, Ian MacLaren, Peter McGuigan, Pixie

Parker, Dan Rawlins and Peter Wynn. I am very grateful to them all, as indeed I am to Alex Ward and John Harding of the Army Historical Branch, Jonathan Lloyd my literary agent, Roland Philipps and Angela Herlihy at Hodder and Roy Gasson, the copy-editor.

Finally, my family needs a special thank you. The book came with us on every holiday we took from 1991 to 1996!

P.C.,
York,
10th June 1996

Prologue

'H-hour. It's about to begin.'

But despite being inside an armoured vehicle I had already heard the distinct whistle as the artillery rounds flew overhead. I looked up from the map in front of me and saw that the minute hand of the clock was inching towards the twelve.

'They are spot on for time,' I said out loud, and looked down again, trying to fathom out what, if anything, I had not covered in my orders.

'I'm sure they are complete,' said Euan, 'but I'm just going to ask Robbie . . .'

His next words never reached me. They were drowned out by a series of colossal explosions as the artillery rounds from nearly a hundred guns erupted less than a thousand yards to our east. The command vehicle shook alarmingly and I momentarily prayed that the gunners' calculations were correct. But my confidence quickly returned. For five months the 7th Armoured Brigade had trained in the scorching heat and pouring rain to drive out Saddam Hussein and liberate Kuwait. For five months we had talked about and exercised and planned for the violence we were unleashing. It was going to work.

The back door swung open and Mark's face appeared.

'You've got to look at this,' he shouted above the thunder. Rather unwillingly I stepped outside; it was no longer pitch black despite being one o'clock in the morning. There was an eerie orange glow and the sky immediately above us was alive with white streaks. I walked a few yards away from the cover of the vehicle and froze, dumbstruck by the violence of the barrage. Nothing could have prepared any of us for what we were witnessing. You did not so much see the explosions as feel them – the pressure waves on your face, the shaking ground.

But it was the Multiple Launch Rocket System that was the most fearsome. The rockets streaked across the darkness and, over the target, with a bright flash, burst apart like deadly seed pods showering their lethal contents to the earth. Then there was a noise almost like a machine gun and the ground boiled with fire as the hundreds of tiny bomblets exploded. Again and again came the salvoes.

Time seemed to stand still as the man-made inferno continued. 'I can't believe anyone under this onslaught can do anything but surrender, if they survive. Poor bastards,' I said to no-one in particular.

The air was rank with a smell like fireworks. I think it was this that shook me out of my trance. I had a job to do. In a few minutes the advance would continue against an enemy position, perhaps of several thousand men. After the entire might of our artillery had been brought to bear on a few square miles of Iraqi desert and the men defending it, our job was to complete the destruction.

I clambered on to my tank and picked up the radio headsets. 'Right then, let's go.'

Chapter 1

Friday 3rd August to
Sunday 16th September 1990

'Seven o'clock on Friday the third of August . . . Super-powers are united in their condemnation of Iraq's invasion of Kuwait. The United States has ordered the aircraft carrier *Independence* and six escort ships from the Indian Ocean into the Gulf . . . Witnesses said the first sound of artillery and machine-gun fire was heard around four o'clock this morning.'

Breakfast was the same as ever. Rushed. In the background I could just make out the headlines on Radio 4 relayed through a transmitter at Hohne; the reception that day was worse than usual. Anyway, such dramatic events seemed a long way from northern Germany and the pleasant small town of Soltau where my wife Melissa and I lived, joined in the school holidays by our two teenage daughters, Antonia and Miranda. And, besides, there were other more immediate concerns. The *Burgermeister* had complained yet again of diesel spills from tanks using the Soltau–Luneburg training area and wanted to see me, the local military commander, as soon as possible.

Such problems had occupied a disproportionate amount of

my time since I had taken over command of the 7th Armoured Brigade, the vestiges of the World War Two Desert Rats, some nineteen months before. Soltau, which had been the home of the brigade headquarters since 1945, was dominated, or rather overwhelmed, by the adjacent British training area, the largest such facility we had in Europe. This domination was a bone of contention with the townsfolk as we used the area, despite the ending of the Cold War, on three-hundred-and-twenty days each year, putting mud on the roads in winter and dust in the air in summer.

Priority, however, went to training the brigade. It was part of the 1st Armoured Division, itself one of four divisions that made up the 1st British Corps, Britain's contribution to NATO's central front. The brigade comprised two tank regiments, the Queen's Royal Irish Hussars and the Royal Scots Dragoon Guards, each manning fifty-seven Challenger tanks; one armoured infantry battalion, the 1st Battalion, the Staffordshire Regiment, with fifty-two Warrior armoured infantry fighting vehicles; a gunner regiment, 40th Field Regiment, Royal Artillery; an engineer squadron, and numerous other units in support. The total complement was over five thousand soldiers; wives and children took the overall responsibility to nearly twelve thousand. Our mission, once simply to defend western Europe against Soviet aggression, was now to be ready to react to any NATO-assigned task. We assumed this would be in Europe.

Our routine altered little as August continued hot and sultry. The brigade kept training. Despite rumours, it was not until early September that there was the first genuine indication we might possibly be deployed to the Gulf. By then the government had already announced it was reinforcing the Armilla patrol, the naval presence in the area, and sending a squadron of Royal Air Force Tornados to Saudi Arabia. These forces were to be commanded by Air Chief Marshal Sir Patrick (Paddy) Hine from High Wycombe, with Air Vice Marshal Sandy Wilson as the British forces' man-on-the-spot in Riyadh. The operation was to be codenamed 'Granby'. At this point the army's contribution consisted of some advisers

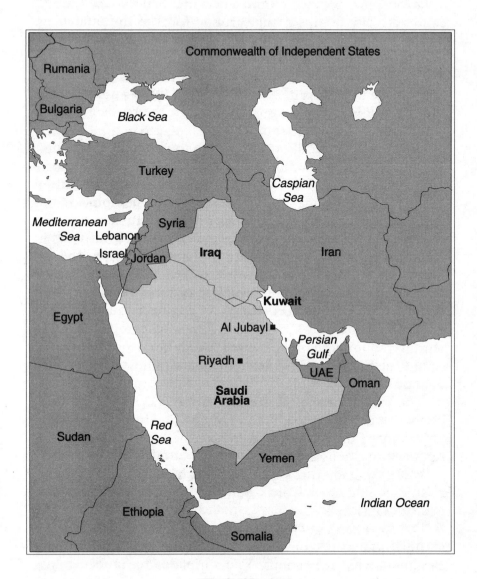

The Gulf Region

to the Saudi National Guard and a large contingent of signallers, communications being so crucial in times of crisis.

As the weeks progressed and it became clear that the Americans were dispatching a huge ground force to the defence of Saudi Arabia, it became equally clear that Britain was likely to offer more than just ships and aircraft. Throughout the British forces in Germany rumour ran rife. Our regiments seemed to know more than anyone else. The Irish Hussars were certain they were going. Their commanding officer, Arthur Denaro, confided in me that a friend of his, well placed in the Ministry of Defence, had told him 7 Brigade had definitely been chosen. With Arthur's contacts that was a very strong rumour.

The Scots Dragoons Guards appeared to have other collateral intelligence. A contractor's lorry carrying paint for a sand-coloured barrack block got lost in their camp and ended up in the area where the regiment's tanks were parked. By some incredible coincidence a pot fell off the tailboard and burst, spilling its contents on to the concrete. None of the soldiers were prepared to believe this was anything other than paint for their tanks.

During the evening of Tuesday 11th September I was in the stables at home when Antonia came running across from the house.

'There is someone on the phone for you, Daddy. I told him you were about to go riding but he said it really was very important.' I thrust the grooming brushes into her hands and ran back to the house.

'Hello, Brigadier, it's Ben Bathurst here. The corps commander would like a word.' Ben was Lieutenant General Sir Charles Guthrie's ADC.

'Patrick, I can't say very much but we'd like to see you here at the headquarters tomorrow morning. At nine o'clock. You can guess what it is about. Your brigade is probably going to the Gulf.' I replaced the receiver and sat down. My mind was racing, thoughts tumbling over each other. However, the heady mixture of excitement and concern was soon swamped by practicalities and then completely drowned the next day.

No author writing an exercise for students at the Staff

College could possibly have produced a more fanciful scenario than that given to me by the corps commander. He told me that during the next twenty-six days our establishment would double in size. We were then to move the brigade and its one-hundred-and-seventeen Challenger tanks to Saudi Arabia in order to counter Iraqi aggression. We would be operating under the tactical control of the United States Marine Corps. Oh, and by the way, the first ship leaves in two weeks' time,' he added.

The rest of the morning went by in a whirl of activity as I was shunted from one staff officer to the next and given more and more information. There was intelligence on minefields, the size of enemy forces, numbers of tanks and a myriad of other assorted crucial facts about the threat we were to face, a veritable information assault repeated at every subsequent briefing I attended. Everyone wanted to tell me all they knew about their speciality. Obviously they thought it would be helpful, but they were trying to impress as well. People also love to impart bad news and at this stage of the crisis the majority of the news was bad.

As I was trying to absorb all this, a key principle formed in my mind which was to stay with me throughout the hectic preparation phase. We would not take one more soldier than we needed for the job. The pressure to do otherwise was going to be immense. Every officer, non-commissioned officer and other rank in the army would want to join the brigade. We were going to have to fight hard to keep the numbers down.

By lunchtime the briefings were over. I felt lonely as I travelled back to Fallingbostel, just south of Soltau, where the majority of the brigade was stationed. The magnitude of the undertaking was clear to me but I had to make light of it; it was my job to be positive and give confidence. If there were concerns of an unusual nature they were mine to seek a solution to and not to share unnecessarily with my subordinates. Command is an isolated position, however I had been trained to cope when running my own regiment for three years. But then we had been guarding western Europe; now it was going to be harder.

*   *   *

The commanding officers were waiting for me and it was impossible not to share their sense of exhilaration. John Sharples, who commanded the Scots Dragoon Guards, was the first I greeted. He had taken over his regiment as I had assumed command of the brigade, indeed we had travelled out to Germany on the same ferry. Not a typical cavalry officer, quiet and slightly self-effacing but with a wicked sense of humour, he epitomised dependability. Next to him sat Charles Rogers, brought in from the Devon and Dorsets to command the Staffords. I had known him since he was a captain and he was wonderful company, although some of his lightheartedness had gone with the increased responsibility. Another interesting character was Rory Clayton, the gunners' commanding officer; it was rumoured he had been a bass guitarist in a rock band and a male model before joining the Army. For the past nineteen months we had worked together on training exercises plotting defensive tactics to be used against an unknown enemy.

John Moore-Bick was next; he commanded 21 Engineer Regiment. Normally only a squadron from the regiment supported the brigade and consequently I did not know him very well, but he had the reputation of being an intellectual. Rod Croucher, the commander of the divisional workshops, was also there. I knew him best as the highly effective manager of the large military camp at Fallingbostel. Finally there was Arthur Denaro, the charismatic commanding officer of the Irish Hussars; at times his enthusiasm made him difficult to rein in.

I confirmed we were definitely off to the Gulf. Silence greeted my corroboration of what they had already guessed. No-one moved or said anything. I told them about my ghastly morning being bombarded with facts at corps headquarters. Despite that I had little useful information to give them, except that we were likely to be placed under the command of the American Marine Corps because they were short of good tanks and we had plenty. I said I knew little of them beyond their reputation of being exceptionally hard fighters. I commented that their air wing alone had more aircraft than the entire Royal Air Force. However, as their primary role was amphibious warfare, our procedures and training methods were likely to be quite different to theirs. I said we would be joining them at full war establishment and had been promised anything we wanted, but I urged the commanders to be sensible with their requests, adamant that there was to be no mad spree chasing after long-sought-for military kit. I finished by saying I was off to Saudi Arabia in three days' time but I promised to brief them fully immediately I returned. In the meantime the process known as Transition to War would begin.

The next three days were marked by a most unpleasant series of injections against practically every disease imaginable, the largest, most painful one being saved for the night before our first press conference.

At the same time the anticipated personnel inflation began. Headquarters went from a staff of twenty-three to nearly eighty. It was the same in the regiments. The Staffords were to grow by over two hundred and the tank regiments would both have to import extra sixteen-man tank troops to bring them up to a war footing. But the gunners had the largest headache, increasing from five hundred to over a thousand. On top of all this the daily bombardment of information – we received about a thousand signals a day – left us in no doubt about the complex nature of the task ahead.

I was in Soltau on the Friday preparing for the next day's press conference when the government made the official announcement. I was still uncertain about what to expect from the press, but as all the mainstream media were attending it seemed an ideal opportunity to show both my own countrymen and the Iraqis what the Desert Rats were made of.

I had, as a result, ordered the regiments to get as many tanks, armoured fighting vehicles and artillery pieces as possible to Fallingbostel where the conference was to take place. When I went to inspect the tableau, it looked magnificent. Dozens of huge, threatening, green and black Challenger tanks were packed together. Near them were the M109s of the artillery regiment, their 155mm barrels thrusting skyward. In one area a Lynx helicopter sat, anti-tank missile racks clipped to its stubby brackets. And, amid them all, the army's newest fighting machine, the Warrior. These huge infantry-carrying vehicles with their 30mm Rarden cannons looked almost like tanks. I left encouraged by the image the world would have of us.

By ten o'clock the next day, Saturday 15th, I was furious. I had arrived back at the tank park to find it bare except for a few soldiers dressed in fatigues pushing brooms around. I grabbed the sergeant in charge. 'Sir, some chap from the public information team told us to put them all away, said it made the place look a mess. We've been here since eight o'clock tidying up.'

The impressive arsenal of twelve hours ago was gone, replaced by a line-up that looked like a local Territorial Army display at a country fête. It was too late to do anything about it.

An hour later the place was swarming with journalists and television crews all searching for their own particular angle on the news. 'Welcome to the 7th Armoured Brigade, the Desert Rats,' I started. 'I'd like to say how very proud we are to have been chosen for this task. Ahead of us lies a professional challenge, one that this brigade is well suited to tackle.

'We are fully manned and equipped with the very best equipment in the army. The Challenger main battle tank is without parallel. The Staffords, our infantry battalion, will fight from the Warrior, the newest addition to our arsenal. At war establishment this brigade will be the most powerful such force in the British Army.' And so I went on.

There is something of a ritual with press conferences. You make these prepared statements, which are solemnly recorded though seemingly never actually reported. But it is during the question and answer session afterwards that the press try to find their story. To know that large numbers of the population are going to read what you say, or see you on television, is exhilarating and perhaps even seductive; personal pride and vanity make you want to appear in control. Under these circumstances 'no comment' is no answer. It was therefore with interest I looked at the papers the next day, wondering what would be reported. The coverage was very positive; the first media hurdle had been cleared.

The last of the initial briefings was to take place on Sunday 16th September in England at the Joint Force Headquarters, known as the bunker, in High Wycombe. Leaving Soltau early I arrived at Hanover airport to find the place empty of soldiers, although I had been told I would be met. I sat in my staff car listening to Radio 4 and laughed to hear one of their pundits describing how Brigadier Cordingley was even now in the Gulf studying the ground and planning the deployment of his forces.

Eventually a member of the movements staff turned up and led me out on to the runway to the RAF Andover. Already on board was the reconnaissance team coming to Saudi Arabia with me. The first face I saw was that of Brigadier Mike Walker, chief of staff of the 1st British Corps and a long-time friend from our Staff College days. The rest of the fifteen-strong team were logisticians, because our priority at this stage was solving the practical problem of how to get to, and then live in, Saudi Arabia; tactical considerations were secondary.

The High Wycombe bunker was perhaps a disappointment. I had been expecting something along the lines of the Pentagon's war room, of which I had seen countless pictures. In its leafy encampment, from the outside it looked much like any modern office building, although most of the facility was buried deep underground. Inside it had an almost nautical feel, like being on board a warship; it was bustling with activity. Purposeful-looking people from all three services, with security passes hanging from their necks, were hurrying about their business down windowless corridors lit by fluorescent lighting.

We were escorted into a briefing room lined with huge maps of the Middle East. I was then taken from the rest of my team to meet the Joint Force Commander, Air Chief Marshal Sir Paddy Hine. His was an undistinguished, functional office.

He outlined the day's events and we discussed areas we would have to concentrate on during the reconnaissance. It was clear at this stage that only the sketchiest plans had been made for Britain's contribution to the ground defence of Saudi Arabia. It was going to be very much up to my team to fill in the gaps.

After twenty minutes I returned to the rest of the group for yet another onslaught of information, a full and highly detailed brief on the Iraqi biological and chemical capabilities, on their artillery and on what was known about the defences.

Biological weapons were a real concern, being cheap, readily available and easy to deliver. Intelligence sources predicted that Iraq was capable of producing a wide range from anthrax through to plague.

'We believe he might consider either long-range attacks against ports and airfields by putting biological warheads on Scud missiles, or using fifth columnists to mount attacks in Saudi cities by poisoning water supplies, or releasing microbes into the air from specially adapted trucks,' said the RAF briefing officer.

Chemical attack was even more likely. Saddam Hussein was known to have all three main types of lethal chemical weapon: blood, choking and nerve agents. Blood agents, such as hydrogen cyanide, are so called because once inhaled they are rapidly absorbed into the blood stream. Death comes quickly, in minutes if not seconds. Choking agents attack the lining of the lungs, causing them to rupture. Our forefathers knew only too well from the trenches of the First World War chlorine gas and the horror of 'dry land drowning'. The most deadly of the three is nerve – a colourless, odourless gas or liquid that can enter the body either through the lungs or the skin, interfering with the central nervous system by inhibiting the action of the chemicals that cause nerves to stop twitching and reacting. Once a nerve is stimulated it carries on reacting out of control. The body effectively overloads itself. Death is caused usually by heart and respiratory failure.

In addition the Iraqis were known to have blister agents, and in particular mustard gas. Blister agents, as their name suggests, cause painful, slow-healing blisters once in contact with skin. They are most effective in moist areas of the body – armpits, groin and eyes. Although mustard is not classified as a lethal agent, it had killed, either directly or indirectly, hundreds, if not thousands, in 1915 and 1916.

All types of agents can be divided into two categories, depending on their persistence. Non-persistent agents, such as hydrogen cyanide and some of the nerve gases, will dissipate in only a few seconds after an attack. Persistent agents, like mustard and other nerve agents, have an oil-like consistency. They are slow to evaporate and can contaminate an area for hours or even days, depending on the weather. The Soviets were known to have thickened persistent agents with a glue-like consistency that could pollute an area for months.

Saddam Hussein had used chemical weapons. In March 1988 his air force sprayed the Kurdish town of Halabjah with either nerve gas or cyanide, killing at least four thousand people, mainly civilians. He had also used them in the battle to recapture the Fao peninsula in 1988, when Iraq retook that strategic feature from Iran in one of the greatest victories of the eight-year Iran–Iraq war. Iraq's tactic was to shell the Iranians with both conventional artillery and chemical weapons. This forced them to don their old-fashioned rubber chemical suits in temperatures of 40°C (104°F) and higher, which in a short time rendered them useless for further combat. But by using quick-dispersing, non-persistent agents the Iraqis were then able to attack the area without the need for suits themselves. In addition they used persistent chemical agents. By shelling Iranian rear areas, which housed logistics, command and control and reserves, they played havoc with Iran's ability to fight the war.

And the Iraqis certainly had the weapons to deliver the chemicals – huge numbers of artillery batteries, albeit of greatly varying quality. Their best was very good, the South African made 155mm G-5 howitzer. It has a range of twenty-five miles, considerably more than that of our own M109. They also had large numbers of Katyusha BM-21 multiple rocket launchers. Old though still potent weapons, they were capable of landing a vast amount of explosive on a small area in seconds. They too could deliver chemical weapons.

Of some comfort to us was the efficiency of the British nuclear, biological and chemical (NBC) suit. A two-piece charcoal-impregnated cotton suit, it was lighter and far less cumbersome than the Iranian covers. It was still very hot to wear and dramatically increased the necessary water consumption, a serious problem in the desert. And we did have a wide variety of chemical detectors; also every soldier carried antidotes on him at all times.

Next an enthusiastic engineer informed us about the sixteen million Italian mines Iraq had laid, and the twenty million more he thought they were either going to lay, or had already laid, in minefields several miles deep for the defence of Kuwait.

The latest intelligence was no more encouraging. It confirmed that the initial invasion had been spearheaded by forces from the Republican Guard Force Command, the elite troops of the Iraqi army. They were not, however, occupying Kuwait City. Follow-on forces had been used to subdue the capital while the Republican Guard pushed south to the border.

The colonel briefing us pointed out the area on a large-scale map. 'They are now in positions along the border with Saudi Arabia. However intelligence from the Americans suggests some pulling back by these forces and regular forces taking their place. This would seem to indicate that an immediate invasion of Saudi Arabia is unlikely. At the same time the number of Iraqis in Kuwait is growing daily, which could mean either that Saddam is massing his forces before invading, or digging in to defend what he has already taken.'

The Americans had estimated the Iraqi force in Kuwait to consist of 150,000 men in ten divisions with 1,300 tanks and 600 artillery pieces. In addition there were perhaps another twelve divisions just over the border in Iraq. American troops were deploying as fast as they could, arriving at around one thousand a day, but they were still relatively lightly armoured. The rapid deployment troops of the 82nd and 101st Airborne Divisions were in theatre, alongside part of the US Marine Corps, but neither had any tanks. However, what the Americans lacked in ground troops they more than made up for in air power. Incredible numbers of aircraft had flown to airfields in the Middle East or were on aircraft-carriers out at sea.

Our mission was starkly clear. We had to be prepared to fight a defensive battle against a potentially huge force equipped with chemical and biological weapons and no doubt led by the battle-hardened Republican Guard. I went to bed that night in the Gateway Hotel at RAF Brize Norton deep in thought. I managed to ring Melissa at home, although it was very late. It was somehow comforting to hear of her problems with the horses, which seemed much more real than the thought of fighting a quarter of a million Iraqis thousands of miles away.

Chapter 2

Monday 17th September to Wednesday 10th October 1990

The day, the 17th, started badly. Having finished my telephoning well after midnight, I was woken at five o'clock by the alarm clock, set by the previous occupant.

We left Brize Norton for Riyadh on an RAF VC-10. With us came Sir Paddy Hine and Lieutenant General Sir Michael Wilkes. The latter, a powerfully built ex-gunner and commander of all United Kingdom-based troops, I knew quite well; we had both spent many years serving with the British Army of the Rhine. Their job was to obtain an audience with King Fahd and get his permission for us to continue with the reconnaissance and, in particular, talk to the Americans already in Saudi Arabia.

I had flown in countless RAF VC-10s, but never one in VIP configuration. Like a train carriage, it had groups of four large seats arranged around tables either side of the aisle. The general and air marshal sat at one table and throughout the flight they worked. I sat across the aisle with Mike Walker. I was uncomfortable, feeling it necessary to do something, but until I had spoken to the US marines and seen the ground there really was little I could achieve. Rather than get out my

Jilly Cooper, I did the small amount of work I had, debating with Mike the principles for our order of arrival into theatre, and then whiled away the rest of the flight by dozing.

We were told the temperature on arrival at the Riyadh Military Airport was 39°C (102°F), but as we walked out on to the aircraft steps it was like walking into a wall of heat. The hot, clinging air left you fighting for breath. The prospect of fighting in such a climate was daunting.

We drove to our hotel in air-conditioned mini-buses. Riyadh is an impressive, clean, modern city, with wide tree-lined boulevards. Wealth was evident from the Mercedes and BMWs that shot past us on the smooth multi-lane highway and the opulent public buildings, standing back from the roadside in their own oases of green grass and trees. Almost all of the Saudi men were dressed in the traditional white gown with a headdress secured by a black cord; the women were heavily veiled in black.

We pulled up at the Intercontinental Hotel, a red brick modern building designed in anonymous international hotel style. Ostentatiously liveried bellboys opened doors and carried cases as we were escorted into the lobby. White marble and an abundance of plants were set off by the extravagant gold and mahogany fittings. Groups of white-robed Arabs sat about in enveloping white leather sofas. Around raced scores of children, ambushing fathers who wandered the lobby aimlessly. And tucked away, almost out of sight, were gatherings of veiled women in heavy black *chowdras*. These were Kuwaiti refugees who had fled the invasion. There was nothing for them to do but sit and wait for their country to be returned to them.

I would have felt self-conscious, being in combat clothing, but for the presence of scores of smart-looking armed American soldiers in their sand-and-chocolate-coloured cotton fatigues. I made a mental note about procuring desert-camouflage uniforms for the brigade. We looked out of place, in a uniform designed to blend into jungle, in a country where almost every tree had been planted by hand. It was some while before I discovered that the Ministry of Defence had recently sold its entire stock of desert camouflage uniforms – it was rumoured to Iraq.

While waiting for the formality of checking in and sorting out our bags, I strolled around the lobby. The newspaper stand had a selection of English papers and I picked up a copy of *The Times*. The *mutawa*, the religious police, had censored with a thick black pen almost every picture of a woman. I looked for a copy of the *Sun* but there was none there. Nearby was an impressive looking computer that promised to tell one the weather in any city in the world. No matter what I typed in, it had only one answer: it was cloudy and raining in London.

As we waited for royal approval to continue with the reconnaissance, the one decision it was possible to make was on the order of arrival of our troops and equipment into theatre. The first American combat troops to arrive went straight into the desert because of the immediate threat of an Iraqi invasion of Saudi Arabia. Their logistics followed behind them, which meant they initially had very little support. Our arrival behind the American defensive screen could be conducted at a less frenetic pace. Consequently, the first British troops could be the Royal Engineers and local resource sections of the Royal Army Ordnance Corps. Their priority would be accommodation. Either we would have to build our own covered areas, which would be a job for the engineers, or else hire whatever was available, a task that would fall to the resource sections.

Once this was completed the force would have somewhere to live and work from. Then we could start to send in the logistics infrastructure to handle the thousands of combat troops. Dispatching combat troops was not simply a matter of lining the brigade up alphabetically and filling up aeroplanes. They had to be sent in a logical order which minimised the time soldiers were sitting around with nothing to do both in Germany and Saudi Arabia. The plan would be complicated by the fact that all heavy equipment would come by sea, taking three weeks, while the troops would fly, taking seven hours.

On Tuesday the 18th, our first full day in Riyadh, Mike and I were invited to the British Embassy for a working lunch. When we arrived at the ambassador's residence our hackles

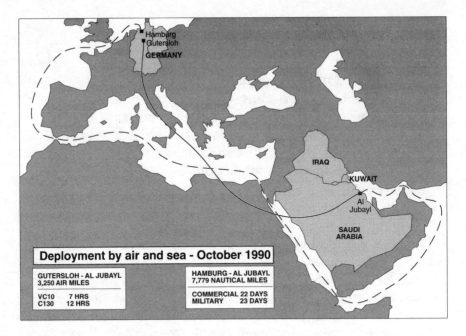

Deployment by air and sea - October 1990

GUTERSLOH - AL JUBAYL	HAMBURG - AL JUBAYL
3,250 AIR MILES	7,779 NAUTICAL MILES
VC10 7 HRS	COMMERCIAL 22 DAYS
C130 12 HRS	MILITARY 23 DAYS

rose – there, laid out in front of us, was a dining table set for a formal lunch for twenty. 'I thought we were supposed to be fighting a war, not having a bloody garden party,' I muttered to Mike as we went in.

However, I was wrong and the lunch period was certainly not without its use. The ambassador, Sir Alan Munro, a former cavalry officer whom I had first met in Libya in 1966, was full of useful advice on life in Saudi Arabia and how to handle our hosts. His gut feeling was that the Iraqis were not going to invade. It was one thing to storm Kuwait, not a popular country with its neighbours, but to attack the Saudi royal family, keepers of the Holy Cities of Mecca and Medina, the holiest sites of Islam, was altogether different. It would be certain to unite the Arab world against them. Although the Arab League, under the skilful hand of the Egyptians, had condemned Iraq's invasion of Kuwait and were sending troops to Riyadh's defence, it was an uneasy position. Saddam Hussein was certain to increase that unease and attempt to split the Arabs away from the rest of the coalition. He could not do that if he invaded Saudi Arabia.

*   *   *

Late on the afternoon of 19th September royal consent was received for the reconnaissances and discussions with the Americans to start the next day. We set off early next morning. On leaving the hotel I could hear a muezzin in a mosque near the hotel calling the faithful to the first of the Muslims' five prayers a day. 'Prayer is better than sleep,' he wailed, 'prayer is better than sleep.'

A flight in the back of a C-130 Hercules is always cramped, noisy and extremely uncomfortable and this one was made worse by the heat, which even early in the day was oppressive. Inside, the aircraft is very basic. Rows of red netting seats, hanging off metal frames, line each side of the hull, with another row down the middle of the aircraft. There is very little leg room. Facilities are non-existent. There is a funnel attached to a plastic pipe that goes straight out of the back of the fuselage for the call of nature. Food is normally whatever you take on board with you.

We landed at the military airport to the north of Al Jubayl, which had been taken over by the Americans. It was frantic with activity. As one huge C-5 Galaxy transport aircraft was coming into land, its cavernous hold packed with spares, others were preparing to take off. One entire runway was full of helicopters – hundreds of them, looking, with their rotor blades folded, like giant insects hatching and about to stretch their wings out to dry. American troops were everywhere. Some were unloading the tons of cargo, while others patrolled the barbed wire fence or were building sandbag emplacements. There were yet more soldiers manning the Patriot anti-aircraft missile batteries that dotted the landscape.

A mini-bus escorted by two large Humvees, the American equivalent of the Land Rover, came speeding up to us. A smart-looking closely shorn young officer with a Military Police armband over his desert combats came up to me and saluted. 'General Cordingley, sir, on behalf of the 1st Marine Expeditionary Force, welcome to Al Jubayl. If you and your party would like to board the bus, sir, we'll drive straight to the headquarters in the docks. General Boomer is expecting you, sir.'

21

Al Jubayl was a scruffy place, smaller and less developed than Riyadh. The characteristic smell of a Middle Eastern town hung in the air, a mixture of spice and incense with a strong hint of animal dung. A market spilled out over the streets with stalls selling everything from cheap fabrics to water melons. One stall was piled high with bamboo cages crammed with scrawny chickens.

We arrived at the port on the edge of the town. The Americans had heavily reinforced the approach road. It was a lesson bitterly learnt in Beirut after a suicide bomber had driven a lorry packed with explosives into the Marine Corps barracks. More than two hundred marines had perished in the blast. They had now devised a series of tight chicanes and concrete barricades that were almost impossible to break through and had to be negotiated very slowly, all the time under the gaze of half-a-dozen heavily armed guards. In a watch tower above the main gate I saw two more marines, with M60 machine guns, cover us as we approached.

The port was a vast, sprawling compound, at least four times the size of the docks at Dover. Whole quaysides were taken up with bumper-to-bumper sand-coloured vehicles – tanks, guns, trucks, the fat-bodied Humvees. Pallets of supplies, hanging from huge towering cranes, swung through the air. Forklift trucks scurried by ferrying kit to loading bays, into enormous container trucks or to stockpiles in vast warehouses. As at the airport, security was paramount. Vehicle parks were ringed with triple-concertina barbed wire and guarded. Overhead you could see vapour trails from fighters on constant air patrol.

The marines' headquarters, a large white two-storey concrete building, was heavily guarded and ringed with barbed wire and sandbag emplacements. We were shown into a conference room, empty but for a long table and boards covered in maps. In one corner, neatly folded, were several camp beds, sleeping bags and other personal kit. While the others were briefed on the day's activities, Mike and I were taken upstairs to meet Lieutenant General Walt Boomer, the commanding general of the 1st Marine Expeditionary Force.

General Boomer was not at all what I had expected. Instead of a bull-necked marine, we were introduced to a tall, wiry and rather quiet man, perhaps in his early fifties, with an almost contemplative air about him. 'General Cordingley, General Walker, I can't tell you how happy I am to see you here,' he said in a Southern accent.

His office, like the building, was bare and functional. Behind his desk were two flags, a Stars and Stripes and the 1st Marine Expeditionary Force's colours, from which hung dozens of silk streamers, each inscribed with a battle honour.

After making our introductions he walked over to a flip chart and gave us an outline of how the marines were organised. The 1st Marine Expeditionary Force was the US Central Command's marine element, known as MARCENT. General Boomer reported directly to General H. Norman Schwarzkopf, the commander-in-chief.

Ashore, the marines had one ground formation of about thirty thousand men, the 1st Marine Division commanded by Brigadier General Mike Myatt. Accompanying them was the team that provided the logistics, the Force Service Support Group. The ground troops were supported by the 3rd Marine Air Wing, under Major General Royal Moore, with forty Cobra gunships, forty Harriers, forty-eight F/A18s and nearly eighty support and utility helicopters.

At sea were another eleven thousand men – the 4th Marine Expeditionary Brigade and the 13th Marine Expeditionary Unit, with another twenty Harriers and seventy helicopters.

'But my real problem, and that's where you gentlemen come in, is tanks,' General Boomer said. 'I just don't have enough of them. My division is twelve battalions strong, but only two of them are armoured; that's only one hundred and twenty tanks, total.'

Until 24th Infantry Division arrived in Saudi Arabia with its hundreds of M1A1 Abrams tanks, the Americans were short of firepower. They were relying on either the marines' M60, an old, poorly armoured tank with only a 105mm gun, or the M551 Sheridan, a vehicle with so little armoured protection it could hardly be called a tank at all. Two regiments of

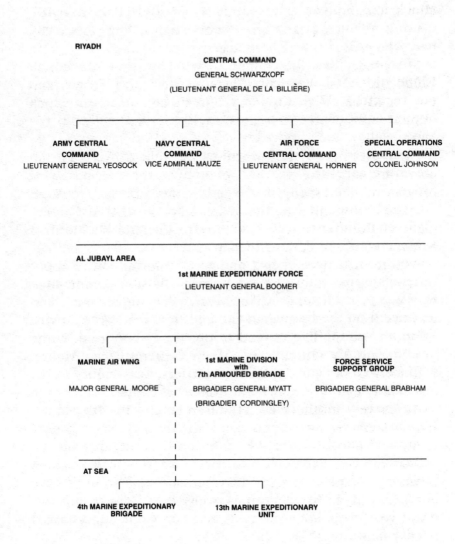

RIYADH

CENTRAL COMMAND

GENERAL SCHWARZKOPF

(LIEUTENANT GENERAL DE LA BILLIÈRE)

ARMY CENTRAL COMMAND	NAVY CENTRAL COMMAND	AIR FORCE CENTRAL COMMAND	SPECIAL OPERATIONS CENTRAL COMMAND
LIEUTENANT GENERAL YEOSOCK	VICE ADMIRAL MAUZE	LIEUTENANT GENERAL HORNER	COLONEL JOHNSON

AL JUBAYL AREA

1st MARINE EXPEDITIONARY FORCE

LIEUTENANT GENERAL BOOMER

MARINE AIR WING	1st MARINE DIVISION with 7th ARMOURED BRIGADE	FORCE SERVICE SUPPORT GROUP
MAJOR GENERAL MOORE	BRIGADIER GENERAL MYATT	BRIGADIER GENERAL BRABHAM
	(BRIGADIER CORDINGLEY)	

AT SEA

4th MARINE EXPEDITIONARY BRIGADE	13th MARINE EXPEDITIONARY UNIT

Chain of Command for US Marine Expeditionary Force

nearly sixty of the Chobham-armoured 120mm Challenger tanks were going to be very welcome indeed.

He outlined another worry, should they be ordered to attack into Kuwait. He only had five mine ploughs, and, bearing in mind the size of the obstacles they were likely to cross, they needed any help we could give them with combat engineers. I explained that the British Army of the Rhine did not have a large armoured engineer force, just one regiment, 32 Armoured Engineer Regiment, and some of their equipment was frankly ancient, based on Centurion and Chieftain tank hulls. But if 7 Brigade brought with it all the armoured engineer equipment that normally supported the entire corps in Germany we would have a potent force. Mike was taking copious notes.

It was an encouraging meeting because together we seemed to dovetail strengths with weaknesses: they needed tanks and engineers, which we had; we needed logistic support and air power, both of which they had in abundance. We left the general's office with a real sense of achievement. Our next stop was to meet their intelligence and operations staff and be briefed on the Iraqi threat and the marines' deployment. Then we were to fly out for our ground reconnaissance.

The operations brief lasted about thirty minutes. The first map showed the latest intelligence on the Iraqi dispositions. It had changed little since we left High Wycombe. Defences along the border continued to be built up, with heavy mining and large tank traps being dug. There were unconfirmed reports of chemical mines. The next chart showed the planned deployment of the Coalition forces, which at this stage consisted only of Arab forces and the Americans. On the border was a lightly armoured Saudi reconnaissance screen. Their job was to watch and, should the Iraqis invade, fight a delaying battle to slow them up so the Coalition air forces could engage them. Behind the Saudis were the other forces of the Coalition, with most of the Arab troops, the Egyptians, the Syrians and the remainder of the Saudis in the west, and the US forces, the US marines, the 24th, 82nd and 101st Divisions, in the east.

The last chart showed the marines' area, stretching from

just south of Al Jubayl, north to a town on the coast called Ra's Karmah and from the coast west about fifty miles. The 1st Marine Division had been divided up into four task forces to cover the area. Just behind the Saudi reconnaissance screen was Task Force Shepard, their own reconnaissance screen. Behind them were the two main forces, Task Force Ripper in the west and Task Force 3/9 covering to the coast. In reserve was Regimental Combat Team 3, made up of two infantry battalions and one mechanised battalion. The air wing had Harriers forward with the task forces, who in turn were well supported by Cobra gunships. The F/A18s were flying constant combat air patrols throughout the sector.

The mission was to defend north of Al Jubayl. The 'red line' was stretched very thinly. If the Iraqis invaded in strength I doubted if the marines would have been able to hold them for long. It was a sobering brief.

Our helicopter was waiting on the pad with the rotors turning. The doors had been taken off and a gunner, festooned with ammunition, sat with his feet hanging out, his machine gun in front of him. It was like something out of a Vietnam film.

The land that opened up before us was classic desert, flat and featureless. It was bisected by one dark grey tarmac road down which trundled endless American convoys, with the odd Arab pick-up weaving in and out. After twenty minutes or so we approached the first position. The tanks were in shallow protective scrapes, with camouflage nets over them. I could make out a battalion command post by the forest of antennae sprouting from another camouflage net. As we flew on we could see how well dug in they were, but the positions were miles from each other. The line clearly was thin and needed reinforcing as soon as possible. There were simply too few troops and too much ground to cover and defend.

Back at Al Jubayl for a final de-brief with General Boomer there were two key issues to be finalised – how would 7 Brigade slot into his command and when? There were two options. We could operate as an independent brigade within the force reporting directly to the general, or we could be placed under command of the 1st Division and Brigadier General Myatt.

The first option gave us more independence and politically it looked attractive – we would seem to be less reliant upon the US marines. The second option was militarily neater. My brigade was not designed or equipped to operate as an independent command; plus we would be able to take advantage of the 1st Division's logistic support for items such as fuel and food.

General Boomer was amenable to both plans, although it was apparent he preferred the second, a view I shared. The only problem, more political than military, was that I would be placed under the command of an American of equal rank. Nevertheless we agreed to it.

Mike Walker added one important caveat. 'The British government will place 7 Brigade under your tactical control. But you must realise the brigade will remain under national command through Riyadh and the British Joint Force Commander at all times.' The general nodded his agreement, clearly understanding how sensitive the subject of national control is for any nation.

The second issue was when could we be expected to be up and running in Saudi Arabia. 'Frankly, gentlemen, as soon as damn possible,' said General Boomer. On the back of a scrap of paper we did a quick time appreciation. If the brigade started to load by the end of September, until say the beginning of October, then we could have most of the heavy equipment in Al Jubayl by around 25th October. Allowing a week for modifications and repairs, I thought, and two weeks work-up training, then, 'We'll be operational by 16th November,' I said.

That evening back in Riyadh the team assembled to go over the day's events. Before we started I reiterated my concerns about manning.

'Gentlemen, none of us have any experience in fighting a desert war, but we are all of us professional soldiers – we have trained for years for armoured warfare. Now is the time to bring that training to bear. Exercise your judgement very carefully over the number of men you each require here. The same is true of equipment. For instance, take attack helicopters; with forty Cobra gunships on call, why bring our own?' Most nodded their agreement.

But the key to this operation was going to be the logistics. Nearly everything we needed we would have to bring with us and that meant at least forty-two days' supplies. In turn that meant ships to carry it on, people to unload it, store it, account for it, issue it, and re-order low stocks. It meant an armada of trucks to carry supplies and stores forward to the soldiers, and to carry broken equipment back for repair.

The work continued. Because the brigade would not have its usual support, indeed no plan existed for this or a similar eventuality, we agreed to re-structure it. Normally it would be split into the fighting element – the tanks, soldiers, guns and headquarters – and the logistic element. Logistics were then further split – urgently needed stores and the mechanics were grouped in the Brigade Administrative Area and the remainder went to the Divisional Administrative Area. Since we would have no division of our own we looked again at these arrangements, eventually agreeing on a Brigade Maintenance Area some fifty miles behind the fighting element and a Force Maintenance Area at Al Jubayl.

We then tackled the medical aspects. With the threat of chemical weapons we would need a large medical force. Every front-line unit would have its own medical post with a doctor and stretcher bearers. Behind them would be the better-equipped dressing stations, where we would also have surgical teams capable of performing emergency operations. Back in the port we would need a full-size, fully equipped hospital, with at least four hundred beds, the size of a small county hospital. With the huge distances from the front to the port we felt we would need RAF support helicopters. In this instance we did not choose to rely on the Americans. If a question of priority arose we could hardly expect the Americans to put us first.

After several hours' discussion we had the outline of a report. We had rattled through the necessary decisions: yes to Al Jubayl and its airports; yes to our order of arrival – logistics, workshops and movements people first, tanks and fighting troops when they were ready. Accommodation was going to be tight at the port and, although the huge sheds would hold some of the men, we would have to build a tented camp for two thousand soldiers on the quayside.

Switching to operational matters, Mike and I outlined our conclusions. Air defence was superbly covered by the Americans. We would bring a battery of Javelin hand-held anti-aircraft missiles to cover us if we advanced, but the combination of Patriots, Hawks and the hundreds of aircraft flying constant patrols made any further contribution we might offer to area air defence irrelevant.

The meeting broke up well after midnight. At eight o'clock the next morning we had to brief Air Vice Marshal Sandy Wilson, the British commander in the Gulf, on our findings before catching a VC-10 back to England two hours later. On board would be a clerk who would type up our report as we wrote it. We were to deliver it to Sir Paddy Hine and his staff in the bunker the next day.

I got up at five o'clock to finish the work. At seven Mike and I went to the embassy to see Sandy Wilson. He accepted all our points and wished us well. Waiting for us was a car and escort to whisk us to the airport. But from then on things went rapidly downhill, for on the tarmac at Riyadh Military Airport stood not the promised VC-10 but an all-too-familiar grey and green Hercules – the fat-bodied, four-engined, and decidedly slow RAF transporter. For some reason the VC-10 was delayed. We were to fly the first leg to Cyprus by Hercules, where we would meet our intended VC-10, along with a typist, and carry on to England.

It is extremely difficult to work in a Hercules. There is nowhere to write, apart from resting a briefcase on your knee. And on this flight the aircraft was buffeted by turbulence that sent pens and notebooks flying. The noise was deafening. We communicated by half-scribbled jottings on scrappy pieces of paper. Thus was completed the report that formed the basis for Britain's biggest armoured deployment since D-day 1944.

We arrived at Cyprus expecting to rush straight to the VC-10, but no. Waiting for me as I climbed out of the Hercules was the station commander who asked me to follow him. We set off towards the tower. I could sense something was wrong.

'Where's the VC-10?' I asked.

'I'm not sure how to say this, sir,' he said quietly, 'but I'm afraid there isn't one.'

'What?'

'It's all rather complicated, sir, but the aircrew don't have enough flying hours left to get back. They won't be able to fly until tomorrow.'

'That's hopeless. I must get back today. What about a stand-by crew?' I demanded, anger mounting in me.

'There isn't one and, with all respect, sir, you did arrive rather late.'

We had no choice but to continue the flight for another seven hours in the Hercules. We struggled on, arriving back at RAF Lyneham at eleven o'clock that night.

The conference started early the next day. As I was shown into a large panelled briefing room at High Wycombe I was rather taken aback by the size of the audience. I had been expecting thirty or so people. There were well over a hundred.

I spoke initially for about twenty minutes. 'The Americans do not believe an Iraqi attack to be imminent. But they do believe it is inevitable that the allies will attack at some stage.' There was a murmur throughout the room. I could sense people sitting up.

'That prospect was always at the front of our minds throughout the reconnaissance,' I said, driving the point home. I went on to explain, just as General Boomer had explained to us, the organisation and tasks of the marines. When I told them of the air support there were envious exchanges of glances.

I then introduced the report, which had been typed up overnight from our collected jottings. 'The deployment of the Operation Granby brigade promises to be the most complex, dangerous and difficult deployment of armoured forces since World War Two.' I outlined our findings and ended with our list of recommendations. The use of Al Jubayl, being placed under the tactical control of the 1st Marine Division, our proposed order of arrival and key timings were all accepted. The only fly in the ointment came when I was probed aggressively by some civil servant from the Ministry of Defence. I had no idea who he was. What had apparently set off alarm bells was when I said we complemented the marines, particularly with our engineers. From the nature of his questions I could sense an unease with the idea of large numbers of British casualties.

The High Wycombe meeting had focused on strategic considerations, such as relations with our allies and political repercussions of various aspects of the operation. The brief at corps headquarters in Germany the following day was concerned with the nitty-gritty, and hence to us much more real. How many tanks would we be taking? How large a reserve? What about air defence? What were the ammunition requirements? Throughout both conferences, and not for the last time, I had this nagging feeling that, despite my best efforts, people were trying to bump up the numbers.

Escaping from the endless talking I flew back to Soltau that afternoon. Euan Loudon, a major and the brigade's chief of staff, was there to meet me off the helicopter. It was good to see him. On his shoulders had fallen the responsibility of preparing the brigade, in my absence, for its new role. But we could not have had a better person for the task; he was a serious, highly intelligent and professional officer. We had been posted to the brigade at the same time and we had struck up a strong friendship almost immediately – we shared a very similar outlook on life. Perhaps this outlook was a weakness, as both of us would go out of our way to avoid having a row with anyone.

'You've been sent a deputy commander, Brigadier,' he told me as we walked towards the headquarters building.

'Oh really, who?' I asked.

'Chap called John Milne, a gunner colonel. Corps thought you'd need one. He turned up the other day and just cracked on with it. He's taken over liaison for movements and manning.'

It is a curious fact of the British Army that, although regiments have second-in-commands, brigades, divisions and corps do not. Having John, therefore, initially felt awkward – but what a blessing it turned out to be.

The last, and for me, the most important conference of the day was with my own staff and the commanding officers, all of whom were there waiting for me in a lecture theatre at the top of the headquarters. The relief that their commander was back again was evident. Since I had been away they had all set about preparing for war, but for a war they knew little about. What were we going to do? Where? And with whom? After I had spoken to them you could sense the enthusiasm for the work ahead. Euan, with his two principal staff captains, Maurice Gibson and Ron Powrie, would continue to train and to work out the complex movement to get us to Saudi Arabia, while preparations for our logistics would fall to the deputy chief of staff, Major Robbie Burns, helped by Captains Peter McGuigan and Mick Simpson. We were all very aware of the huge and unusual task that confronted us.

The period between 24th September and 9th October, when the first of the brigade departed for the Gulf, was hectic. The regiments had to increase to a war establishment; in peace, units are not kept at full strength. It had always been foreseen that the reinforcements to bring regiments to a war footing would be drawn from the reserves, soldiers who had recently left the army but who remained liable for call-up. However calling up the reserve is politically difficult. So now we were told we had to draw on the rest of the army. Nevertheless, hundreds of volunteers did telephone their old regiments, wrote to them, or simply turned up at the barrack gates.

Preparing our equipment was also going to be a complex jigsaw puzzle. The tank regiments had to swap their Mk1 and Mk2 Challengers for the latest Mk3 where necessary. This was not popular with the crews concerned; most had an affection for their own tank. All our petrol Land Rovers had to be swapped for diesel ones and we were issued with the latest load-carrying trucks.

The Staffords probably had more problems than most.

They had been preparing for a Northern Ireland tour. Now they had to forget months of training for an internal security operation, revert to their Warrior role, and then absorb scores of extra soldiers to bring them to war establishment, which was to include almost an entire company of Grenadier Guards.

One of our first conferences established the priorities for training as we prepared the vehicles for shipping to Al Jubayl. 'Firing, fitness, first aid, and f—ing NBC warfare,' the conference secretary noted. Fortunately we were starting from a high point. Two of the three regiments had been recently to Suffield in Canada, where the British Army runs a huge training area. An exercise there is the climax of peacetime training. It is the only place where tanks and infantry can train together using live ammunition. The least trained of the brigade's regiments was the Irish Hussars, who had only five months before returned from two years in England. They were new to Challenger and had not been to Suffield. But Arthur Denaro had no worries about their ability to catch up.

Soltau and Fallingbostel are next door to NATO's largest firing ranges. Existing bookings for these much-used facilities were thrown out as the brigade moved there *en masse* to test-fire every weapon we had. Training ammunition scales were torn up and we fired decades' worth of rounds in a few days. The 120mm tank guns, the 30mm Rarden cannon on the Warrior, the 7.62mm Warrior chain gun, 81mm mortars, Milan anti-tank missiles, the 94mm LAW anti-tank weapon, grenades and the infantryman's 5.56mm SA80 were all put through rigorous testing. Down the road, at the artillery ranges at Munsterlager, Rory Clayton's gunners, their manpower swollen by a hundred per cent, were doing much the same with their twenty-four 155mm M109s.

Between firing and vehicle maintenance, first aid and NBC training were paramount. The Falklands War had shown how vital even the most elementary first aid was. Since then every soldier had been trained in the basic skills, and many to a much higher level. One real life saver was the saline drip. The Israeli army, I was told, teaches every single soldier how to insert one, even rectally if there is no other way, so we did the same. Chemical and biological training had taken on a new urgency. We went over and over the drills until they became second nature. Close your eyes, hold your breath, turn your back to the wind, pull your respirator out of its haversack, always by your side, stick it on, breathe out hard shouting 'Gas, gas, gas!' You had to do it in less than nine seconds.

Then there was instruction in recognising symptoms of gas poisoning, both in yourself and others, using the various detection equipments, administering antidotes, and simply living in the chemical suit. Even the most simple task becomes a major challenge when wearing a respirator, thick rubber gloves, rubber overboots and a heavy two-piece charcoal-impregnated suit. How do you eat, drink, go to the loo, or fire a gun?

This was also a time of innumerable visitors, from the Secretary of State for Defence, Tom King, to endless senior officers who came to advise, help or just offer their best wishes. It was also the first time I met my new commander, Lieutenant General Sir Peter de la Billière.

He had been appointed, on Mrs Thatcher's insistence, as the Commander British Forces Middle East, taking over from Air Vice Marshal Sandy Wilson on 29th September. He came to us on 4th October. A quiet man with piercing, clear blue eyes, he wore his sandy coloured SAS beret and had the distinctive blue and white SAS wings on his right arm. Like every one else in the army, I knew his reputation, his involvement in the Iranian embassy siege, his time in the Falklands, his experience of working with the Arabs. Britain's most decorated soldier was not what I had expected; he was much quieter and much more thoughtful. However he made us feel confident.

Our first vehicles loaded at Bremerhaven on 27th September on board the *Dana Cymbria*, with elements of my headquarters (including my driver, Corporal Jameson, and my Land Rover), 7 Armoured Workshops and 16 Tank Transporter Squadron on board.

We issued Operation Granby Routine Order Number 1

on 28th September. 'AWOL. All ranks are reminded that having been warned for an overseas emergency tour, any period of absence without leave is liable to result in a charge of desertion and will be punished accordingly.' What is the punishment for desertion in these circumstances I wondered? But it was a salutary reminder of the seriousness of what we were undertaking. We also ordered that everyone should make out a will. Fortunately, as for most things in the army, there is a form for it. I was not exempt from these personal matters. Trying to get my life insured, I discovered only two companies were prepared even to consider us, and then the premiums were absurd.

The days slipped away until on Wednesday 10th October it was time for me to leave Germany.

It was a cold day. I got up early, just as dawn was breaking, and slipped downstairs to finish yet more paperwork. Breakfast was a tense, rather stilted affair, with the family trying to keep a stiff upper lip. I drove myself to work and was able to keep busy for most of the day. At the end of the afternoon I was told my helicopter had arrived. I signed the few remaining papers, cleared the in-tray and put my pen away. I said a rather inadequate goodbye to Gerardine, my secretary, whose sapper husband Chris was also going to the Gulf. I looked around the office at the familiar pastel-green walls. It was neither an attractive nor a particularly spacious room, but I was fond of it. I wondered how long it would be before I would see it again.

Chapter 3

Thursday 11th to
Monday 29th October 1990

The evening helicopter flight to RAF Gutersloh was unusual because it was pitch black and raining. As we climbed I could see nothing in the gloom but malevolent storm clouds, dark grey against the black night. I was glad to land an hour later.

About fifty or so journalists packed into a large room at next morning's press conference. Television lights shone into my face, making it hard to read the prepared statement – prepared rather hurriedly. Then followed a rather hesitant question and answer session, some of it in German. We finished it as soon as possible, and I went out on to the runway where General Sir Peter Inge, the Commander-in-Chief of the British Army of the Rhine, was waiting for our photo-opportunity. We made small talk look like military secrets while scores of photographers scurried around us snapping avidly. We shook hands, saluted and I walked up the stairs on to the aircraft, turning around at the top to wave goodbye to no-one in particular. As I walked into the aircraft I thought to myself, 'I'm glad that's all over'. But no, to shouts of 'Brigadier, could we do that again?' we had to go through the whole rigmarole once more. I do not remember seeing a single picture of the morning's activities in any paper.

The VC-10 taxied to its take-off and I felt the surge of power as we hurtled down the runway. As the wheels lifted off the German soil I pondered the problems that lay ahead. I wondered if I, and perhaps those above me, really understood the nature of what we were going into. I felt uneasy about the course the brigade might have to pick alone through political minefields. Our only companions once in Saudi Arabia would be the fair-weather friends of the media, who would be only too happy for us to stray off the path.

In military theory there are four levels of conflict: grand strategy, military strategy, operational and tactical. The highest level, grand strategy is the stuff of government. It is the application of national resources to achieve policy objectives. This includes the full range of diplomatic and economic resources as well as military. Military strategy is the application of military resources to achieve grand strategic objectives. In the Gulf campaign the British military strategy would be decided by the Ministry of Defence and the Joint Commander, Sir Paddy Hine.

The operational level is the link between the fighting, the tactical level, and military strategy. It is a rather nebulous concept, but in essence it requires one to consider the political aspects of one's actions as part of the strategic objectives and not just the fighting. For those of us brought up in the sterile atmosphere of the Cold War, the operational level of conflict barely existed below commander-in–chief's level. Our training and deployment were fixed and almost unchanging and, as a consequence, the political ramifications had long ago been sorted out. As a result I had no experience of the operational level of command.

What was clear to me, however, was that we were going to have to operate and run 7 Brigade at the operational, and not just the tactical, level of conflict. But as far as the Coalition, and perhaps our government, was concerned, we were simply one brigade among many and so spoke with the limited authority of that position. But to the British public, unused to military structures, whatever we said in the Gulf would be taken as government policy and thereby we could circumvent, if we were not careful, the higher command and political staff. There was of course the headquarters in Riyadh, hundreds of miles away, but on a day-to-day basis it was round 7 Brigade that the press would be hanging. I was beginning to understand this and the responsibilities it placed upon us, but I needed to make certain all commanders and our public relations staff in the brigade did as well. So on this flight there was no need to pretend to work, for I was inundated with papers to read, briefing notes to prepare, and the mental process necessary to sort out the wheat from the chaff.

When we landed at Riyadh some six hours later, and stepped out into that debilitating Middle Eastern heat, my first call was to General de la Billière. He had arrived in Saudi Arabia only two days before us, but seemed in his element. We had dinner that night in the hotel he was being forced to use as temporary accommodation. Our conversation was confidential, and had to be conducted in muted tones, broken off whenever anyone passed our table. Every now and again one of us would make furtive glances around the crowded room to see if anyone was paying too much attention to our talk.

We met once more in the morning to discuss our plans for the next few weeks. While waiting for the ships to arrive the commanding officers would get as many soldiers as possible into the desert to help the acclimatisation process. Once the tanks and Warriors arrived, my priority was to get the brigade to test-fire all its weapons. We wanted every soldier to have confidence in his equipment, from the 155mm artillery guns down to the hand grenade. We would need to construct our own ranges, and so would want an area, preferably near Al Jubayl, not being used by the marines and uninhabited by Arabs. General de la Billière gave me his promise to do what he could.

For the onward flight to Al Jubayl he lent me the RAF HS125 seven-seater blue and white executive jet assigned to him. The four-hundred-mile flight took just under an hour and there to greet me was Colonel Martin White.

Martin had been appointed to command the Force Maintenance Area. He was a perfect choice for the job as he had
spent his military career in the Royal Corps of Transport and
he was just the sort of man one would want to go to war with.
Utterly reliable, and a first-rate logistician, he would tackle
any problem with dogged determination and thoroughness.
He had been in Saudi Arabia now for a week having insisted
he be there to oversee the brigade's arrival.

Facilities in the port were basic. Lieutenant Colonel Barry
Aitken and the advance party of engineers had done well to
acquire anything at all, operating in the wake of the huge,
and richer, American resource teams. We were left with two
of the cavernous warehouses on the quayside to use as our
transit accommodation, each of which could hold up to five
thousand soldiers.

The warehouses, known as Sheds 4 and 5, were vast
hangars, dimly lit with no air conditioning. Their metal walls
and concrete floors offered no respite from the heat. It was
rather like living in a sauna. Without their equipment there
was little for the soldiers to do except sit around and wait and
go through time and again their NBC and first-aid drills.

The engineers from 39 Engineer Regiment had also
constructed a tented camp for another two thousand on
some hard standing in the port to house logisticians who
were likely to remain there after the rest of us deployed into
the desert. This quickly became known, first unofficially and
then officially, as Baldrick Lines, after the hapless manservant
in the *Blackadder* television series. (The soldiers adopted
Blackadder as something of a mascot. Baldrick's catch-
phrase. 'I have a cunning plan', became a running joke
for the next six months and later on in the campaign the
logisticians even adopted a *Blackadder* arm badge.)

The third site, known as Camp 4 and situated out of
the port towards the north of the town, was much more
promising. Built to house migrant workers, it was to prove
ideal as a temporary headquarters during the deployment
phase and as more accommodation. Later we were to use it
as a fitness and training centre. The camp comprised dozens

of accommodation blocks, sort of cream-coloured Portakabin affairs, each of which had ten rooms running off a central corridor. These four-man rooms had electricity and were air conditioned. In the centre of each block were showers and lavatories of a Western style. The major drawback was the state it was in after being hurriedly evacuated in August by the foreign workers. No fewer than two thousand soiled mattresses had to be burnt.

Sanitation, a problem we had prepared for when we moved into the desert, raised its unwelcome head in the port. The lavatories on the quayside were of Arabic design, and we quickly discovered their plumbing was altogether different from ours. The only clue you got was the curious tap, and the rubber pipe attached to it, beside the hole. Paper is unusual in the Arab world. In its place you use water and the left hand, hence the tap. You use your right hand to eat with. However the niceties of Arab customs in this respect were lost on the soldiers of 7 Brigade and in no time at all, between ourselves and the US marines, we had blocked the port's main sewer.

Very quickly the resources team managed to get hold of a few dozen Portaloos. But it was a brave soul who ventured into one of these in the midday sun – the stench was more than off-putting. Soldiers quickly became adept at finding out when they were going to be emptied, and would then make a dash for them as the now sweet-smelling hut was returned to action. They were also moved from time to time and inevitably one unfortunate chap got it wrong and was still enthroned when it was carried off.

Washing was equally a problem, both in the absence of showers and in meeting the huge demand for fresh water. Between our own engineers and the resourceful US marines and their 'Seabees' we managed to manufacture some shower stalls. The showers themselves were nothing more than watering can roses screwed into the bottom of red fire buckets, but they worked. But at the port's busiest, soldiers were managing perhaps not more than one shower every two days.

With nothing to do but sit around and wait for the ships,

mealtimes took on a huge importance. We were still at this stage being fed by the marines, both with their MREs (Meals Ready to Eat) and the once daily 'chow waggon' that served the hot food. It was a strong constitution that could cope with an MRE cold chicken curry for breakfast so the evening meal was for most the highlight of the day. Whatever I was doing I tried to make a point of making my way back to the port for it. The informality of a meal queue was the perfect opportunity to chat to the soldiers; I have never known one to miss the opportunity of quizzing senior officers in these circumstances. 'How long have we to put up with this crap food?' was the question asked most often, with a quickly remembered 'sir' tagged on the end as an afterthought. Despite the grim living conditions, morale seemed high.

Life in the port was something of a phoney war as we waited impatiently to move out into the desert. Each day the force built up, as aircraft ferried soldiers from Germany and, after 17th October, more and more ships arrived at the impressive Al Jubayl port. Each week a multi-national armada docked, flying all sorts of flags – Panamanian, Nigerian, Scandinavian, but few British. The first tanks arrived on board the landing-ship *Sir Bedivere* on 20th October. This Falklands veteran docked slowly, its square stern-doors opened and there in the hold we could see the sand-coloured Challengers.

The soldiers told varied tales of their sea voyage. Some had clearly enjoyed their time on their 'world cruise' with swimming pools and sun loungers, while others had had to make do with the cramped and austere life on a roll-on-roll-off container ferry. We had even managed to acquire an extra recovery vehicle. At Bremerhaven, where most of the vehicles loaded, a Foden recovery truck had been on stand-by for breakdown work. The driver, feeling a bit peckish, went in search of something to eat. The enthusiastic loading staff, seeing a truck on its own assumed it was ours and drove it on to the next available ship. The unfortunate driver returned from his lunch as the ship, with his truck in the hold, was just sailing.

*   *   *

As soon as every tank and Warrior had gone through a modification programme to cope with driving in fine sand we planned to move into the desert to start training as squadrons (fourteen tanks) or battlegroups (a mixture of tank squadrons, probably two, and infantry companies). The first few days would be for getting used to desert life and driving in sand. Once people were confident, then the regiments and battalions would have a few days of their own separate squadron, company and battery exercises. I and my headquarters staff would get involved at the battlegroup and brigade level. Then we would be ready for field firing. And of course deserts are a tactician's dream; nowhere else, not even at Suffield, in Canada, because of lack of space, could we exercise as a brigade.

Through this training we hoped to meld the disparate group 7 Brigade had now become into a team once more. Although the core of the brigade was used to working together, the tanks, infantry, artillery, and engineers, there were scores of other units now under my command for the first time. It was vital that they should all feel part of one team in this respect. One of the first things we had done was to give each man a 7 Brigade Desert Rat arm badge. Arm badges had been common in World War Two, and were still very much a feature of the American Army. However the British Army, not wishing units to be easily identified during the Cold War, had phased them out. We obtained permission to phase them back in.

The Royal Electrical and Mechanical Engineers, our mechanics, presented me with one of the biggest melding problems. The tank manufacturers Vickers, who had taken over responsibility for Challenger when they bought Royal Ordnance Leeds, were making a quite extraordinary effort to support us, putting their factory almost totally at the army's disposal. They had sent out an advisory team to help us. John Slade, and later Brian Trueman, the men in charge and both former Royal Tank Regiment officers, could not have been more helpful. Challenger, having been hurriedly brought into service to replace some of the ageing Chieftain tanks, was not a tank without problems. But Vickers, who had not designed it, maintained that some of the reliability shortfalls were due to poor maintenance. This made them unpopular with the REME, who had ultimate responsibility for the maintenance. As a result they were reluctant to talk to the Vickers team. For some time this was a ticklish problem and I could see the efficiency of the brigade was being put at risk by sensitivities. However, slowly there was an accommodation and they began to work together. The results were then quite excellent.

The RAF support helicopter squadron also gave me worries. Although the airmen were under my command I seemed to have no authority over the number of people they could bring with them, and inevitably they brought more than they had originally said they would. I was incensed to hear that their excellent commander had signed a million-pound contract to hire air-conditioned cabins for his pilots. And this at a time when the American helicopter pilots were quite literally living in holes in the ground next to their aircraft. Despite his bitter protestations, I cancelled the contract.

Unfortunately they were not the only people we upset. Our first battle with the Ministry of Defence happened rather sooner than I had expected. Not surprisingly, and predictably, it was over the media. At one of the press conferences, we were running one every second day, a photographer from *The Times* slipped away from our minders. It took twenty-four hours to find what he had done.

About eight o'clock on the evening of 19th October, the day before the tanks arrived and about a week into the campaign, a breathless Major James Myles, my public information officer, came dashing up to me, obviously agitated.

'Brigadier, I'm afraid there's been a bit of a problem back in London with our media coverage yesterday.'

'What exactly do you mean?' I asked anxiously.

'You had better read this,' he replied, handing me a signal from Brigadier Bryan Dutton, the Director of Army Public Relations, and a fax of the front page of *The Times*. It showed a photograph of two soldiers dressed in T-shirts and shorts carrying weapons. There was nothing particularly upsetting in that, I thought, until James read out the caption: 'Dressed to kill; Corporal Myles Sharman and John Shonfield on patrol in Saudi Arabia.'

I then read the signal. The whole Ministry of Defence seemed to be after my blood. Even Number 10 wanted to know what we were up to allowing soldiers to go on patrol dressed like that. My heart sank. Everything we had been striving to achieve in showing the army in a professional light seemed to collapse in an instant, all thanks to a photographer. I tried to telephone General de la Billière, but he was unavailable. So I called the Ministry of Defence direct and found Bryan Dutton in his office.

'What the hell do you expect, Bryan?' I shouted down the telephone. 'I've got a thousand bloody journalists breathing down my neck. Of course there're going to be mistakes. A photographer doesn't know when a soldier is on patrol and when he isn't. It's the editor's fault or the caption writer; I can't control that from here. That's your job.

'It seems also a gross distortion to accuse us of painting the army in a bad light. The truth of the matter is that the two soldiers were not on patrol when photographed. But because we haven't got an armoury everyone carries their gun with them. The same goes for the respirator.'

'Calm down, Patrick, it's all right. You and I know that, but they're a bit twitchy on the sixth floor [where the Secretary of State's office is]. It's all very early days and I think they were just flexing their muscles a bit.'

'You sent the message,' I retorted.

'Well, I rather had to; I am the Director of Public Relations.'

There was little that either of us could do except try to ensure it never happened again. To that end the first thing I did was to strengthen my public-relations team. I liked and trusted James, and knew that he knew his job, but he needed help. I decided to bring in someone senior so James could concentrate on the nuts and bolts of press relations. Chris Sexton, an extremely bright engineer major (and the army cricket captain) from John Moore-Bick's engineer regiment, was not commanding a squadron and I knew John could spare him. (The plan was later to cause me even more problems. To give him the authority he needed I made Chris a local lieutenant colonel. I later discovered I did not have the authority to make field promotions, but by then it was too late. He remained a lieutenant colonel for the duration of the war.) From that moment on and for the next two months public relations was first on the agenda at brigade conferences.

Within a week of the *Times* incident Sir Paddy Hine visited us. The party to meet him assembled at the sheds before driving to the northern airport. I had Mark Shelford with me, a 5th Royal Inniskilling Dragoon Guard captain I had seconded from the headquarters to act as my personal staff officer. I had known Mark for several years; he was an affable and very friendly officer who had transferred from the Royal Marines to the army. He was to prove exceptionally useful in arranging programmes for our constant stream of visitors and co-ordinating our work each day.

Travelling with us as well was Sergeant Thomas, the escort the military police insisted I had. It was felt, because of the terrorist threat, that I needed close protection. I originally balked at this waste of manpower but was over-ruled both by Riyadh and London, who did not want any embarrassing incidents.

The drive out to the airport took us through the outskirts of town. The Arabs, having been excited when we first arrived, now seemed oblivious to our presence. We passed through the US marine security at the airport just as the air marshal's aircraft came into view.

As we sped back to the port in Corporal Jameson's two-day-old Range Rover (Land Rover had given us two), Sir Paddy Hine and I chatted. He was irritated by the *Times* picture, the fall-out from which was still in the air. The only good thing to come from it, he said, was that the Secretary of State was keen to get the brigade into desert combat clothing as soon as possible.

Our first visit was to General Boomer. I sat in as the two men talked tactics. What had been planned as a twenty-minute office call turned into a major operational debate, the two feeding off each other's vastly different experiences. The rest of the morning was taken up visiting soldiers, talking to commanders and a quick flight around the marines' desert defences so that the air marshal could see for himself the problems we were going to encounter. When he departed he left behind his army chief of staff, Brigadier Philip Sanders, to conduct a more detailed reconnaissance, and with him Colonel Jo Gunnell, General de la Billière's chief of staff in Riyadh.

First we toured the newly erected 33 Field Hospital set up in a Goodyear tyre factory on the outskirts of Al Jubayl. Then, when travelling in convoy with the military police car behind us and speeding back to the port, disaster struck. Driving fast down a tree-lined avenue, where we had the right of way at each crossroads, I saw to our right a blue Mazda heading to challenge us at the junction ahead. It was one of those moments when time slows right down. I knew he was going to hit us. For most Arabs it is a case of 'Allah Rules' when driving. If Allah is with you, particularly at crossroads, you will be safe. The driver, without so much as a glance at his brakes or the give-way sign, smashed straight into our back wing with a sickening crunch. The road appeared to slide to one side. It took a few moments to realise what was happening, but then I calmly said to myself, 'We're rolling over.' The Range Rover flipped on to its roof and careered down the road with a screech of metal on tarmac.

'My God, they're trying to kill the commander,' shouted Jo Gunnell, travelling in the escort car behind us. The military-police driver of the back-up car suddenly realised his moment had come. Years of training were to culminate in this one instant. No terrorist was going to kill his charge. Swinging his white Sierra towards the now stationary Mazda he stamped his foot on the accelerator, smashing straight into the side of the car and sending it too reeling down the road.

When it came to a halt the Arab driver leapt out and ran to the Range Rover. I was hanging upside down. I remember clearly him looking through the shattered glass of my window and saying, in English, 'Oh shit', before lifting up his white robes and sprinting for the nearest building.

Suddenly Philip Sanders shouted 'Petrol – get out quick.' We fought our way through the shards of glass scattered everywhere, tearing palms and knees as we did so. Meanwhile, Jo, seeing the would-be assassin escape, drew his pistol and gave chase. The Arab, who we later discovered was an honest citizen who simply wished to call for an ambulance, had by this stage dived into an enormous white building, which happened to be a bank, with Jo hot on his heels. Bursting through the swing doors, Jo stumbled into a hall full of locals in identical white robes and red headdresses. Our man was nowhere to be seen. Pandemonium broke out. The bank guards, seeing the drawn pistol, set off the alarm.

Meanwhile, back on the road, the four of us – Corporal Jameson, Sergeant Thomas, Philip Sanders and myself – crammed into the smashed Sierra and limped back to the hospital we had left only a few minutes earlier, there to put a brave face on our wounds. But I did ask for the help of the physiotherapist, Mr Smith, and a trough full of painkillers.

Eventually, and with the sheds and tents overflowing, we left Al Jubayl and made for the desert. Not all the equipment had arrived. Ships had been held up because of storms in the Mediterranean. Almost unbelievably, one storm had washed some lorries, lashed to the upper deck, overboard. Nevertheless, to meet our commitment to General Boomer of being operational by 16th November, we could wait no longer. I also felt the media, and indeed the US marines, needed to be reassured that delays were not going to deflect us now or later.

There were other practical considerations as well. I knew from my two years spent in the Libyan desert when I first joined the army that skills, such as dead reckoning and desert navigation, would have to be learned. The maps looked like sandpaper. The countryside was featureless and disorientation could happen in seconds in a tank where the hull can point in one direction, the turret in another and the commander's sight in a third.

M109 guns of 40th Field Regiment, Royal Artillery loaded at the railway sidings at Hohne before being taken to the port of Bremerhaven near Hamburg in northern Germany.

Saturday 15th September 1990. The first of countless press facilities, this time at Fallingbostel, the home of most of the 7th Armoured Brigade.

Lieutenant Colonel John Sharples, commanding officer of the Royal Scots Dragoon Guards.

Lieutenant Colonel Arthur Denaro, commanding officer of the Queen's Royal Irish Hussars.

Lieutenant Colonel Charles Rogers, commanding officer of the 1st Battalion, The Staffordshire Regiment.

Lieutenant Colonel Rory Clayton, commanding officer of 40th Field Regiment, Royal Artillery.

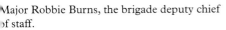

Lieutenant Colonel John Moore-Bick, commanding officer of 21 Engineer Regiment, Royal Engineers.

Major Robbie Burns, the brigade deputy chief of staff.

Major Alun Price, our senior padre.

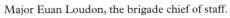

Major Euan Loudon, the brigade chief of staff.

Visitors came in their droves but we were always pleased to see them. On the left I am making a point to Paul Wolfowitz, the Under Secretary for Defense Policy in the Pentagon, Dick Cheney's second-in-command. On the right Admiral Bader and I greet our own Secretary of State for Defence, Tom King.

HRH Lieutenant General Khaled bin Sultan commands my tank during an exercise. Behind him is Major General Salih al-Muhaya, the Saudi Arabian Eastern Area commander.

Lieutenant General Walter Boomer, the general commanding the 1st Marine Expeditionary Force.

Air Chief Marshal Sir Paddy Hine, a frequent and most welcome visitor, who was the commander of the British forces. His headquarters was based at High Wycombe.

An unpleasant experience on the outskirts of Al Jubayl. Four of us crawled unhurt from our two day old Range Rover. Rumours circulated as to why the accident actually happened.

The fateful press briefing on 28th November 1990. Lieutenant Colonel Chris Sexton and I felt we had the situation in hand but the results, including an Iraqi propaganda leaflet, were surprising.

TONIGHT'S WEATHER: CLOUDY

WEST END FINAL

Evening Standard

LONDON, THURSDAY, 29 NOVEMBER, 1990   25p

British commander's warning as Gulf forces go on alert

'PREPARE FOR A BLOODBATH'

from Tim Barlass in Saudi Arabia

THE COMMANDER of the Desert Rats warned the British public today to prepare itself for a bloodbath if war broke out with Iraq.

Brigadier Patrick Cordingley said: "The public should be told that there will be a lot of casualties and that unpleasant things will unfold.

"When two armies of this size line up against each other, it is inconceivable that casualties are not going to be large."

As he spoke, allied forces in the Gulf were placed on alert for an Iraqi strike for the first time.

Troops were ordered to Air Raid Warning State Yellow—just one below full-scale attack—because of

Defiance of the hostage wives: Page 14

DEAR SOLDIERS :
YOUR COMMANDERS HAVE SAID THAT THE WAR WILL TAKE FEW DAYS WERE THEY CORRECT ? AND CONVINCED YOU THAT LOSES WILL BE MINIMUM IN THE GROUND COMBAT. WE ASSURE THAT THEY WONT BE CORRECT

SUNDAY EXPRESS

Cummings

SUPER GUN

Churchill didn't hide the truth

by ROWENA WEBSTER
the first British newswoman in the Gulf

BRIGADIER Patrick Cordingley has obviously had enough. For weeks the gangly commander of the Desert Rats has kept his Ministry of Defence bosses happy by keeping his lips tightly sealed about the horrors of war.

He had been told before leaving for Saudi Arabia in October to accentuate the positive aspects of Britain's role in the Gulf — and leave the negative questions about death and injury unanswered.

It is the MoD's belief that talking openly about the

So he broke the MoD conspiracy of silence, telling reporters at the 7th Armoured Brigade headquarters near the port of Al-Jubail that Britain had to brace itself for a very unpleasant war with heavy loss of life. "When two armies of this size line up against each other, it is inconceivable that casual-

aggressor who will one day threaten the world with nuclear weapons if he isn't stopped now.

It is a worthy cause.

But the MoD has kept us in the dark about the price our armed forces and the nation may have to pay.

The Brigadier knew blame be that did not lie with the media. A few weeks

of war can never be made public for reasons of safety and tactics but, as the Sunday Express has argued, the Ministry of Defence should take the public into its confidence, not seek to hide unpleasant truth from us.

Churchill did not hide the truth from Britain 50 years ago. He told the nation of the terrible price it would have to pay against Hitler — and the country rallied round him.

The Brigadier seems to be alone in understanding that. All we can hope is that he

I'm so proud of being Mrs King Rat

WIFE IN VIGIL

EXCLUSIVE from Kim Bartlett in Fallingbostel, Germany

THE wife of King Rat Patrick Cordingley spoke last night of her relief when told her "big man" had been spotted alive and well "somewhere in Kuwait."

Hoping . . . Melissa Cordingley with pet Muffin   Picture: IAN DERRY

20 FACTS TO PUT ON PARADE ABOUT OUR KING RAT PAT

By JOHN KAY

UR legendary Desert Rats were last night cked in battle with Saddam's troops in the Gulf nd war.

The 9,500 men in the 7th Armoured Brigade — e Rats' official name — have a key role in the ttle to free Kuwait.

Here are 20 things you never knew about King Rat — eir leader **BRIGADIER PATRICK CORDINGLEY**, 46:

▶ He once wore ORANGE pyjamas on NATO manoeu- vres in Germany. The rest of the Rats slept in their ilitary fatigues, but the Brigadier insisted on changing

▶ He is a brilliant mimic with a special line in impressions of politicians — former Prime Minister d Heath is his best. If he had not gone into the Army.

He puts on orange pyjamas and takes off ex-Premier Ted

Desert leader . . . Brigadier Patrick Cordingley

As time went by the embarrassment factor, especially in the tabloids increased, but the soldiers greatly enjoyed my discomfort.

The press, our constant companions. We laid on facilities for them on an every-other-day basis once we had deployed into the desert.

My tank, *Bazoft's Revenge*, was used to ferry visitors across the rugged terrain. Above, The Prince of Wales commands.

Below, the Secretary of State, Tom King, takes over with Lieutenant General Sir Peter de la Billière, the commander of the British Forces Middle East, in the loader's position.

On my first reconnaissance in early September I had been introduced to an entrepreneur, Peter Lenthall, who had persuaded me of the importance of satellite navigation. I had put in a request for a few trial sets. Using signals transmitted from satellites, a computer in these hand-held devices could give a ten-figure grid reference anywhere on the earth's surface. In layman's terms this meant you could always be within ten yards of the desired spot. They worked so well I put in a request for hundreds more, my aim being that every infantry platoon and tank should have one. By the time the ground war started there were at least two in every infantry company and nearly all the tanks had them.

I lived a peripatetic life, flitting from our training area to the port to Camp 4. Brigade-level exercises and, most important, firing were still a few days away and I had other matters to deal with. We had daily meetings with the marines to sort out endless problems; I had the inevitable hounding from the media, although I did get some respite when Chris Sexton packed them all off to the desert to watch the training; but most of all we had a constant stream of visitors.

On 28th October we were surprised by Paul Wolfowitz, the Under Secretary for Defense Policy in the Pentagon, the number two to Dick Cheney, the Defense Secretary. It was a scorching day, the sun was crashing down on our necks as Euan and I stood by one of the Challengers still in the docks, waiting for him. Coming towards us I could see a convoy led by a Humvee with a flashing yellow light and behind that a large mini-bus, behind which was another Humvee.

They came to a halt and heavily built bodyguards dressed in fatigues, wearing the ubiquitous dark glasses and carrying M-16 rifles, poured out. They stood around the mini-bus scanning the area while out stepped our visitor accompanied by an entourage of at least fourteen people.

We showed them over the tank. I pointed out the various key features, how we loaded the gun, the sort of rounds we used, their ranges. He was interested in the thermal night sight and wanted to know details of its specifications, but the heat was getting to us all so we headed for a small office in the shed where we could talk, and which was at least air conditioned. As soon as we got in he made his opening bid. 'General, how do you think we should go about getting Saddam Hussein out of Kuwait?'

I was surprised by the question. I had been prepared to talk about the Challenger or what we were doing and how we fitted in with the US marines, but it was clear he wanted to talk about the strategic issues. It was an unusual moment for a British brigadier with no authority for policy.

'Well, sir,' I said, rather hesitantly, 'I think the marines' plan of an attack straight into Kuwait is not such a good idea.'

'How so?'

'Two reasons. The odds are appalling. There are something of the order of thirty Iraqi divisions in Kuwait now. The Marine Corps has, what? – one large division. There's the US Army 24th Mechanical Division and a few others. Say five, maybe six divisions in all.

'In addition,' I went on, 'as soon as we hit that obstacle belt and start to bunch up behind it, he'll hit us with everything he's got, artillery and chemical. I don't think we are in any position to attack that way unless it is a diversion for something else.'

'How would you do it?'

'Go round the obstacles. Attack from the open flank, way out to the right, and cut through Iraq.'

'Through Iraq?'

'Yes, sir. Two very good reasons. Firstly, we don't have to go through the minefields, and secondly it draws him out of his dug-in defences and into the open. There we have the room to manoeuvre properly and we can fight on our own terms.'

I explained my reservations to this plan. I did not believe there was the political mandate to take the war into Iraq, and the move west was way beyond the logistic abilities of the force in Saudi Arabia at that time. It was doubtful, in my opinion, that, with what we had there and then, we could actually fight any kind of war save repelling an invasion.

When he left I got on to the secure telephone and called Riyadh, to tell them about the visit. About two hours later

I got a call back. They wanted to know exactly what I had said.

I woke early the next morning; we were expecting the Chief of the Defence Staff, Marshal of the Royal Air Force Sir David Craig. His was only a fleeting call, but as Britain's most senior serviceman, and one who had daily access to Mrs Thatcher and the Cabinet, he was a very important player. It was a cooler day, which was a shame. I had wanted him to experience at first hand just how oppressive it could be for the soldiers. We set off to meet him along the now familiar route from the port to the airport, but this time in a borrowed Toyota driven by Lance Corporal Dye. Sadly Corporal Jameson had not fully recovered from the Range Rover crash. As we went Mark Shelford briefed me.

'There has been a slight change in the plan, Brigadier. Sir David is arriving about ten minutes earlier. Apparently Admiral Badar wants to meet him, so I have squeezed him in right at the start.'

I had yet to meet Admiral Badar Saleh Al-Saleh, although as commander of the local naval base he was the senior Saudi service representative in the area. I knew we would be dealing with him to get permission to test-fire the tanks, so I was pleased he was to meet the Chief of Defence Staff.

'Then we will go straight from the airport to the port, where Euan will be waiting,' Mark continued. 'After your half-hour briefing the marines will fly us out to see the Scots Dragoon Guards. We need to be back at the airport by midday.'

We drove straight on to the tarmac. Sir David Craig's aircraft was not due for a couple of minutes. I looked around, but no Admiral Badar. 'I think your admiral must have better things to do, Mark,' I said, and thought no more of it.

I learnt later that forty miles away, on the other side of Al Jubayl, at the King Abdul Aziz Military Airport, the town's other airfield, Admiral Badar's blue Mercedes had pulled up. He had got out and brushed himself down. This was an important day, and one he was determined would go without a hitch. The VIP lounge, an enormous hall, had been redecorated; the beautiful fifteen-foot crystal chandelier had been cleaned, and the luxurious deep red carpet relaid the day before.

Across town, Sir David Craig's aircraft appeared in the distance, small and flying low. It taxied in, its bright white and red paint scheme glaringly out of place. He climbed out dressed in tropical combats with his blue peaked RAF hat and tan desert boots. Like all of us, he carried a gas mask around his waist. During the car journey back to the port I had thirty minutes of his undivided attention. There was one thing I wanted to talk to him about more than anything else – the media. 'I am concerned about the press,' I said as we sped past the familiar oil terminals. 'I am not at all convinced we are getting the right message put over or even if the press is behind us. I had a lot of problems with that picture in *The Times*, for instance.'

'Yes, so I've been told. But I think I can put your mind at rest,' he replied. 'As far as I am concerned we've had nothing but excellent coverage. Let me worry about reaction to the media, you worry about the Iraqis. That business over *The Times* was a storm in a teacup. You are bound to get one or two silly incidents, but the overall effect is extremely good. The press are definitely on our side.'

It was a great relief and it assuaged one of my major concerns. We talked about other lesser worries on the drive back. I was disturbed to hear that the Ministry was getting involved in some very low-level matters such as what soldiers wore when they boarded aircraft to fly to Saudi Arabia. Apparently they did not like to see them carrying briefcases, preferring rucksacks and rifles. It was better for the cameras.

Meanwhile, at the Abdul Aziz Airport, Admiral Badar realised something was wrong. He dispatched an aide to find out what had happened to this senior British officer. A few minutes later a nervous man returned. There had been a terrible mistake; the Englishman's airplane had changed airports and had already landed at the international airport. He was now on his way to the port. Furious, Admiral Badar got back into the car, slammed shut the door and shouted at his driver to get him to the international airport, where he would see the air marshal before he left.

Sir David Craig's visit was a success. The brief went smoothly; our flight out to the Scots Dragoon Guards was impressive. In the desert we were met by Mark Ravnkilde, a Dane by birth and one of the Scots Dragoon Guards' squadron leaders. He and his squadron were training in full chemical suits, masks included. The good impression that made on arrival was slightly lost when Mark took off his gas mask to reveal a beard. The poor chap was suffering from some kind of complaint which made it impossible for him to shave.

After a short interruption by the press we flew Sir David Craig back to the airfield. Following a few pleasantries on the tarmac, we waved him goodbye. As I walked back to the car, congratulating the staff on what I thought was a successful morning, I stopped short. I had completely forgotten about the admiral. Unfortunately he had not forgotten about us.

As I left the tarmac I noticed a large dark blue Mercedes waiting just outside the apron gate. It didn't occur to me for a few moments that this was the missing admiral. As we went through the gates I watched a smaller white car draw alongside and a number of Saudi naval officers start to shout at each other. Then the penny dropped.

This was potentially serious. The admiral had been at the airport but we had failed to see him and, more importantly, he had failed to meet the Chief of the Defence Staff. If he treated it as a snub it could cause problems. We were learning that matters of Saudi honour were not to be brushed off lightly, so I went straight over to make profuse apologies and try to ease a potential diplomatic incident. As I approached the huge Mercedes sped off, leaving only the white car, full of perturbed naval officers. Fortunately a Saudi naval captain spoke excellent English. I suggested I go immediately to the naval base, introduce myself to the admiral, and make my apologies on behalf of Sir David Craig. This, the captain thought, was a good idea, and he would lead us there.

The base was about as far away from the airfield, and the port, as one could get and still remain in Al Jubayl. Even following the white car, driven I could only imagine with the guidance of Allah, it took us over an hour to get there. An enormous arch leading to the base was set back from the road leading to Dhahran. The headquarters, like every government building in Saudi Arabia, was immaculate. The lawns in front, clearly constantly watered, were a luxuriant green. We followed closely behind the captain's car in our Toyota and drove under the arch, on the top of which flew a huge Saudi flag. About two hundred yards on the right-hand side we pulled up outside a white, flat-roofed, two-storey building.

I was then escorted by the captain to the admiral's outer office. Behind a large desk sat an even larger officer. Despite the air conditioning he was mopping his brow with a silk handkerchief. After a muted exchange between the two, I was asked to wait while they went through another door into what I guessed was the admiral's office. Although the door was closed I could hear raised voices. A few minutes later I was shown in.

It was probably one of the smartest offices I had ever been in. Lining the walls were white leather chairs above which, almost obscuring the decoration, were plaques and photographs of passing dignitaries and visiting ships, and assorted certificates and awards. In the middle of the room were three white leather chairs and a glass-topped table. In the far corner was a mahogany desk at least eight feet across. Behind it sat the admiral.

I waded through the carpet and saluted him. A small man, perhaps five foot six inches tall, he was dressed in Saudi summer uniform – light khaki shirt with a name tag and several rows of ribbons, and trousers with a thin web belt. On his shoulders lay the opulent gold epaulettes of a rear admiral.

He spoke very good English, with a faint American accent. We sat down and I was offered a cup of coffee, just one, which I took to be the rebuke. He could not have been more charming. In typical Saudi way we made small talk before getting down to business. I apologised as best I could for our unchivalrous behaviour and promised if Sir David Craig were to visit again I would do my best to ensure they met.

He took it all with good grace, assured me there was no ill feeling, and after about twenty minutes I left. Unexpectedly I felt I had made a good friend, and one who would be very useful to us. I hoped he felt the same.

I did not realise then how quickly I was to need this friendship.

Chapter 4

Tuesday 30th October to
Tuesday 6th November 1990

There were few tears shed when the fighting element of the brigade finally left Al Jubayl. The monotony and appalling conditions were soon forgotten. The Saudis had given us a huge area of rolling desert in which to train. Al Fadili, as the area was called, was barren – mile upon mile of sand dunes, broken only by small gorse-like prickly bushes a couple of feet high. In fact this was prime camel-grazing land at that time of year and there were hundreds of camels in herds all over the area. A herd is allowed to wander, sometimes as much as a hundred miles, and is rounded up only occasionally, either to be checked over or to be milked. Arabs drink the milk either fresh and warm, or else allow it to curdle slightly, rather like a yoghurt. In the former state it is, as I found to my cost, an effective laxative.

We were briefed that there were no wild camels in Saudi Arabia so if we injured one – when, inexplicably, only the owner could put it out of its misery – we would have to pay compensation. An average camel was valued at around £1,000 but we guessed a racing one, which the soldiers reckoned it was bound to be, could be ten times that amount.

We laid down strict rules on what to do if camels strayed into the range once we were given permission to start firing. If it was a herd then all firing was to stop immediately and the herd would have to be cleared. If individual camels were seen, then firing could continue but soldiers were to exercise extreme caution. This sort of policy was not new to the British army. The live-firing range in Canada is a wildlife reserve and home to several herds of wild horses as well as to pronghorns and numerous other animals. Firing is always suspended for the horses.

While the regiments busied themselves with low-level training I had more visits to make. I had been told it would be politic for me to tip my hat to three local dignitaries. Admiral Badar I had already met, but I had yet to visit either the Emir of Al Jubayl or the chairman and chief executive of Yusuf Bin Ahmed Kanoo. This was the tenth largest firm in Saudi Arabia. It dealt with travel, import, export and seemingly pretty well everything else. I became acquainted with the name of its chairman, Abdulla Ali Kanoo, almost from the minute we landed. Nearly every contract we signed, from accommodation to bottled water, had made some reference to the company.

Mark and I, accompanied by a British interpreter, Major John Rigby, went to his office in Damman, about an hour's drive from Al Jubayl. There we were met by an elegantly dressed assistant who carried out the introductions. Our host, dressed in traditional robes, stood up and greeted me in English, shaking my hand. While we chatted we had the inevitable coffee. He told me proudly of his eight houses in London and how much he enjoyed visiting them.

'Really the finest of all Europe's capitals I believe,' he said with the certainty of one clearly in a position to judge.

'Well, actually I live in London as well,' I said.

'Oh,' he replied, 'I'm sure it must be a lovely house, big and spacious.'

'Oh . . . Something like that,' I replied, a mental picture of our very modest three-bedroomed, subsidence-prone terraced house in Fulham forming in my mind. 'Quite large.' After more small talk, he made a speech and presented me with a lavishly illustrated book about Saudi Arabia. In return I gave him a NAAFI-produced '7th Armoured Brigade in the Arabian Peninsula' plaque, making a mental note that we really had to do something about our presentations, especially as 'Peninsula' had been spelt with an 'r' at the end. We all then went across the road to his apartment to eat.

The dining room was large and traditional. The table was covered with a finely embroidered red and gold cloth; the floor was laid with heavy Persian carpets. I sat next to our host.

'As this is only lunch,' he said, 'it is a small meal. We are not having the whole sheep, only four legs of lamb.' Servants carried in enormous trays piled high with food – the promised lamb, rice, salads, all manner of other dishes – and laid them on the table. Abdulla took a plate for me and piled it with food.

As the meal went on, and on, I began to feel more and more bloated. At each course, and I lost count of how many there were, our host would explain what it was, how it was made and how we should eat it. The lamb came and went, as did a sort of couscous and an array of salads and various fruits. And each time I forced the last few mouthfuls down to clear my plate it was replenished.

'I see you have a fine appetite,' my host complimented me.

By three in the afternoon I was defeated. Inventing an excuse to get back to work, I bade him farewell. As we drove north, John said, 'I say, sir, you did do rather well there. You don't normally eat like that do you?'

'You must be joking,' I replied. 'He wouldn't stop piling it on; what could I do?'

'Oh,' he replied knowingly, 'were you not briefed about Arab meals? It's quite acceptable to leave food, in fact it's expected. What we didn't eat will go to the servants. Traditionally, when an important guest visited a village the finest animals would be slaughtered. The rest of the village wouldn't have minded because they would be sure to get their share of the food. But if a visitor ate all the food it would leave the villagers with nothing at all. As you cleared your plate every time, he obviously thought you were just unusually hungry.'

*   *   *

A few days later I was better prepared when we paid a call
on the Emir of Al Jubayl. With Mark and Sergeant Thomas
in tow, I set off from the port to the emir's compound. With
us came Bill Knight-Hughes, one of many infantry officers on
loan to my headquarters, who was acting as a liaison officer to
the local dignitaries. He had already been to see the emir,
to set up this meeting. It was the emir, along with Admiral
Badar, who had allowed us to use the training area and was
clearing it of Bedouin, or trying to.

The emir's compound was near the edge of town. As we
went through the gate a short datepalm-lined drive opened
up before us; on either side were luxuriant green lawns, not
of grass, but of a much coarser, almost round-leaved plant
that looked like a weed.

We pulled up at the heavy front door, guarded, as every
public building was, by armed sentries. As we entered the
surprisingly crowded hall I was talking to Bill and almost
walked straight into someone. Turning to make my apologies
I saw standing in front of me an ancient Saudi in flowing
brown Bedouin robes. His gnarled face, the colour of a
ripe chestnut, was almost hidden beneath his red *ghotra*
(headdress); across his shrunken chest hung two bandoleers
of ammunition. Over one arm was slung a wooden-stocked
bolt-action rifle, probably as old as he was. He seemed
delighted to see us. '*A-salaam 'alaykum*,' he greeted us
repeatedly, baring his few remaining blackened stumps of
teeth while taking my hand in both of his and shaking it
enthusiastically. '*W'alaykum a-salaam*,' I replied, with one
of the few snatches of Arabic I knew. It was the traditional
greeting.

Still smiling broadly he walked out, his numerous family
following him. Right at the back was a beautiful girl I
assumed to be his daughter. What surprised me was that
her face was totally uncovered. She looked at me unsmiling
as she walked past.

'They must have just been to see the emir,' Bill said.
'Everyone in the town has the right of audience. The emir
sets aside two days a week to hear grievances and will then
rule on them. They just turn up and are shown in. There're

no appointments or anything like that.' It turned out that the family had been evicted by their landlord and had come to the emir for help. He had promised to find them money to stay in their home.

The emir's office, unlike Abdulla's, unlike Badar's, was modest. And, unlike the other men, he was surrounded by heavily armed guards. The emir himself was a smallish man, dressed in a well-cut Western-style suit. After the introductions we moved over to one of his sofas as the coffee arrived. The waiter, if that's what he was, was obviously not to be out-gunned. As he bent down to offer me a cup his hunting rifle slipped off his shoulder and fell forward, gently grazing my nose.

The emir spoke excellent English – he had, I later discovered, been educated for two years in England. I was amazed and embarrassed when he told me just how many people had to move to make way for our training. I had understood the area was almost uninhabited, save a few camel boys. But there were apparently hundreds of nomads who had, he assured me, been happy to move. Arab culture demands that guests be made at home, so much so that an Arab would give way without protest to anyone who wished to move on to a piece of ground where his home or tent was. The emir's main concern, as was mine, was that we might start firing while someone was still in the area – with the obvious awful consequences.

It was with that admonition that I opened the training conference the next day to discuss the firing programme with the five commanding officers – Arthur, Charles, John Sharples, John Moore-Bick and Rory – along with Euan, Bill Knight-Hughes, Robbie Burns and my deputy, John Milne.

The firing was to be done in phases. Armour, infantry and artillery would first of all practise on their own. Next we would get squadrons, companies and batteries working and firing as teams. Then we could start the business of live firing in battlegroups – all-arms units made up of tanks, infantry, engineers and artillery, each battlegroup being commanded by one of the three regimental headquarters.

By the end of the conference we had a timetable. We had committed ourselves to being operational by 16th November, a date the Secretary of State had already made public, so time was not on our side. Live firing was scheduled to start on 6th November and continue to the 13th. After two more maintenance days, we would be operational by the 16th.

The aim in this period was to raise confidence – confidence of the men in their equipment, of the regiments in the brigade, of the marines and the general public back in England in us. Although we got on well with the marines, it was clear the American Army had doubts about our capabilities. They knew, for instance, about the Challenger's reliability problems. We had to show it was a war-winning tank and demonstrate our professionalism and preparedness.

I was also under the impression that the marines thought we were a slightly undisciplined lot. They were incredibly smart and highly professional. Everything seemed to be done at the double, everyone looked good, everyone had an air of determination. We, on the other hand, liked to present a more casual appearance which I suspected they took the wrong way. It did not help that we were pretty scruffy at times, with tank soldiers in their overalls, the infantry in jungle camouflage and others in all manner of dress. Desert fatigues, which had started to arrive, would solve the uniform problem; a really aggressive and hard-hitting training programme would show them what we were capable of.

Firing would also inspire confidence in the men in their own abilities. In peacetime safety on ranges is of paramount importance and there are very strict rules. We were going to break almost all of these, for two reasons. First, I simply did not have the manpower to provide safety staff. The second reason was psychological. There are no safety staff in war. Each soldier had to become his own safety officer – it was going to be up to him to judge whether to pull the trigger or not. We needed to drive out our peacetime thinking and procedures and inculcate an aggressive, determined fighting spirit. All of us had to realise that each one of us was responsible for his own actions, right or wrong.

One of my earliest conversations with General de la Billière had been on just this subject. I felt it was inevitable soldiers would be killed in training, particularly when we started firing, and I could just imagine the field day the press would have when it went wrong. 'What an incompetent army we have; they can't even train without killing each other; heaven knows what will happen when they meet an enemy that shoots back, etc.' What this would do to public morale and confidence in us was obvious. The general was completely supportive. With his SAS background he of all men knew the importance of realistic training. He gave me his word that he would stand right behind me. Nevertheless it was another unwelcome but unavoidable pressure.

I had put Bill Knight-Hughes in charge of organising and setting up the range. It was big, although not as big as I would have wanted. About twenty miles long east to west, and, at its widest, about eight miles wide north to south, it was an area of some eighty-five square miles, room enough for all the infantry ranges, with their mortars, anti-tank missiles and small arms, and also for a limited tank battle run, an artillery impact area and an engineer demolition area.

Then there was the problem of targets. What would we shoot at? For the infantry this was not too much of a problem. The standard military target, a 'figure 11', is a man-sized figure printed on paper, glued to plywood. It was not difficult for the engineers to construct these. Some tank targets are also simply plywood, or hessian screens with tank figures painted on them, and these we could construct as well. But tank crewmen like to have something more solid to shoot at. Hitting a plywood screen at two miles' range is not very satisfactory.

Tanks fire both kinetic-energy rounds and chemical-energy rounds. A kinetic round, known as a fin, is in essence a large, very dense dart made of tungsten. Later variants use depleted uranium, which are not radioactive, but are even denser. Fired at over three thousand miles per hour, it simply smashes through tank armour, but it makes only the smallest of holes in a screen.

Chemical-energy rounds are so called because they contain high explosive. The British round, High Explosive Squash Head (HESH), has a 'soft' head. When the round hits a tank the head 'pancakes' or flattens out. An instant later the shell is detonated from the base, sending a shock wave down the round and, because of the pancaked soft head, into the armour. Inside the tank the shock wave rips off a scab of razor-edged metal, sending it flying around at very high speeds, destroying anything in its path.

On established tank ranges 'hard targets' are provided. These are either old tanks that have been bought for scrap, or something similar. For a long time the army tank gunnery school in Lulworth Cove used the armour plating from HMS *Ark Royal*. When you hit a 'hard' target with a kinetic round it produces a blinding burst of light, a chemical round erupts in a ball of flame. These effects are what tank crewmen want to see. I threw the problem at the engineers. What could they provide? On the day Bill started to set up the range they turned up with fifty rotting car hulks. Someone had been round to the local scrap dealer and bought half his stock. They made excellent targets.

It was not long before I got a call from General de la Billière, who was keen to see what we were up to. We arranged a visit for 1st November. At the same time, and by pure chance, we had discovered the existence of a number of Kuwaiti helicopters and pilots in Al Jubayl sitting around with nothing to do. About a dozen pilots has escaped the invasion in their Gazelle and Puma helicopters – similar helicopters to the ones the British Army use.

The night before the general's visit I had made some tentative calls to Riyadh and the Army Air Corps, with whom I was still unpopular for not including them in the original order of battle, and told them of my change of heart; I was now thinking about requesting four Gazelles in theatre. They were astonished, but delighted. What I did not tell them was the real reason. A flight of helicopters would deploy with its own support in the shape of specialist aviation mechanics and supply staff. Once they were here there would be no reason why they should not maintain the identical Kuwaiti Gazelles as well as our own. That way I would have a much larger force and, more importantly, we would execute a neat political coup, very good for Anglo-Kuwaiti relations. Stage one of the plan was to win over the general, who was rather surprised when I turned up at the airport to meet his HS-125 in a Kuwaiti Gazelle and not the usual Marine Corps Huey. I introduced the pilot, a charming captain who spoke excellent English. He told the general how he had been forced to leave his wife and family behind when the Iraqis came. He nearly blew my delicate plan when he went on to say how pleased he was that he would be able to fight alongside the British. General de la Billière looked puzzled but said nothing. As we climbed into the Gazelle he turned to me and muttered 'I say, Patrick, I hope this chap doesn't decide to fly north.'

'Don't worry, General,' I replied. 'My pistol is loaded.'

The general had had his own political coup. He had managed to persuade Prince Khaled bin Sultan, the joint commander-in-chief of the Coalition forces, to pay us a visit. A lieutenant general and Chief of Air Defence, Prince Khaled was also a son of King Fahd's brother, the Defence Minister, Prince Sultan. His connections were impeccable. We were both very aware of the potential for sales in the region after the war, however distasteful this seemed while preparing to fight.

I sounded General de la Billière out on my plan for the Kuwaiti helicopters. He liked the thinking, but did not believe it would be feasible. The Coalition had agreed that all Arab forces would fight together. He would raise the matter with Prince Khaled, but doubted he would agree.

The visit went well. The general's quiet manner and slow, deliberate delivery when talking to me or General Boomer changed totally when he was with the soldiers, with whom he became totally relaxed and at ease. They, in turn, warmed to him. His SAS beret and wings, which he always wore, earned him enormous prestige and admiration, but his demeanour was his most powerful asset.

As I was saying goodbye at the airport, after a day in which we had visited every regiment in the brigade, he dropped his bombshell. 'Oh, Patrick,' he said in passing as we walked over to his jet, 'I would like your staff to work out how we could reinforce 7 Brigade should the Cabinet think it a good idea.' I didn't think this was necessary but said, 'Of course, General, we will get on with it straight away. But what sort of reinforcements are we talking about?'

'Oh, I don't know, say up to a division.' And with that he boarded his airplane and left.

'Reinforcements,' I said to myself as I walked back across the tarmac wondering why this should be thought necessary in the present circumstances. Try as I might I couldn't put the curious idea out of my mind.

On one of the evenings in when I was not in the desert but at Camp 4, General Boomer invited me to a small dinner at his headquarters. At about six in the evening as the sun began its rapid descent, I drove through the port to the familiar two-storey headquarters building. The thought of dinner was appealing. Also I enjoyed the company of the marine generals. The 1st Marine Expedition Force commander was an affable man, unpretentious, intelligent and thoroughly likeable. Like all the senior officers he had served in Vietnam, and he had earned two Silver Stars, a Legion of Merit and two Bronze Stars. His obvious ability had been spotted early on and he had rocketed up the command structure to make lieutenant general at the age of fifty-one.

My immediate superior, Mike Myatt, a forty-nine-year-old Californian with an angular face and silver-white hair, was perhaps more as one would expect a US marine general to be. He was clearly one for leading from the front. I picked up a slight tension between him and his boss. I think it was felt that he could be a bit impetuous. He, too, was delightful company and I suspected would be a real friend. A quiet dinner with them seemed the ideal way to spend the evening.

So it was something of a surprise, as we rounded a corner, to see the helipad behind the headquarters packed with helicopters, and not just the usual Marine Corps Hueys but Blackhawks as well. 'But surely only the US Army use those,' I said to myself.

'Over here, Patrick,' a voice shouted in the fast-descending gloom. It was Mike. 'We were just beginning to wonder where you were.'

I looked at my watch. I was about ten minutes late – politely late, I thought. I walked over to Mike and we shook hands. 'The dinner is in here,' he said, leading me into a building I had not noticed before. As we walked in it struck me that there was an awful lot of noise for just a handful of officers. The room was packed. At first I wondered who they all were, as every one of them was dressed in identical US-issue 'chocolate-chip' fatigues. But then I started to pick out the ranks, and most of them were generals.

The Americans have wonderfully simple insignia for their generals. Brigadier generals have a single star on each lapel, major generals have two, lieutenant generals three, full generals four. A general of the army (the equivalent of a field marshal), if they had any (the last was Eisenhower), would wear five. I could see an awful lot of stars. I soon learnt that gathered in this one room was every senior formation commander in the US Army in Saudi Arabia and their chiefs of staff.

During dinner I sat between Major General Ed Scholes, chief of staff of XVIII Airborne Corps, and Major General Binnie Peay III, commanding general of the 101st Air Assault Division. It was a humbling experience mixing with these men, even more so when they told me of the sort of firepower and equipment they had available. The 101st Air Assault Division, 'The Screaming Eagles', had four-hundred-odd helicopters, more than the British Army and RAF combined. During a chat after dinner with Major General Barry McCaffrey, the commanding general of the 24th Mechanised Infantry Division, the only really heavy force the Americans had in Saudi Arabia, I discovered we were not really comparing like with like when discussing capability. An American division like his, although it had about the same manpower, had considerably more combat power than a British armoured division.

But despite the force now deployed, the overwhelming impression I got was that no-one was properly balanced. Lieutenant General Gary Luck, commanding general of XVIII Airborne Corps, which comprised the 101st, the 82nd Airborne ('The All Americans') and the 24th Mechanised Divisions, admitted a Coalition attack was not a possibility at that moment. He was, he said, barely ready to defend Saudi Arabia. His soldiers had nicknamed themselves 'Iraqi speed bumps'; they could only hope to slow down Saddam Hussein on his drive towards Riyadh. But reinforcements, such as my brigade, were arriving all the time, I argued. The Coalition would certainly be ready to stop any further Iraqi aggression by 16th November. The date seemed important to us all.

I flew out to the ranges next morning via Mike Myatt's headquarters. Unlike my own headquarters, which was housed in armoured vehicles, much of the 1st Marine Division's was in tents and lorries. It had a large area under canvas, the Combat Operations Centre (COC), around which were the various supporting units, such as a communication centre and a cookhouse. The whole affair was circled by triple-decked barbed wire. Marines in trenches, armed with machine guns, were on guard.

Near the COC was Mike's tent. As I walked up to it I saw him sitting outside, his helmet and webbing by his feet. The tent was under a huge camouflage net to provide shade. In front was laid out a bright green square of Astroturf. An aluminium table, upon which was the inevitable bottle of iced water and a tray of biscuits, was covered in maps and papers. Beside the tent was a trench with a field telephone sitting in the bottom, the wire running towards the COC.

We went over details of our firing programme and of an exercise immediately after for which he had agreed to lend me troops to act as enemy. Sticking to the policy of trying to give confidence, I deliberately laid it on thick when talking about the firing programme. I knew they had just completed firing, but their tanks had only fired when static at static targets. We were planning tactical exercises, passing one squadron through another, then bringing in the infantry to clear trenches, while targeting artillery fire to within fifty yards of the advancing troops.

'That's some programme, Patrick,' he said when my presentation was over. 'I'd sure like to watch some of that.' He was clearly impressed. And I hoped it was going to work.

I awoke early the next day, just before dawn, and watched the sun rise, feeling its rays drive out the chill of a desert night. We stood to and every soldier not manning radios was in his trench, gun loaded, and watching. Twice a day at dawn and at dusk the brigade would stand to. Historically these are the most likely times for an attack, and although we were miles from the front line it was a good routine and good training. It was also a daily reminder that this was not an exercise.

When stand-to was over and after a cholesterol-laden breakfast of fried everything served in oil I made my way over to my tank. The last time I had commanded from a tank was when running my own regiment. It was usual for brigade commanders in Germany to control their brigades from the back of a command vehicle designed specifically for the purpose. In the Gulf I believed a tank was going to be more appropriate, but this needed some justification. In war, when you know where you are going but have very little idea what the enemy will do, a distinction between command and control very quickly appears. The control measures are given out in the opening orders; command is coping with a fast-moving fluid battle.

Clearly, while initial orders were being prepared I needed to be with my staff to direct and advise. Once the operation was under way I had to be able to talk to the troops and also to my staff, which meant I needed to be on a radio net. I had to be able to see, or sense, the battle the brigade was fighting. If I could not actually see it I had to be poised to go to a problem area so that people would not have to waste time describing the ground to me. This would expose me to danger so I needed protection.

The obvious solution was to be in a tank. It has excellent protection, speed, communications and sights. I could get anywhere on the battlefield yet remain in contact with my staff and commanding officers. Having been 'brought up' in a tank and commanded a regiment of fifty-seven from the cramped commander's seat with a map on my lap and a pair of headphones over my ears, I was confident I could command my brigade from one as well.

My crew – the driver, Trooper McHugh, Corporal Smith, who commanded the tank when I was not in it, Lance Corporal McCarthy, the gunner, and Lance Corporal Shaw, the radio operator and loader of the gun – had taken down the camouflage nets as soon as stand-to was over and had the tank ready. I walked round to the front, put one foot on the towing hook and hauled myself up. Avoiding McHugh's head, I walked up the glacis plate. As I did so I noticed two words painted in black on the side of the fume extractor in the middle of the 120mm gun – *Bazoft's Revenge.*

'What's this all about?' I asked McHugh.

'Brigadier, you said all tanks were to be named by the end of the week.'

'But I meant names like Wellington or Montgomery, names of towns where you live. Anyway, who on earth is Bazoft?'

I felt embarrassed when I was given the explanation – I should have remembered that in March 1990 Farzad Bazoft had been hanged by the Iraqis for spying. At the time of his alleged offence, photographing a military installation near Baghdad, he was working for the *Observer* newspaper. His death, I recalled, had caused indignation at home but the stir had subsided quickly.

'That's brilliant,' I shouted back. 'We will keep that name.'

As I climbed into the turret I could hear the whine of the cooling fans inside the radios, the laser, the air filters and the hiss of static from the headphones in the helmet Corporal Shaw handed me. Dropping through the open hatch I stood on the commander's seat and pushed the helmet microphone in front of my mouth.

'Morning, team,' I said as I adjusted my sun-goggles.

There were various replies and from that I knew they could all hear me. After a check to make sure we all had our guns with us, and a look round to ensure everything was correctly stowed I said, 'Right, McHugh, lets go.'

I felt the clunk of the handbrake releasing and slowly the sixty tons of tank crept forward, the 1200-horsepower Perkins diesel engine bursting from a rumble to a roar with a cloud of blue-grey smoke forced out of the exhaust. As we picked up speed I dropped down into the turret so that only my head and shoulders were exposed. It was exhilarating. For the first time for ages I was on my own, just me and my crew. I could forget the worries of the media, and the pressure of decision-making. For the next few hours I wanted to get used to commanding a tank again and to advise on the setting up of the range. The sand was surprisingly thick and as the sun warmed it it expanded, making it even heavier going. It took us two hours to go only twenty-two miles.

The range area was softly rolling, with small valleys. Unfortunately the battle run lay across the grain, which meant one was for ever slewing from side to side to get round berms and high ground. But I had a clear idea of where I wanted the targets to go when firing started in a couple of days' time and I found the work relaxing despite the heat. Halfway through the afternoon I had an urgent call. I was needed in Al Jubayl. Mike Myatt wanted to see me there. I drove the two hours back and went straight to General Boomer's headquarters. I found Mike in one of the planning offices. He looked up as I came in.

'I think you have a big problem,' he said. 'When do you start firing?'

'Tomorrow,' I replied. 'Why?'

'I don't think you'll be able to. I've just heard that you have not been given permission to fire.'

'What do you mean?' I demanded.

'Just that. You can't fire. Someone has screwed up.'

My first thought was what was this going to look like to the media. They would make mincemeat of us and the Saudi Arabians. So much for a Coalition all pulling together. We had to resolve this now.

I drove back to Camp 4 where I had secure communications with Riyadh, and tried to reach General de la Billière, but he was out. I spoke to various staff officers, each one getting more and more of an earful as time went on. It had been quite clear where our responsibilities lay, and what the headquarters in Riyadh was going to do to help us. We had set the range up, moved all the camels and tribesmen out, spoken to the emir, arranged the safety patrols. They had been responsible for the political liaison.

To my utter frustration the problem rattled on for the rest of the afternoon without resolve. I seemed unable to re-trace the circuitous path by which permission had to be given. By ten that night I was still no clearer. I got hold of Euan on the radio. 'Tell the regiments to stand down,' I said. 'There will be no firing tomorrow.'

At six o'clock the next morning I started to try to resolve the problem again. I planned to go straight round to the marines. On my way I bumped into Jerome Nunan, a captain who was our liaison officer at Admiral Badar's base.

'What do you know about this monumental cock-up over firing?' I asked. I wondered if the naval base was involved in any way.

'Has that still not been resolved?' he asked.

'You know about it?' I demanded.

'Yes, Brigadier. The Saudis told the marines last week you wouldn't be able to fire. Some problem with the aircraft. They told the American training officer, a colonel I think, about three days ago. But since they didn't hear anything back, I guess they figured you weren't bothered.'

'Come with me,' I said. 'We're going to find this man.'

The colonel occupied a small office tucked away in the port. 'You do realise,' I said as I walked straight in, 'that you have single-handedly buggered up the training of my entire brigade?'

After an acrimonious, and mainly one-sided debate I at last had a clue as to where the problem lay – in the air-space control above the range. Someone had failed to issue a NOTAM, a notice to airmen warning them of the danger.

'How did we do that?'

'I think you had better speak to the Saudis,' the colonel suggested.

We drove as fast as we could to the naval base. The Saudi liaison officer was a delightful man called Commander Ghazi. I explained our problem to him.

'Oh dear,' he said. 'We had better speak to the admiral.'

Once again I found myself in the cavernous office. The admiral was clearly irritated by the affair.

'Why should anyone want to stop you firing? Someone is making a lot of fuss over nothing,' he said, clearly upset that everything had not gone well. I explained the problem with the aircraft.

'Well, what do you want me to do about it? I'm an admiral, not an airman. You must talk to the air force,' he said, but by now smiling.

'Sir, I would be delighted to. Where do I find them?'

He turned to Ghazi and fired a question at him. Ghazi thought for a minute and then turned to me. 'We must go to Dhahran.'

As quickly as I could I found Major John Rigby and Captain Yusuf bin Musa'id bin Abdul Aziz, our newly appointed Saudi interpreter, and with Ghazi we set off on the hour's drive south.

Ghazi directed us to the Dhahran International Airport, home also of the Eastern Command Air Forces. Pulling up at a rather shabby building in the military area we piled out of the cars and were shown upstairs into a conference room. We were already expected, for there to meet us were two Saudi air-force officers, one a lieutenant colonel and a royal prince, Saad bin Fahd Abdul Aziz, the other a major; both were dressed in flying suits.

The air-force prince explained the situation. First, the Saudis were, quite understandably, controlling the air space over their own country. Secondly, our range lay right beneath the main flight path for aircraft coming and going to patrol along the border with Kuwait. These would not be able to overfly if we were firing and as aircraft were going up and back every half an hour this was a considerable problem. They were insistent that we would have to move our range.

Argument ensued. Ghazi, arguing on our behalf, made an emotional plea about how many families had been moved, and how the honour of the emir was at stake, and so on. I tried to give way as much as possible. I kept reminding everyone that we were all here to do the same job, defend their country, and we had to work together. After about thirty minutes the two airmen backed away from the table and conferred. The air-force prince then turned to me and said, this time using the interpreter, although he spoke immaculate English, 'I think we can compromise. What is the ricochet height of the rounds you are firing?'

I stared blankly at him. I didn't have the faintest idea. Without obviously betraying my position I looked at John Rigby. With the smallest of gestures, he shrugged his shoulders. Then, staring straight at the colonel, I said, 'Five thousand feet for tank rounds, two thousand feet for small arms.' The two airmen leaned back and started to debate this in Arabic. Turning back to John, I whispered into his ear, 'Nip out and get on the phone to Riyadh and find out what the ricochet height really is.' He made his excuses and left.

My made-up heights seemed to have broken the ice with the Saudis. 'This is not such a problem,' the prince said. 'I am sure we can work this one out.' As they argued among themselves and with Ghazi, John came back. 'Sir, a word,' he whispered in my ear.

'Would you excuse me?' I said as we both went outside. 'What is the real figure?'

'You were a bit out,' he answered. 'The ricochet height for tank ammunition on this terrain is fifteen thousand feet.'

'Blast!' I said. 'Right, not a word about this. They'll never agree if we tell them that.'

We went back in.

'We will recommend that you be allowed to fire twice a day, an hour in the morning and an hour in the afternoon,' the prince said.

'Make it ninety minutes and we have a deal,' I answered.

'Fine, we will recommend ninety minutes. We will let you know as soon as possible; it will be later today, I promise.'

That would suit us fine, I thought as we drove back to

Al Jubayl. I did not want to fire in the heat of the day and we could stretch the ninety minutes either way. The ricochet height was a worry but as we knew the route the air patrols would take we could put out sentries to warn of any approaching aircraft. When I got back to Camp 4 there was a stack of messages waiting for me but nothing about firing.

The next morning, 6th November, I set off early for the ranges despite having heard nothing from either Dhahran or Riyadh about permission to fire. I arrived expecting to find everything ready, with the Scots Dragoon Guards in place and the targets laid out. John Sharples had his regiment there waiting and as we still did not have permission to start I decided to take a squadron down the range and go through the motions, without firing.

It was a fiasco. I had left strict orders as to how I wanted the targets laid out. I had spent at least an hour poring over the map with my staff, discussing how there should be targets right across the front to force the tanks to spread out, and some placed so that tanks on one side of the range could see them, but the others could not. The idea was to make it challenging and surprising. Most of all I wanted it to be dynamic.

But every time we came to a rise there would be a row of targets looking like a line of parked cars, slap in the middle of the range, all facing the same direction, all at the same sort of distance. We carried on to the end of the range, and then I called John Sharples to my tank. When he arrived I explained the problem, explained what I wanted and left it to him to sort it out. I knew he understood what I was on about.

At ten that night, with another day wasted and our 16th November deadline for being operational looking extremely uncertain, I got a call. We could fire tomorrow, for two periods of ninety minutes, at eight fifteen in the morning and three o'clock in the afternoon.

Chapter 5

Wednesday 7th to
Friday 16th November 1990

'Fire!'

An explosion shot through the Saudi morning. For the merest instant a ball of white flame burned brighter than the already blazing sun. A cloud of black smoke billowed out from where the flame had burned.

Seconds later another explosion, another ball of flame, and then a third. Previously drowsy vultures frantically beat their huge wings and flew in a panic.

'Hello Zero, this is Delta Two-Zero, targets destroyed, over.'

'Zero, roger, Delta One-Zero push on, out.'

Even before the words had left Arthur Denaro's mouth the fourteen tanks of Major Hugh Pierson's A Squadron of the Irish Hussars moved as one. Engines roared and the sixty-two-ton Challengers reversed back off the slope which only minutes earlier they had occupied. Building up speed in high reverse they were engulfed in a cloud of smoke and sand. Seconds later, still racing backwards, they burst through it. Suddenly first one tank, then another, then a third and then all of them veered hard left and right, braking heavily as they did so. They stopped momentarily as drivers threw their gearboxes from reverse to forward. Then, with engines screaming, the Challengers raced along the low ground. As their hulls spun, flattening mounds of sand under the tracks, the turrets remained locked on their axes, the guns pointing at the now out of sight burning car hulks destroyed by Major David Swann's B Squadron, some one thousand yards to their front.

Driving hard, A Squadron's two leading troops of three Challengers each raced in a pincer movement, emerging at opposite ends of the gully, before turning and roaring towards the next slope. As they passed B Squadron the net burst into life again.

'Zero, Delta One-Zero, contact, tank, wait out.'

On the left, as it cleared a small dune, one of Pierson's leading tanks saw the target. It slowed fractionally . . . another explosion. The tank rocked and a cloud of dust and smoke was kicked up in front of it as the shell exploded from the gun and an instant later tore through the plywood screen, sending a shower of charred wood splinters high into the air.

'Good target,' came Arthur's voice over the radio. 'Crack on. Delta Two-Zero prepare to move.'

A Squadron's tanks slowed down as they approached the next ridge line, creeping the last few yards into fire positions. As soon as they were there they fired. Two thousand yards ahead and right across their front was an 'Iraqi position' of plywood and car hulks. The crump of 120mm shell after shell, each following a laser-plotted, computer-projected path with deadly accuracy, was interspersed with the staccato barking of machine-gun fire. Orange tracer arced through the air; the ground seemed to spit sand where it landed.

In the distance was another thunderclap, louder, even more menacing. Moments later, high and whistling, artillery shells came careering overhead. Right in the heart of the position burst a huge explosion and then another and another, each hurling towering plumes of sand and smoke into the air, leaving gaping, smoking craters. This was the work of the 155mm guns of Rory Clayton's artillery regiment.

'Rounds on target, end of mission, over,' the net crackled.

'Rounds on target, end of mission, out,' came the reply.

But even as A Squadron continued to pour shells into the position, the first tanks of B Squadron appeared to their flanks. One last shot went just over the top of a racing Challenger and A Squadron's battle was put on hold.

Inside their turrets tank commanders hastily grabbed maps to check their position as their loaders, in the sweltering interior, re-stowed shells and their charges. There was no time for anything more. Over the radio came the squadron leader: 'Prepare to move.' Experienced drivers already had their tanks in gear, poised with both feet pressing hard on the central brake pedal, just waiting for the word to go. Their commanders meanwhile were checking where other tanks were; in the dust it would be easy to collide. Straining to look over a shoulder through the letterbox-sized periscopes at the rear of the cupola, each man was planning his reverse, too well trained to forget the essentials. Always reverse out of a fire position, never go straight forward once off the back of the slope, head for the low ground, use the ground to mask your movement. When you break clear of cover, do it at top speed, with the gun pointing at the enemy. Fire on the move if you have to and choose your next fire position on the reverse slope quickly. Race towards it, but slow down as you near. Do not kick up a huge dust cloud announcing your arrival. Crawl in those last few yards, remembering to keep your hull covered. But there was no time for revision now.

'Move, move, move,' came the order. Once again A Squadron was rolling forward. As they began, I too advanced in my own Challenger, keeping out of their way but watching as the first minutes of our first battle run began to flow. After six miles of this gruelling activity we hit the end of the battle run.

'All stations,' I radioed, 'stop, clear guns. Well done, that was magnificent. Commanders come to see me on return to the start line.'

I got there first and clambered to the ground in front of my tank, rubbing my stiff back, which was still uncomfortable from the Range Rover crash. I watched as the two Irish Hussar squadrons roared past into the low ground then peeled off,

A Squadron to the left, B to the right, into a well-formed box-leaguer, like a Waterloo-era hollow square, their guns pointing out in all directions.

Tank hatches were thrown open, letting in the fresh air and out the sulphurous cordite fumes. Arthur led his twenty-eight excited tank commanders up the small slope to me. 'Did you see that target?' 'I swear rounds were firing over my turret.' 'I could hear shrapnel pinging off my hull'. A cacophony of pure adrenalin.

They knew they had done well. This was the least-trained regiment in the brigade, and they had put on an outstanding performance. I took great delight in telling them so.

A roar overhead and a white vapour trail in the clear blue sky, two American F18s flying high northwards towards the border, told us firing was over for the morning.

As we spoke the well-practised routines of the tank crews were swinging into action. Camouflage nets were up, and sentries posted. On the tanks the loaders and gunners were scrubbing the barrels with long wooden-handled brushes. Although just mid-morning it was already nudging 38°C (100°F). We had hours to wait before firing could start again. It was intensely frustrating.

By half past two Arthur had his remaining squadrons in place, those commanded by Nigel Beer and Toby Maddison. Fifteen minutes later I made a quick call to our makeshift range control, which was in touch with our lookouts.

'Any sign of aircraft?' I asked.

'Patrols report all clear.'

'Roger. We are going to start again.' Range control hoisted a red flag up the makeshift flagpole. Even if the goats and local camel boys did not have the faintest idea what it meant, the rest of the brigade did. The range was live.

The second battle run was slightly disappointing. It started badly when a herd of camels drifted on to the range. Firing stopped while one of the Kuwaiti helicopters, whose pilots were thrilled to be helping us, chased them away. It was also much hotter and tempers were beginning to fray. And then Arthur joined the front line of the battle and he instantly got bogged down in the minutiae of controlling one tank not twenty-eight. The squadrons got out of sync. The result was nothing like as slick as the morning's performance. It was an important lesson for me as well, having made the decision to command the brigade from a tank.

Overall it was a most satisfactory day; we were working well. The next day's firing should be even better. To increase the pressure not only was General de la Billière visiting, but also Mike Myatt, Major General Jeremy Blacker, the Assistant Chief of Defence Staff (Operational Requirements), the man in charge of the British Army's equipment development and also the press.

The Scots Dragoon Guards had probably the finest reputation for tank gunnery in the army. They did not let us down. With spectators present, there was no cheating on the clock and the first round went down the range on the dot of eight fifteen. Following on, my own tank became something of a spectator platform. I had given up my commander's seat to General de la Billière and clinging on to the turret were the BBC's Martin Bell and ITN's Paul Davies. The morning was another success. Tanks thundered down the range, bursting out of clouds of smoke and dust. Artillery rounds whistled overhead and detonated only yards from other tanks. Tracer arced through the blazing sky. I knew from the look on the reporters' faces that they were impressed. It was perfect footage and just the image we wanted portrayed at home.

When the tanks finally finished and after the inevitable television interview I headed back to range control for a discussion with Generals de la Billière and Blacker.

I emerged two hours later much concerned. Right in the middle of this live firing I could have done without an irritating combination of news.

First it was General de la Billière. 'Patrick, you ought to know that things are in the offing. Thank you for your notes on reinforcing the brigade and your comments are noted. You should know we are now planning not just the defence of Saudi Arabia but an attack to liberate Kuwait. President Bush is about to announce a massive reinforcement. They're sending another entire corps, VII Corps, from Germany. I stress that no decision has yet been made, but it is highly likely that we are going to be reinforced.'

'Who by?' I asked.

'Well, as I said, the formal decision has yet to be made. But it's going to be another brigade, 4 Brigade under Christopher Hammerbeck, plus a medium reconnaissance regiment, the 16th/5th Lancers, helicopters, a whole lot more artillery and a divisional headquarters, probably commanded by Major General Rupert Smith.'

As requested, I had already told the general I thought forming an independent division would be a mistake. I believed it was a political decision, not a military one. My brigade had the fire power to do the job and we were a perfect fit with the US marines. Another brigade would make only a marginal contribution. Also I had argued we needed all the American firepower we could get to support us. If we were independent we might be cut off from this advantage.

We argued the point. He listened, but it made little impression. At last I said, 'I don't think the marines need another division.'

'You won't necessarily be fighting with the marines.'

'What?'

'No. I am going to press hard that we should be with VII Corps when they come.'

'Why?'

'Two reasons: first they are NATO forces and we'll share a common doctrine. You know it's quite difficult in that respect when working with the marines. And secondly they are going to be the main show, or, as the Americans say, the point of main effort.

'Patrick, I know you won't like this but politically and militarily we have to be where the action is. If VII Corps is there, we want a part of it with them.'

'What about roulement then?' I asked, as it was clear I was making no headway on that tack. '4 Brigade is supposed to be relieving us in six months' time. If they are coming out now who will take over from us and when?'

If ever there was a subject dear to the soldiers' hearts it was when would they be going home: either get on or get out – or, in this case, either go to war or go home.

The general looked awkward. 'Well, as you know,' he said in his slow delivery (and by now I had got to know him well enough to understand that meant he was not going to give me the answer I wanted to hear), 'roulement policy has yet to be decided, but I would not imagine you'll be here for more than six months.'

'Six months from when, though?' I asked. 'From the first deployment, from being complete in theatre, or from being declared operational?' There was more than a month between the first and last of these dates.

He could not give me an answer, but I knew this topic would need to be handled carefully once the reinforcement news broke with the brigade. The soldiers were sharp. They would realise that an armoured division was the complete modern British Army. There were no more Challenger Mk 3 tanks or Warriors. The soldiers trained to fight them would all be in the desert as well. The commitment could be open ended. This should not have mattered but we had become, for twenty-five years, used to half-yearly tours in Northern Ireland. We had a six-month-roulement mentality. But my main worry was the marines, who had been so good to us and who actually needed our capabilities. One thing was certain: VII Corps did not.

The second piece of news created another awkward situation. Jeremy Blacker, who had come to brief me on a number of equipment matters, told me of a problem with the tank ammunition. To put it simply, under certain circumstances it could blow up. British tank ammunition is unique in being split – the shell is separated from its charge, called the bag-charge. The bag-charges are stored in the hull in either water-cooled or armoured bins to minimise the threat of an ammunition fire if the tank is hit. Or so we hoped. In other tanks, such as the Iraqi T72, far less care has been taken in ammunition design and stowage. There is a strong chance that if the T72 hull or turret is penetrated the ammunition will spontaneously combust. The tank, with the crew inside, will explode or in the soldiers' terminology, 'brew up'.

But, in war, sitting in any vehicle packed with ammunition, however carefully protected, is unquestionably dangerous and all our tank crews were well aware of this. What Jeremy Blacker had to say was that we could reduce this danger if we altered the stowage layout just in case a tank was hit during our realistic work-up training. He urged me to do this straightaway.

I was in two minds as to the best course of action. As we were carrying out the most dangerous live-firing programme short of actual war, it was certainly possible that one tank might shoot another by mistake. The loss of a tank crew would be tragic, and if we had a spontaneous detonation of a Challenger it would be seen by everybody, with horrendous morale consequences for the remaining crews. On the other hand, if we stopped training to do the suggested re-stowing the soldiers would want to know why and it could cause unnecessary concern. On balance I decided it was best to continue and say nothing. Later, with the help of commanding officers, I would get the crews to go against years of training to stow their ammunition in a different way.

The afternoon battle run was nothing like as good as the morning's. Several times I had to shout at people not to be so cavalier. I was preoccupied by Jeremy Blacker's brief; the thought of a tank 'brewing up' in front of our soldiers and the BBC cameras was not a happy one. That would have made an interesting item on the nine o'clock news.

It must have been obvious that I was relieved when the day was over.

'I have been watching you carefully,' said Captain Abu Abdullah Khalid, one of our Kuwaiti pilots. 'I think you need these more than I do; they were my father's.'

He handed me the most beautiful set of black worry beads.

Friday 9th November was a very special day. It started with the Staffords practising their first mounted attacks against 'an Iraqi defensive position'. A company of the huge Warrior fighting vehicles thundered towards the nearest position.

Overhead came the now familiar whistle of artillery, the shells exploding less than a hundred yards in front. The Warriors' 30mm Rarden cannon and 7.62mm Hughes chain guns were rattling away, filling the air with tracer rounds.

Then over the radio net came the countdown. 'Three hundred metres . . . two hundred metres . . . one hundred metres . . . debus, debus, debus.' Every one of the company's fourteen Warriors skidded to a halt, their fronts almost ploughing into the sand. I watched one vehicle as the hydraulic rear door flew open and out poured the eight-man section in a well-rehearsed and slickly choreographed movement. Four men dashed down each side of the vehicle, throwing themselves to the ground as they cocked their SA80s. All the time the Warrior continued to pump rounds into the targets. Suddenly it was all shouting. The two four-man teams split into pairs. One pair was up and running while the other sprayed the area ahead with fire. A ten-yard zigzag dash and the first pair threw themselves to the ground. Then they started to fire as the first pair zigzagged past them and on.

Again and again, each pair was up. Within moments the first men had reached the edge of the 'Iraqi' trenches. One man knelt up. 'Grenade!' he shouted, throwing himself to the ground. A muffled explosion and the white smoke and sparks of a white phosphorus grenade billowed out of the trench. A second later he followed it in, bayonet glinting in the sun. They now had a toehold on the position.

This was fighting at its most basic. Not for them the laser range-finder and ballistic computer of a tank. The drill is a controlled use of brute force. First the hand grenade into the trench. Wait just long enough for the explosion and then jump in. Anyone in the trench who survived the blast will be too stunned to fight. At that range there's no room to fire your weapon, so the bayonet is used. Once the trench is taken, it is used as a base to put down fire for the attack on the next trench.

And so it went on, trench by trench. Watching, it seemed over in minutes but in the 38°C (100°F) heat, weighed down by webbing, a helmet, a rifle and hundreds of bullets, it must have felt like hours. When finally it was over the soldiers were sodden with sweat.

I was sorry to leave them, but I had a prior engagement. After a quick word with Charles Rogers, simply to congratulate, I headed back to range control to be picked up by a Kuwaiti helicopter to take me to celebrate the most important day in the US Marine Corps' year, the Marine Corps' birthday. Every year, as near as possible to 10th November, no matter where they are, each Marine Corps battalion celebrates with a cake-cutting ceremony. Tradition then dictates that the 'honor guest' and the oldest and youngest marines on parade eat the first three pieces. That they were in the middle of the Saudi desert on the edge of war would not stop the marines' celebration.

I arrived at the 1st Battalion, 7th Marines about three minutes early. The entire battalion of one thousand one hundred men was formed up, as, inevitably, was the press corps. Each year the ceremony is the same. The adjutant reads out a message from a former commandant, General Lejeun, and then a letter from the current commandant. This is followed by the cutting of the cake. As I joined the marine celebrities at the front of the parade I heard the band of the 1st Queen's Dragoon Guards, resplendent in sand-and-khaki fatigues, strike up.

Several weeks before, back in Al Jubayl, at one of the many command conferences, I had arrived to find General Boomer and his commanders in serious debate about the celebration.

'Can we do the cakes?' asked the general.

'Sure, no problem,' replied Royal Moore, the commander of the air wing, 'but music, that's going to be the tricky one.'

'Yeah,' agreed another. 'One year in Vietnam we had to use a tape deck and loudspeakers – it's not the same. But with only one band here . . .'

At the mention of bands I chipped in.

'Bands, did you say?'

'Yeah, Pat,' said General Boomer. 'We were talking about the Corps' birthday. We need bands for the day, but I guess we're going to have to do without them this year.'

'Far from it,' I said. 'I've got sixteen of them. How many do you need?'

In war bandsmen act as medical orderlies. When we deployed to the Gulf we took a large number of them to man dressing stations and ambulance exchange points. Most of them, but not all, had also brought their instruments. The marines were delighted. By ferrying our bands in their helicopters over a two-day period we were able to make sure that every birthday celebration had music. The Queen's Dragoon Guards band was a hit with 1st/7th Marines.

Once the formalities were over the cake was marched out. It was delicious, a perfect sponge cake. How they did it I have no idea. I then made my speech. What no-one had told me was the particular way the marines show their appreciation. They do not clap, they grunt. As soon as I was introduced this chorus of grunts broke out. It went on for a minute. It sounded just like an enormous gathering of seals. My speech took rather longer than planned, interrupted as it was by grunting, but I think they liked it. I certainly, for once, enjoyed giving it.

Two days later it was time for our own poignant contemplation. On 11th November we marked Remembrance Day. During the short service held at the brigade headquarters and conducted by Alun Price we sang a few hymns and laid a wreath at a hastily made cross held up by stones. As a trumpeter played 'Last Post' I wondered how many of the twelve thousand men in the command would not be going home, but would, in the words of the service, 'grow not old as we that are left grow old'.

It was at this time, in the run-up to being declared operational, that I received from Riyadh a sealed envelope stamped 'SECRET – UK EYES ONLY – EXCLUSIVE FOR COMMANDER'. It contained the official policy directive assigning forces to my command and detailing exactly what was expected of me and them.

Strategic objective: To secure the effective imposition of United Nations Security Council resolutions including the status quo ante in Kuwait as economically as possible.

UK military objective: Priority in conjunction with Allies is to deter and if necessary to repel further Iraqi aggression in the area of the Arabian Peninsula . . . If so directed to assist Allies in achieving the withdrawal of Iraqi forces from Kuwait.

Tasks: Commander 7th Armoured Brigade is to prepare 7th Armoured Brigade Group for combined operations, to deter or repel an Iraqi invasion of Saudi Arabia or to achieve an Iraqi withdrawal from Kuwait.

Be prepared to conduct operations under TACON Commanding General 1st Marine Expedition Forces. You will be given support for an initial deployment of six months. You will receive weapon stocks for thirty days expenditure at NATO planning rates, and a further twelve days stock as in-theatre reserve. A total of forty-two days at normal planning rates or fourteen days at intense rates.

You are responsible to me for: the conduct of operations of 7th Armoured Brigade Group; for the defence and security arrangements; the administrative, logistic, medical and support arrangements; for keeping me informed of US plans for deployment of the Brigade Group; during hostilities keeping me informed of the operational situation in 1 MEF Tactical Area Of Responsibility, and in so far as they affect 7th Armoured Brigade Group, future intentions of Commanding General 1 MEF.

Command and Control: Operational control. I will operate OPCON of all UK in-theatre Land Forces. If I subsequently delegate TACON of land forces to any other national commander you are to consult me on all policy matters. Specifically this will include any military action or operation other than exercising the right of self-defence; redeployment or planning for offensive operations; rules of engagement requests; proposals for changes to this directive; and politically sensitive issues relating to co-ordinating of land operations with other allied forces. Tactical control: If I delegate TACON of forces assigned to you it is likely to be passed to CG 1MEF who may in turn delegate TACON to CG I MD. You are also to be prepared to take OPCON or TACON of such forces allocated to you by myself or any other commander.

Administrative control: I shall administer overall administrative control of all UK land, air and sea forces.

P. de la Billière
Lieutenant General
Commander, British Forces Middle East.

Information:
Chief of the Defence Staff
Joint Commander
Commander-in-Chief BAOR
Commander-in-Chief UKLF.

Exercise Jubayl Rat was our last exercise before declaring ourselves operational, when we would come under command of the marines. It was to start on the same morning as a visit by the Secretary of State for Defence.

The day before the exercise the commanding officers and I walked through and discussed the opening phase, breaching a mock-up of the Iraqi border defences. This mock-up was as close to the real thing as we could make it. It had taken a team of Royal Engineers under Chris Goddard five days to build. Arriving for the first time at the site with Euan, I was amazed at both the size of the defence belt and its complexity. Between the first triple-roll concertina barbed wire and the final anti-tank ditch and sand berms were over four miles of obstacles.

Once through the barbed wire you entered an anti-tank minefield four hundred yards deep. After that was an anti-tank ditch, about ten feet deep and twelve yards across. Span that and several hundred yards later came another belt of thick barbed wire and booby traps. Then followed a particularly nasty combination: a sand wall behind which was another anti-tank ditch, and in between an oil pipeline – not much of an obstacle at first glance, until you remembered oil burns. At last you came to the enemy, a company-size defended position of well-dug-in infantry in bunkers and trenches, protected by tanks and minefields. It appeared uncrossable.

Rather than simply talk our way through the problem we had our full engineer contingent available to see if we had the equipment for the task. It was a motley collection of armoured vehicles that were assembled. They were christened the Antiques Roadshow, since some of them were more than thirty years old. We had armoured bridgelayers that could lay a scissor bridge across a twenty-five-yard gap and a mine-clearing system called the Giant Viper, a one-hundred-and-fifty-yard hose of plastic explosive attached to a cluster of rockets. The rockets were fired over the minefield, dragging the hose behind them. As soon as the hose hit the ground it detonated, clearing every mine in a path one hundred and fifty yards long and eight yards wide. We had Bangalore torpedoes, the infantry equivalent of the Giant Viper, but in this case to blow holes in the wire obstacles. We had armoured bulldozers. But did we have enough?

Obstacles are built so that anyone trying to breach them can be attacked either directly, by dug-in infantry or by a tank counter-attack, or indirectly, by artillery fire. So breaching an obstacle is more than just an engineering task, it may take a whole battlegroup or more to support the engineers in a highly controlled and tightly planned operation.

First one must make sure the projected crossing site has no enemy capable of firing at it. Once secure the engineers can start breaching. However, they will need protecting by infantry and tanks. With the first breach in the obstacle open you will need soldiers on the ground and tanks to secure it against counter-attack. With the breach secure, the tanks pass through up to the edge of the next layer of obstacles, when the whole laborious, time-consuming and extremely dangerous procedure must be repeated again. And again for each one of the obstacles, be it minefield, tank ditch, or oil pipeline. And all the time this is happening you are likely to be under artillery fire and, perhaps, chemical attack. It is no wonder that the Royal Engineers have won a disproportionate number of VCs in past wars.

We found after our trial that the limiting factor was not, as had been expected, the engineering equipment, but rather the lack of infantry. You need at least a company to secure a breach and with only one battalion in the brigade it would be quickly used up. We would have to call on the marines for support.

On the morning of 14th November I watched the exercise start and then flew to Al Jubayl airport to meet the Secretary of State. With him were a number of journalists, including an old friend – John Keegan, the *Daily Telegraph*'s defence editor and a former lecturer at the Royal Military Academy, Sandhurst. A more charming and informed man it would be hard to find.

After a noisy flight in a Puma we arrived at my tactical headquarters and went straight into a briefing. The Secretary of State had been well prepared and asked several surprising questions. There was a bit of a sticky moment when he asked about Challenger's reliability.

'We're very pleased with the tank and with the support we are getting, particularly from Vickers. But the tank's engine is not without problems,' I said.

'For instance?'

'On average we're losing one tank whenever the brigade drives four miles.'

'What? Every four miles?'

'Yes, sir, about that.'

He looked shocked and made a hasty note. It was only later I discovered he thought I had meant that every tank broke down every four miles, and was stunned that I should consider this an acceptable performance. What I had meant to explain, but clearly had chosen my words inadequately, was when our entire fleet of one hundred and seventeen Challenger tanks moved four miles one would break down. This was an acceptable, but not encouraging, statistic. In simple terms it meant we needed a good stock of spare engines.

We then rumbled across the desert to inspect the obstacle belt, just as a company of Staffords were pouring out of their Warriors to secure a minefield breach. Over the radio came a constant stream of reports and orders. Suddenly there was a huge explosion and a massive cloud of dust and smoke was thrown up about two hundred yards to our front, simulating artillery. It was rapidly followed by half-a-dozen more explosions as the engineer team detonated small charges of plastic explosive.

We followed as the brigade attempted to tackle the obstacles, fighting off a counter-attack by Nigel Beer's squadron acting as enemy, setting off simulated Giant Vipers and clearing enemy bunkers. Our visitors were amazed by what was happening; the complexity of breaking through a massive obstacle belt was made very clear.

We flew back to the port after lunch to visit Martin White and the Force Maintenance Area. Our first stop was at the port's tower, a viewpoint which would give Mr King a good impression of the magnitude of the operation taking place there.

I had arranged that the port director, 'His Excellency' as he liked to be known, would meet us at the top. So into a tiny lift crammed Martin White, Tom King, Sir Alan Munro and myself. It was one of those lifts where you have to stand that little bit too close to each other for comfort. And up we went. We reached the twelfth floor. The lift stopped. We waited. Nothing happened.

'What's the matter with the doors?' asked Sir Alan. I found a control panel. 'It's all right,' I said, 'I've found the controls.' I pushed a button. Nothing happened. I pushed another. Nothing. I pushed every one. Nothing. The doors remained shut. The lift would not move.

'It looks like we're stuck,' I said, laughing but just a little concerned.

'You do think someone knows we're stuck in here?' asked Mr King.

After four minutes I was getting worried. It was hot in the lift and slightly airless. I was not certain how to get out of this one.

After five minutes the joke had worn off completely. There were airplanes to catch and schedules to meet, and it was getting extremely hot.

After six minutes I tried all the buttons again. Still nothing.

After eight minutes we heard a grinding noise, and then a

banging. Suddenly there was a jolt and the lift rattled before very slowly starting to move upwards. Another jolt and it stopped. Another jolt and we went down again.

As the doors opened on the ground floor the four of us tumbled out. We never did meet His Excellency, the Port Director.

The next morning, the 15th, General de la Billière and I met General Boomer in his office for the formal hand-over of the brigade. He told us the marines were about to embark on a major amphibious exercise, about one hundred miles south of the Kuwaiti border. He was, however, in fine form. But the meeting was not to be a happy one. General de la Billière was laying the groundwork for changes afoot, talking about the options for the British and hinting that it was not a foregone conclusion that the British brigade, or indeed a division, would remain with the marines.

General Boomer looked concerned. He clearly had no idea that changes were being planned and since we had been put under his command he had not unnaturally assumed we would stay there. I felt desperately uncomfortable and wished I was elsewhere.

Back in Camp 4 there was a message waiting for me. It was from Sir Paddy Hine:

I have greatly admired the energy and determination you and your staff have applied to ensure the timely deployment of your brigade from Germany to Saudi Arabia. Since then you have completed a vigorous in-theatre training programme and I warmly congratulate you on hitting the original operational date of 16th November. Now that 7th Armoured Brigade is under tactical control of 1st Marine Expeditionary Force you are entering a new and testing phase of your task. I have no doubt you will meet the challenge with the same professionalism that you and your officers have shown from the outset.

And so the formalities of handing command of the brigade to the marines were completed and, in turn, we were assigned to Mike Myatt and his division. This was to happen at twelve o'clock on Friday 16th November.

On the Friday I was with Mike Myatt, sitting outside his tent discussing future training and waiting to meet General Schwarzkopf, when suddenly he looked at his watch and stood up.

'Patrick, it's midday. Good to have you on board,' he said, shaking my hand.

Chapter 6

Thursday 22nd to
Wednesday 28th November 1990

On 22nd November the Secretary of State for Defence got to his feet in a crowded and expectant House of Commons. He announced the decision to reinforce 7th Armoured Brigade with an additional brigade, the 4th Brigade, four more artillery regiments, an Army Air Corps regiment, extra engineers and logisticians, and to dispatch an armoured divisional headquarters to take command of these formations. My independent command was nearly over.

Several thousand miles away at the time he was speaking I was fighting my way through a seething crowd of one thousand identically dressed, closely shorn marines, not one of whom was the slightest bit interested in me, Mike Myatt, who was with me, or any of the other generals or colonels for that matter. The object of their attention was a middle-aged man in a pale blue shirt and fawn trousers who was standing on the back of a Humvee about five hundred yards from us – their Commander-in-Chief, George Bush. He was here among his men to celebrate Thanksgiving Day, and the marines loved him for it.

An hour earlier I had arrived to be briefed at Mike's

headquarters. There were scores of new trenches. Soldiers armed with anti-aircraft missiles were on sentry scanning the horizon. Newly installed radar dishes spun relentlessly, scouring the air for movement. M60 tanks had arrived during the night and were getting into position to provide all-round protection for the whole area. Most conspicuous amid the already huge crowds of desert-camouflaged marines was a large contingent of heavy-looking, square-set men dressed in blue coveralls, baseball caps, impenetrably dark glasses and extravagant weaponry. 'The President's close protection,' said Mike, who had met me as our helicopter landed. 'They've been here for days, checking the place out. They never smile.'

I nodded at one as he walked past, to test Mike's observation. It was true. Quite why so many, and so heavily armed, bodyguards were needed escaped me. After all the President was going to be surrounded by the best part of a US marine division.

The President's helicopter was to be met by General Boomer. He would escort Mr and Mrs Bush the five hundred yards from the helicopter to a stand where a small reception committee comprising Mike, me and some of the other marine generals would meet him. The President would make his speech, then go into the crowd and shake a few hands before sitting down for Thanksgiving lunch. That was the plan.

Exactly on time the President's green and grey Blackhawk appeared low on the horizon escorted by a phalanx of Apache gunships. In a cloud of dust it landed. Out stepped the President and Mrs Bush, into the motor cavalcade, which with flashing lights and amid deafening cheers made its way up the hill towards us.

I could make out the President quite clearly as he waved at the cheering crowd. As he drew level with us I subconsciously pulled myself up. Then, in some amazement, I watched the parade drive straight past us and stop about one hundred yards away in the middle of the now almost ecstatic crowd, leaving the reception committee the wrong side of several hundred cheering marines.

What I had not appreciated was how very egalitarian the Americans are. There is no respect for rank and a private can just as easily shake the hand of the President as can a general. And there was an awful lot of that going on.

'Damn,' said Mike. 'Come on, quick.'

We launched ourselves into the crowd. Military courtesies were forgotten as we literally elbowed our way forward. Surprised marines turned round angrily to see who it was barging their way through. Eventually we got to the front, rather sweaty and slightly out of breath. Moments later I was introduced to President Bush.

'General Cordingley, I would like to thank you, your men and your government, for your contribution. It means a lot to us to have the Desert Rats fighting alongside us.' All the time he was speaking he was shaking my hand.

'Thank you,' I replied, shaking his hand just as hard back. 'It is a privilege to be here, and we could ask for no greater honour than to fight alongside the US Marine Corps.'

He paused, and then quietly said, 'Barbara and I are really sad about the news of your Prime Minister.' And then he was gone, shaking more hands, smiling a lot more and having his photograph taken. It had been a moving, if fleeting, experience; I felt privileged. I was then introduced to the delightful Mrs Bush, who was as charming as she was friendly and approachable. She too said how sorry she was to hear about Margaret Thatcher's resignation. I confessed I had only heard about it a few minutes earlier from the media representatives who had come to cover the President's visit. I was both saddened and a little worried by it.

President Bush's speech was uplifting. I was particularly pleased that 7 Brigade was mentioned several times, it made us all desperately proud. 'Let me just say how pleased Barbara and I are to be here,' he began, 'and I want to thank you all for this welcome.' There was a huge cheer and a lot of grunting from the crowd.

'I want to thank General Myatt for greeting us, Mike Myatt and all his people. I want to thank General Boomer. I want also to thank Brigadier General Cordingley of the famed

Desert Rats who are with us here; you are a long way from home on this day, and your families. But I hope you will forgive me if I focus on the Americans for our very special Thanksgiving Day.'

And so he went on. He explained why the marines were there. He told them of the overwhelming support they had from the American people. He ended with a rousing finale: 'It is Thanksgiving Day . . . year after year on this special day no doubt each of you has given thanks for your country. This year your country gives thanks to you. This has been an unforgettable visit and I leave, and I know Barbara does, with pride in our hearts and a prayer on our lips. God bless you all, God bless our faithful allies of the United Kingdom. God bless the marines and may God bless the greatest, freest country on the face of the earth – the United States of America.'

The cheer was deafening. They must have heard it in Baghdad. The marines had invited one hundred British soldiers to share this moment with them. I was delighted to discover that a further hundred had smuggled their way in as well. During lunch (turkey and blueberry pie, about as traditional as one could get) I hosted Tom Foley, leader of the House of Representatives, and afterwards I was asked to look after Barbara Bush while her husband continued to shake hands as he walked about. She was clearly tired, but still buoyant. Never once did she fail to smile as marine after marine asked for her autograph or to have their photograph taken beside her. It must have been exhausting for her but she carried off her role as her nation's mother figure quite superbly.

Later I was collared by Kate Adie for an interview. When asked a harmless question about the political demise of Mrs Thatcher I said it was really nothing to do with us and to a very large extent it made no difference to us who was in Number 10 as long as we had strong government at this critical time. However, warming to the theme, I said I was personally very sad and had been a great admirer of hers, which was true, and I said how much it would mean to the soldiers, which was probably not quite so accurate. Good friend that Kate became, she did not use my political comments, but suggested others might not be so charitable in future.

As the sun set President Bush flew off to a huge cheer and massive grunting. Mike asked me to stay for some supper but I had to get back. We had our own, albeit more modest, celebration – the Sidi Rezegh dinner.

The battle of Sidi Rezegh was 7th Armoured Brigade's finest hour. On 21st November 1941, in North Africa, against overwhelming odds they had denied a vital piece of ground to Rommel's forces. At the end of the battle the brigade's tank strength, very similar to ours, had been reduced to nine but the Germans were beaten off. It was not a victory but a glorious action.

That evening the commanding officers, most of the brigade staff officers and some invited marines met for pre-dinner drinks in a large tent set up in the middle of the headquarters. The band of the 5th Royal Inniskilling Dragoon Guards, under the direction of Band Sergeant Major Shipp, played for us. Waiters circulated topping up drinks or offering trays of canapés. It was like any other army dinner night except for two things: it was strictly combat dress (no decorations, but respirators to be carried), and there was no alcohol. We had a selection of either orange juice or non-alcoholic beer. For all that, or because of that, it was the most moving guest night I had ever been to. From out of sand and thin air the chefs produced a dinner of roast chicken, potatoes and peas. After months of tinned composite (compo) rations it tasted as if it had been cooked by Delia Smith.

After dinner, during my speech, I quoted at length from the diary of my predecessor, a Brigadier Davy, who forty-nine years before had been in a somewhat tighter situation than I hoped to face.

The tank strength of my brigade had, in ten hours, been reduced from one hundred and twenty-nine to nine. But we had done what we were told and we were holding the ground considered vital to the enemy and defeated his attempts to retake it. We were surrounded. I sent over the radio that evening, in clear for the enemy to hear, this comment: situation well in hand.

I ended by quoting from Winston Churchill's address to the 7th Armoured Division at the end of World War Two:

Dear Desert Rats! May your glory ever shine! May your laurels never fade! May the memory of your glorious pilgrimage of war never die. It was a march unsurpassed through all the story of war.

The band played 'Fare Thee Well, Inniskilling', my regimental march, and then, in honour of the marines present, the Marine Corps march.

Three days later, on 24th November, I met my new boss, the recently appointed commander of 1st Armoured Division, Major General Rupert Smith.

He was a slightly elusive figure. A Parachute Regiment officer did not seem the immediate first choice to command an armoured division, but I knew he had the reputation of being a thinker with wide experience. He had been commissioned into the Parachute Regiment in 1964 and commanded the 3rd Battalion in 1982. In 1978, then a company commander, he had won the Queen's Gallantry Medal for rescuing a fellow officer from a burning car, set on fire by an IRA device. He had suffered appalling burns to his hands and arms. Later, in Germany, he commanded the 6th Armoured Brigade, which he converted to become the army's first helicopter-borne airmobile brigade.

Standing on the tarmac at Al Jubayl waiting for the general's aircraft to come to a halt I thought of the words of a friend who had served under General Smith in 6 Brigade. 'He's very self-contained,' he had said. 'Highly professional and he runs his headquarters like a machine.'

I was somewhat surprised when down the aircraft steps bounced a man who I thought looked rather younger than me, with a shock of black hair, hardly flecked with any grey. He bore a resemblance to the actor Jeremy Irons. He was dressed in jungle combat kit, with a major general's insignia on his shoulders and parachute wings on his right sleeve. In his hand he carried the distinctive maroon beret of the Parachute Regiment, and a map case. He had what I can only describe as an air of authority mixed with fun.

Behind him on the steps was Brigadier Christopher Hammerbeck, tall and blond and wearing the black beret of the Royal Tank Regiment. We had known each other for many years.

Colonel John Reith, the divisional chief of staff, Euan's equivalent one level up, was the next out. He was a highly competent officer, and yet another from the Parachute Regiment. At the back was the smiling face of Colonel Graham Ewer. Graham was the division's deputy chief of staff and a good friend. We had known each other for many years.

There were about a dozen or so others, but as time was pressing I skipped the introductions, shepherding the group towards the four waiting Puma helicopters that were to fly us to our headquarters in the desert. The noise inside precluded conversation; I watched the team staring out of the small windows at the vastness of the area.

In a quiet part of the headquarters, away from the vehicles and generators we had set up a large camouflage net on long tent poles to provide a sort of shelter. Underneath were two dozen or so folding chairs and a series of boards. Some had large maps showing our area, others depicted the deployment of our forces, or those of our allies.

I outlined what we had achieved; our firing programme and later on the almost constant exercises we, unlike the Americans, were running. I explained how we slotted into the marines' deployment plans. We were their armoured reserve, but should we move from the defence of Saudi Arabia to an attack on Kuwait we would be near the front, particularly our engineers. Although I knew that General de la Billière would have explained his ideas about switching to the US Army, nevertheless I made it quite plain that I thought we should stay with the marines.

Later I went into far more detail about the operational plans, including the counter-surprise contingencies should

Iraq launch a sudden attack. I also went over our future intentions. Between the marines and my staff we had decided that our existing range was too small for a division, so we had started negotiations for a new area further north for a much larger complex that we intended to share. And so, under the ever-burning sun, the afternoon wore on. At about four o'clock we all climbed back into the Pumas and flew to Al Jubayl for a tour of the Force Maintenance Area. We carried on the work after the tour at the Holiday Inn on the outskirts of the town. We finally finished at about eleven and went our separate ways, knowing that the next time we would meet all together was still several weeks away.

The next morning, while Rupert Smith and his team conducted their own reconnaissance, I was back at the airfield to meet a planeload of VIPs from the House of Commons Defence Select Committee and various members of the House of Lords. On the drive back into town I sat between Lord Pym, the former Foreign Secretary, and Winston Churchill, the Tory MP. We discussed the Gulf situation in general. But later in the day I broached the subject of an attack into Iraq. The committee agreed that, although bombing Iraq was not politically difficult, if ground troops were to set foot inside Iraq it would unnecessarily widen the war. This time I was surprised – it seemed no-one had told them of the plans being made in Riyadh.

In the afternoon we flew first to the Staffords, who put on an excellent display. The ever-present press made the most of our next stop, the Irish Hussars. The tank the committee was shown was named *Churchill*, after the MP's grandfather, who had been at one time an officer in the 4th Hussars. The photo-opportunity was too good to miss. Michael Mates, chairman of the select committee, was also given special attention. I was rather surprised he had come at all. I had imagined that as Michael Heseltine's campaign manager he would have had other things to do.

While this was happening I had a long discussion with an American journalist about the disappointing coverage of President Bush's visit. I had been incensed by an article in

The Times which claimed the Americans were not happy to see him; from my first-hand experience it was totally untrue.

As I saw the MPs off at the airport a Blackhawk helicopter, sent by the commanding general of the 24th Mechanised Infantry Division, landed to take me some one hundred miles inland to be briefed about their deployment. They were the next-door formation to our west.

As we flew over the vast expanse of nothing I could see the desert change. After the coastal area of rolling dunes and deep fine sand, slowly the dunes flattened and the sand got coarser until the desert was more of a gravel plain.

Landing at 24th Division's vast headquarters I was surprised, and rather touched, to be met by an 'honor guard' and a band. They were dressed identically to the marines – the same chocolate-chip uniform, the same floppy hat. The only difference was that whereas on a marine's right breast a label read 'USMC', these read 'US Army'. I could not help thinking that even in my small brigade no two soldiers, let alone two units, ever wore quite the same uniform.

They had also laid on an equipment display and I was shown round an M1A1 Abrams tank and a Bradley infantry fighting vehicle. There is not much to choose between a Bradley and our own Warrior, except that the Bradley has an anti-tank missile on its turret. Both are well-equipped infantry fighting vehicles which can carry a section of men and their equipment in relative comfort. In some ways the Warrior is a better vehicle, not least because of its size. The Bradley is huge and must present an inviting target, a worrying thought for the men inside.

The M1A1 is a more recently designed tank than our own Challenger. Like the Challenger it has a 120mm gun. This, unlike ours, has a smooth bore which, it is claimed, gives it an advantage in firing some types of ammunition, particularly fin, in that it can fire at higher pressures so the round goes faster and, in theory, will penetrate thicker armour. However you can not fire HESH rounds through a smooth-bore gun, and HESH is an extremely versatile and useful round.

The turret's spacious interior was painted white and was,

unlike Challenger's turret, well organised from an ergonomic point of view. I was shown the self-diagnosis computer from which, just by pushing a button, the tank commander can learn what was wrong when the tank broke down. I made all the right appreciative noises, not mentioning that I thought the armour looked thinner than Challenger's.

What makes the M1 unique among Western tanks is its engine. In tank design there is always a trade-off between the size of the engine and the size of the tank. The bigger the engine the more power it generates, but the larger the tank must be to house it, and the heavier the tank is, the more power it needs, and so on. Every other Western tank is powered by a diesel. The Abrams uses a gas turbine, an engine usually found in a jet aeroplane. A turbine generates a lot of power from a small unit.

However, they traded one set of problems for another. There are two problems with a gas turbine. First it runs at an incredible heat. The exhaust temperature is over 1000°C (1800°F). Looked at through a thermal sight it looks like someone driving around with a searchlight on. Secondly, turbines use up fuel at an alarming rate. I did try and find out how far the M1 would go on a full fuel tank. The escort officer either did not know or wanted to keep this fact close to his chest.

Then on to the briefing in the headquarters compound. This was a mixture of wheeled and tracked command vehicles gathered in small groups and linked together, some under canvas awnings. I was escorted to the heart of the complex for my brief. From the outside this looked like a huge mobile office stuck on the back of four lorries. I went up a flight of metal steps and through a door and was amazed at what I found.

Our own headquarters normally has a small area under canvas, out of the way of the officers and operators manning the radio sets in the vehicles, where we set up a trestle table and a few folding canvas chairs and which we use for planning purposes. The inside of 24th Division's headquarters was like something out of a film. It was about thirty feet by twenty feet. There were fluorescent lights overhead, it was air conditioned and serious-looking officers sat on swivel chairs at desks in front of radio sets. The silver-painted walls were lined with huge maps or boards giving the status of each unit in the division, its location, strength, tasks and alert state.

It became clear that Major General Barry McCaffery commanded a huge amount of firepower. The 1st British Division about to form up in the Gulf, two thirds of a normal British armoured division, would have three tank regiments of fifty-eight tanks each, and three infantry battalions; he commanded five tank battalions of fifty-eight tanks and five battalions of infantry.

But it was with helicopters that the real difference lay. Whereas we were planning to bring out an Army Air Corps regiment (twenty-four Lynx anti-tank helicopters and twelve Gazelle reconnaissance helicopters), General McCaffery had over one hundred and thirty helicopters, including fifty Apaches and fifty reconnaissance helicopters.

Once the briefing was completed, the general introduced me to the operator of the overhead projector. 'This young lady,' he said, 'has left her six-month-old baby, so keen she was to deploy with us.' Rather perplexed, I asked her who she had left the baby with. It was her turn to look surprised. 'With her father,' was the simple reply. I didn't bother to explain my rather traditional thoughts on such arrangements. I merely wished her well and hoped the family would be reunited before long. I also made a mental note to check if such a situation existed within our large contingent of women. I did hope not, but I was getting used to surprises; I had recently dealt with the problem of whether married couples could share a tent.

I sat next to the general at supper. He was delightful company. He told me of his time in Vietnam. 'Three tours I did Pat,' he said, adopting, like most Americans I had met, an abbreviation of my name. 'The last time they carried me out, thinking I was dead.

'I was hit by an AK from about thirty yards. Fortunately I took most of the rounds in my arm,' he said. I looked at it; it was a mass of scar tissue. 'I spent two years in hospital while they put it back together again.'

Swopping war stories was never one of my strong points. My military career had been mostly spent close to the East German border, interspersed with rather comfortable tours in Cyprus, Libya and Canada.

On other matters I was intrigued to hear that they had been sent from America a Christmas stocking for every single one of the 18,000 members of the division – presents from the American public. They had also been sent 6,000 Christmas trees.

There was one final opportunity to try and stop us being switched from the marines to the US Army. On 27th November General Wilkes was visiting. He and General de la Billière came to see me together. In the briefing tent the three of us sat round a table with a large map of the Gulf spread out on it. General de la Billière explained what he hoped General Schwarzkopf's planning team would advise for the attack to free Kuwait. He then went on to outline our potential move.

'The plan is that you will remain with the marines until 1st Division is complete, which should be around the New Year,' he said. 'At that time I hope you will be switched to under command of VII US Corps, who by then will be complete in theatre.

'The details of the attack into Kuwait have not been worked out, but in essence VII and XVIII Corps will move west past Hafir Al Batin and attack through Iraq into Kuwait. The US marines and the Arab coalition forces, as a diversion, will remain where they are and attack north directly into Kuwait.

'I am sure you will agree that it is best that we should be part of the main attack and not merely involved in a diversionary role?' He was, I assumed, expecting the answer yes.

'Well frankly, General, you know I don't agree.' I said. General Wilkes looked surprised. 'I don't think it would be overstating the case to say I think it is a nightmare scenario.'

'I think you should explain,' said General Wilkes.

'First, and foremost, to move the brigade, let alone a

new and untrained division, the kind of distances you are talking about is logistically difficult to the point of being unsustainable.

'At the moment we are consuming about a million litres of water a day and our fuel demands are straining the supply chain. Turnaround time to repair major assemblies in Germany or England, such as engines, is already critical. And all of this with us only sitting some eighty miles from the port. If we up sticks and move several hundred miles inland as you suggest,' I said, 'how do you propose to resupply us when we get there? To say nothing of when we go into Iraq.'

Obviously this was not what they wanted to hear, but I was determined to say my piece. I knew that once Rupert Smith was in theatre my advice would no longer be sought, and I also knew General de la Billière had briefed Rupert Smith on the plan and they had agreed to it. This was my last chance to air my concerns.

'Secondly,' I went on, 'do you think we are up to it? Can the 1st Division, a scratch organisation that has never trained as a division, operate effectively attached to a US corps with whom we have never tried out the kind of manoeuvre warfare I imagine is being planned?

'If we stay with the marines, provided we can fight as a division, their tactical battle will be a far easier one, although I grant you likely to be potentially more dangerous.

'Then there is a question of loyalty. We have trained with the marines now for some time. We know how they work, how they think, we understand each other. They need us and I don't like the idea of walking out on them now.'

I knew I probably should just have agreed but I had to say what I felt. I then added a palliative: 'If the plan goes ahead as you have outlined, General, then I promise you that 7 Brigade, the best-trained and best-equipped force in the army, will do whatever we are ordered to do, to the very best of our abilities.'

There was a short silence, broken by General de la Billière. 'Thank you for that, Patrick. I hear what you say and I confess to being rather surprised by your comments about the level of training, but there we are.'

There was not much more to discuss on that topic. Had I known the extent to which our logisticians were to be reinforced I think I might have kept quiet. I knew 7 Brigade was capable of operating over large distances, I trusted that Commander VII US Corps was equally confident about his troops.

I was keen to bring the conversation round to the media. The following day we were to host a two-day visit from British defence correspondents. I hoped to discuss with these correspondents what we described as trivial reporting and also support from the British public of the sort I had seen during my visit to the 24th Infantry Division.

Trivia was rife in the newspapers; the delicate balance of the international situation and the nature of the war that appeared to be inevitable seemed to take second place. One article that particularly incensed us came from *The Times*. Having invited all available correspondents to follow behind a hugely realistic battle run a few weeks before, we did catch the attention of most of the national papers. *The Times*, however, had a trivial slant. Their reporter, when talking to the soldiers afterwards, discovered that one sergeant in the Staffords had not heard from his wife for several weeks. A column was devoted to this problem, with the innuendo that our logistics were clearly poor. Having investigated the matter we discovered that the wife in question had not written to her husband for over a month!

'Frankly, Patrick,' began Mike Wilkes, 'I think you are being over-sensitive. Of course the public are behind you. Stuck out here you won't get the right feel for the coverage. Don't forget there's more going on at home than just the Gulf. We still don't have a prime minister. People have other things to worry about.'

'Are you worried about the defence correspondents' visit?' asked General de la Billière.

'No, not really,' I replied. 'But with a dozen Fleet Street specialists arriving tomorrow to poke around for two days I would like to discuss our view of the reporting. It also seems a good opportunity, as Christmas approaches, to mention next door's trees and stockings.'

'Well, I'm not sure it's quite our way of doing things,' General Mike Wilkes remarked. And there I had to agree with him.

The next day, watching the helicopter carrying the correspondents land, I thought of the exchange of views of the previous day. General de la Billière had looked thoughtful and I felt he was disappointed in me. But I knew he had two reasons for wanting to get us away from the marines. He thought we would take unduly heavy casualties attacking with them straight into Kuwait and he saw it as a sideshow – and he wanted only the best for the British Army.

From our perspective we saw the marines as a highly trained, utterly professional organisation who might give the outward appearance of being macho, but who actually knew the real value of human life better than anyone. There was no possibility of them taking one more casualty than they would have to.

And as to their attack being a sideshow and a diversion, we were not convinced. Who was going to get to Kuwait City first? And where did our politicians really want to see the Union Flag? Flying from the back of a tank driving through a liberated Kuwait City to the tumultuous cheers of the thankful inhabitants, or in the middle of an Iraqi desert surrounded by miles of empty sand? Which would the grateful Kuwaitis remember longer?

However, I had to put all that behind me. For the time being I was briefing the media on the current state of 7 Brigade; the future was not my business.

My brief was the first part of the two-day visit and lasted thirty minutes. 'Right,' I said at the end to the two dozen or so journalists in front of me, 'before I hand you over to my chief of staff, Major Euan Loudon, to tell you about the rest of the visit, are there any questions?'

A number came at once, so Chris Sexton stepped in. 'One at a time, please. I'll point to you. Please give your name and the organisation you represent.'

All started well with a few innocuous comments. Then trouble began.

'Peter Almond, the *Daily Telegraph*. I wonder if you could tell us your future intentions?'

The one thing that they had all been briefed on was that we were not, under any circumstances, going to discuss future intentions.

'Clearly I can't tell you what the plans are but I will gladly go over again our training programme and—'

'I don't think we need that again,' another interrupted. 'You must be able to give us some kind of idea as to what is going to happen. We have been told that you could attack into Kuwait soon?'

That line of questioning went on a little longer but got nowhere so eventually I turned the talk round to my concern over trivia.

'I would like to mention, if I may, the role of newspapers in this conflict. The TV reporting, it seems to us, has by and large been very helpful in preparing the nation for a war. It shows us training in a professional fashion and generally concentrates on making serious comments. I don't believe the same is true of the newspapers.'

'David Fairhall, the *Guardian*,' said a grey-haired man. 'On that theme, then, what sort of casualties do you expect that the British public should be prepared for? We have been told in the Ministry of Defence that casualties would be light.'

A huge alarm bell should have gone off in my head. It didn't.

'I am quite happy to deal with this because I think it right that the British public should be made aware that a war such as we could fight in the Gulf will result in large numbers of casualties. It is inconceivable that if two armies of the size that are facing each other here went to war there would not be considerable casualties.' Suddenly all the journalists were scribbling furiously in their notebooks.

I went on: 'Now clearly the majority of casualties will be taken by the loser, and that will be Iraq. Our casualties will be light because we are better trained and better equipped. But whatever, with the power of modern weapon systems there will be casualties to the forward troops and that cannot be avoided.'

Unwittingly I was now right in the middle of a political minefield. They had picked up the trail and were after me.

'What sort of figures are we talking about?' I was pressed. 'What percentage? Two? Ten? Twenty?'

'It's not really possible to put a figure to it,' I said uneasily, sensing where this line of questioning was going.

'We are planning on about fifteen per cent,' interjected Euan. The minefield had just exploded in my face.

'Fifteen per cent!' exclaimed someone from the back. 'That's over one thousand five hundred men from your brigade alone.'

I shot Euan a look that said 'thank you for giving me time but say no more'. I had to set this straight.

'What you must understand is that that is a total figure and most of the casualties will be taken by the Iraqis because of our overwhelming firepower. Don't forget as well that the more reinforcements we have the quicker we will win the war and the fewer casualties we will take.

'And don't forget that we have an enormous medical back-up here, something like one medic for every six soldiers. So do keep it in perspective.' It felt to me that I had extricated myself from the minefield. The scribbling was continuing, but my points appeared to have been lodged. We had seized back the initiative.

And it was time to stop and press on with the visit. I stood up to hand over to Euan.

'Before I go, I hope none of you are going to go away saying that Brigadier Cordingley says there are going to be lots of casualties in the Gulf. That will not help anyone. What we need to do is work out a way of alerting people to the fact that there will be unpleasant things happening if there should be a war and people at home must be prepared for it.'

I walked out of the tent. Chris Sexton followed.

'Blast, that was grim,' I said to Chris. 'What do you think? Are we in trouble?'

'I don't think so, Brigadier,' he said in a way that clearly meant the opposite.

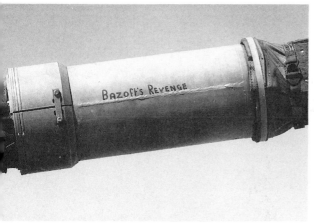

zoft's Revenge, the name chosen for the tank by my crew, s painted on the gun's fume extractor. Farzad Bazoft, an *Observer* newspaper reporter, was executed in March 1990 allegedly spying near Baghdad.

We proudly flew the 1942 Desert Rat pennant from my command tank's radio antenna.

e tank crew in front of *Bazoft's Revenge*. From the left; Corporal Smith who commanded when as elsewhere, the gunner Lance Corporal McCarthy, the driver Corporal Stevely and the loader, en Richard Kemp was away with me, Lance Corporal Shaw.

Challenger. Our main battle tank, mounting a 120mm rifled gun and two 7.62mm machine guns, destroyed enemy tanks at two thousand five hundred yards range and beyond. With their excellent thermal sights they could fight as effectively at night as in the day time. Its protection, Chobham armour, was enhanced by the addition of extra armoured packs on the front and sides giving it a weight of some sixty-four tons. It has a crew of four, commander, gunner, driver and loader/radio operator.

Scorpion. A reconnaissance vehicle, mounting a 76mm gun, was used by the battlegroups for gaining information to their front and flanks. The 16th/5th Lancers were equipped with Scimitars, a similar vehicle but mounting a 30mm Rarden cannon, and Striker which fires a Swingfire guided missile. All three lightly armoured vehicles have a crew of three.

Warrior. Our armoured infantry carrier has a crew of ten, the commander, gunner, driver and seven fully equipped infantrymen. It mounts of 30mm Rarden cannon and a 7.62mm Hughes Chain gun. Like Challenger, extra armour was added to the sides and front, upping the weight to about twenty-six tons. It was capable of travelling at fifty miles per hour on the hard desert.

When the commander and seven infantrymen debussed to assault the enemy they carried with them the SA80 rifle, bayonet and grenades. The only extra help we could give them was an NBC suit and body armour to cover their chests and backs.

The Multiple Launch Rocket System. This awesome artillery weapon system can fire twelve rockets in less than a minute to a range of over twenty miles. Each rocket contains six hundred and forty-four bomblets; these are dispensed from the warhead at a pre-set height above the target. 39 Heavy Regiment, Royal Artillery had twelve MLRS launchers in the Gulf.

The M109 Gun. 40th Field Regiment, Royal Artillery had twenty-four of these guns, capable of firing a ninety-five pound high-explosive shell to a range of over eleven miles. We had five British regiments of artillery supporting us as well as an American artillery brigade. The weight of fire we could call on at any time was quite staggering.

Chieftain Bridgelayer. The bridges carried on the Chieftain chassis can span a gap of seventy-five feet and take only five minutes to put in place. They were invaluable for helping us to cross the numerous oil pipelines.

The Giant Viper. This system, normally towed behind a Chieftain Bridgelayer, was used for clearing lanes through Iraqi minefields. The hose, containing high explosive, is fired, using a rocket, into the minefield where it detonates. This explosion clears a lane one hundred and fifty yards long and eight yards wide.

Martin Bell of the BBC with Major James Myles, one of our senior public information officers.

Lieutenant Colonel Charles Goodson-Wickes, MP. A territorial medical officer who came to our headquarters as the doctor.

Kate Adie discussing events during a period of calm just after the air war had started.

Philip Jacobson of *The Times*, left and Colin Wills of the *Sunday Mirror* were both greatly respected members of the Media Reporting Team. The representation of different newspapers was certainly interesting.

Trying to relax in early February 1991 by playing chess with Richard Kemp. The arbiter is my Land Rover driver Lance Corporal McGuckien.

Lance Corporal Boardman plus desert rat and Lance Corporal Dye were very much part of the team. They acted as a close protection group as well as drivers of one of our more comfortable vehicles. They were affectionately known as the Toyota Cowboys.

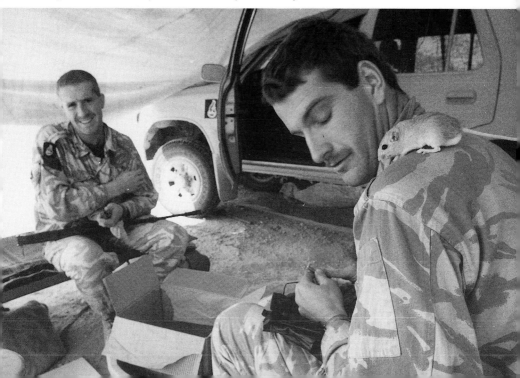

The final briefings. In the middle of February I explained to my commanders how we were going to get through the vast Iraqi minefield immediately to our front. We were to be the first unit into Iraq. The routes, shown diagrammatically on the model, were to be cleared for us by the 1st US Infantry Division (The Big Red One).

On the morning of 24th February 1991 Major General Rupert Smith, the general commanding the 1st British Armoured Division, explained to us exactly how we would advance into Iraq and what objectives he hoped we would be able to reach on the first and subsequent days of our attack.

Chapter 7

Thursday 29th November to
Wednesday 12th December 1990

'Hell, you've got to be joking. Read it to me again.'

'It's on the front page of today's *Evening Standard*. "British Commander's Warning as Gulf Forces go on Alert" and then under that in huge print, in quotes, "Prepare for a Bloodbath". It's written by some chap called Tim Barlass and goes on, "The commander of the Desert Rats warned the British public today to prepare itself for a bloodbath if war broke out with Iraq. Brigadier Patrick Cordingley said . . ." '

'Thank you, Mike,' I said. 'I know what I said.'

I put the telephone down. My brother had just confirmed my worst fears.

I suppose I should have seen it coming because earlier that evening I had had dinner with the authors of my troubles in the Al Jubayl Holiday Inn. After our rather difficult first meeting the day before I had kept out of the way of the journalists and had left it to Chris Sexton and the public-relations staff to shepherd them around. However, I had agreed to have dinner with them, off the record, at the end of their visit.

My day away from them had been most constructive. I had spent it with the marines discussing future plans, notwithstanding the fact that we were not going to be with them for much longer. I was determined to play as full a role as possible and offer as much assistance as I could before we went. So I was in a relaxed mood when we met just after six for drinks (non-alcoholic) and dinner.

The journalists' attitude was now completely different. The aggressive questioning had gone and they were accommodating and at ease. This gave me an opportunity to slip in my thoughts on our perception that we might be forgotten by the British public during the run-up to Christmas. But one thing, to a man, they did pump me about was why, halfway through their visit, the brigade had suddenly gone on alert. The reason was that for a moment we thought there had been a Scud launch. It proved to be a false alarm, but of course I could not tell them that; we did not want Saddam Hussein to know of the Allies' ability to monitor his every rocket launch.

'Routine sort of thing I should imagine; there were either Iraqi troop movements or perhaps an unusual flight somewhere,' I said, dismissing it as if it happened all the time. I hoped no-one would think anything of it. The reporter sitting next to me mumbled something about having to go to the WC and left the table. It was only after he had been away for about five minutes I realised he had gone to call his newspaper and tell them what I had just said.

My first hints that something was amiss came just after the pudding. One of the group lent across the table: 'I'm rather afraid we may not have done you any favours, Brigadier. But I'm sure it will be all right.' What an odd comment to make, I thought, but dismissed it. Only when another made a similar remark while saying goodbye did I begin to get just slightly concerned. So when James Myles took me to one side I was already apprehensive.

'We may have a bit of a problem here, Brigadier,' he said.

'Oh?' I answered, not wishing to give anything away.

'Yes,' he said and sucked his teeth. 'The Director of Public

Relations is a bit concerned about your line on mass British casualties. It may cause a bit of a rumpus.'

'Well, that's not what I said, so I don't think we need worry too much about it.'

So that was what this was all about. Trust the Ministry of Defence to get hold of the wrong end of the stick. Mass British casualties indeed.

But as we drove back to Camp 4, James Myles' words kept turning over in my head. Surely there could not have been a misunderstanding. It was the Iraqis who were sadly going to die, not us. But war is unpleasant and the public must be prepared for some reversals and unpleasant scenes.

At half past eleven, after I had been asleep for about half-an-hour, there was a sharp rapping on the door.

'Brigadier,' came a voice from outside. 'It's the duty clerk, sir. Riyadh wants to speak to you urgently.' I dragged myself into the office and over to the secure link with Riyadh.

'Brigadier Cordingley,' I said.

'Sorry to wake you, sir, it's Nick Southwood here.' This caught my now not so sleepy attention. He was the head of public information in Riyadh. 'I'm afraid there's a bit of a stink been kicked up by some of your remarks to the press.'

'Really?' I asked. 'What remarks and a stink with who?'

'Well, I suspect the Secretary of State. We need a few words of explanation from you.'

'I'm sorry,' I said, realising I had not heard a single word he had said, 'could you say that all again.'

'I said the Secretary of State got wind of some remarks you are reported to have said about mass British casualties and is not terribly happy about it. To be frank you appear to have directly contradicted the official line.'

'This is ridiculous,' I snapped. 'That's not what I said.'

'I'm sure it's not, but we must have an explanation about your remarks so we can put the record straight as soon as possible.'

'For heaven's sake, it's the middle of the night; can't it wait until tomorrow?'

'Not really, no. We must move fast on this. If we hang around it will look like we're trying to hide something.'

115

'I can't possibly give you an answer now, I don't know what they've said I said.'

'This is from the Press Association . . .'

He proceeded to read to me what actually sounded like a fairly balanced report of my comments. There was nothing in it about mass British casualties, but only my comment about a lot of casualties. I was quite happy with it.

'Well, that seems all right,' I said. 'I can't see we have to make any comment about that. If I make some statement now it's just going to make things worse, not better. Leave if for tonight and we'll deal with it tomorrow.'

'But—'

'No buts,' I snapped. 'Tomorrow.' And I put the receiver down. I sat by the telephone for a moment thinking about what to do next. I had to know what was being reported in Britain. I looked at the clocks on the wall. One was set to British time. It showed ten to nine. If I called Germany now I could get Melissa to watch the nine o'clock news for me.

'Hello, Daddy, how are you?' It was Antonia, my elder daughter, who answered.

'Hello, darling,' I said. 'Can't talk for too long. Can you do something very important?'

I explained as briefly as I could. She said she would watch the news. A very long half-an-hour dragged its way across the face of the clock. I could only sit there in the gloom and wait. It was not a good moment for reflection. Had I let anyone down? General Peter, the brigade, the families, most of whom were in Germany with Melissa.

'No,' I said out loud to no-one. I knew what I had said. The press had either misinterpreted my remarks or, more likely, twisted them to make a story.

I looked at the clock. It was now nine thirty in London and ten thirty in Germany. I called Antonia back. 'I can't see what you're worrying about, Daddy,' she said in a cheery voice. 'There was something about casualties but nothing about lots of people going to die.'

'You're quite sure, are you?'

'Oh yes, I watched the whole thing. Do you want me to watch ITN for you?'

'Yes, if you could. Keep an eye on things, will you, darling? I have a bad feeling about this.'

'You worry too much. By the way, why do you always have a fly on your face when you're being interviewed?'

I hung up feeling marginally better.

The following morning there was a message waiting for me. 'Contact Commander at 1000 hours.' It gave me time to prepare. I called Mark Shelford and Peter McGuigan into the office. Fortunately I had taken the precaution of recording the meeting with the defence correspondents. We sat in silence and listened to the tape. When it eventually ran out I felt confident that nothing had been said to contradict the Ministry of Defence line. This was a storm being whipped up by the press.

I asked both Mark and Peter how they had interpreted my remarks and perhaps inevitably they agreed with me. So at ten o'clock I felt fairly confident when I made the call on the scrambler to General de la Billière.

'Patrick, you're probably not aware just how awkward this business has been,' he said.

'Yes,' I replied. I could think of nothing else to say.

'It's a bloody stupid business and quite frankly, Patrick, it shows poor judgement on your part. You laid yourself open. You must think of those at home. They are saying one thing and you, the field commander, are apparently directly contradicting them.'

'Well, actually—' I tried to interrupt.

'I can tell you,' he carried on, ignoring my protestations, 'it took some work persuading people that you had been misquoted.'

'I was misquoted, or rather quoted out of context,' I said.

'I know that, and you know that, and now, thankfully, the Secretary of State knows that. Look, forget it now; you know I am backing you. I think you were perhaps naive. But mind you, Patrick, you have a reputation for speaking out of turn. Make sure it's the last time here.'

While this had been going on perhaps I could have been

117

forgiven for nearly missing one very important piece of news. The United Nations had passed Resolution 678. Unless the Iraqis withdrew from Kuwait by 15th January 1991 all necessary means would be taken to eject them. In the Gulf we were all perfectly clear as to what 'all necessary means' meant. At least now we had a date for the war's beginning.

It was hard to get the media out of my mind but fortunately I was spared the sight of the front pages of every tabloid that followed the *Evening Standard*'s lead. I viewed with some apprehension the visit, on 1st December, of Prince Khaled, the joint commander of Allied forces, to the Al Fadili ranges. General de la Billière had achieved something of a coup in getting him to visit and it was certain to attract press interest.

The press were out in force, but I did my best to keep out of their way.

'A few words, Brigadier,' said one reporter trying to get me to one side.

'Look,' I said, 'you're here to cover the Prince, not me, so please let's just concentrate on the main event.'

I met the Prince, who flew in with General de la Billière, and escorted them both over to my tank. Our plan was to follow a battle run down the range. My crew had been well briefed; at a suitable point the Prince, already in the commander's seat, would order the tank to engage any targets he saw. I would brief the Prince on what to say and when, but he would give the command to fire.

'Brigadier Cordingley, it is a great honour to be with you today,' he said in perfect, if rather formal, English.

'Thank you, General,' I replied, 'but the honour is ours.'

'Tell me,' he said as we walked across the sand, 'when were you at Sandhurst? I mean, which intake?'

'Intake Thirty-five,' I said, 'which formed up in 1963.'

'Thirty-five,' he replied pensively. 'We were not there together then. I was Intake Forty-two.' That would have put him there in 1967.

'Forty-two? Your promotion's been rather faster than mine then.'

He roared with laughter as we set off, he in the commander's seat and I hanging on the back of the turret. We watched the Scots Dragoon Guards do a very impressive battle run, crossing obstacles, firing at targets, calling in artillery. As we came near to the end of the range I said over the intercom to the Prince: 'You take on targets now, sir.'

I gave him a quick lesson in what to say, knowing full well the crew would do the necessary interpretation. However the Prince was very keen to get it right. Two rounds were fired in quick succession and two targets hit.

Corporal McCarthy, the gunner, lined up the next target. It was all going too smoothly.

'Fire!' shouted the Prince.

'Firing now,' replied Corporal McCarthy in strict drill-book fashion and pulled the red trigger clutched in his left hand. Instead of a ball of flame, smoke and a violent explosion there was silence.

A misfire. The drill when this happens in peacetime is quite clear. You have two attempts at firing. If the round still does not fire then you must wait thirty minutes without moving the tank or opening the breech and then take out the dud bag charge. This is a precaution in case the charge is alight and burning very slowly. I looked in the turret. McCarthy was a blur of hands as he checked his firing circuits, circuit breakers and computer readouts. Corporal Shaw, the loader, was likewise furiously checking the breech.

Everything seemed in order. I gave him a look almost of despair. He shrugged his shoulders.

'Give the order again, sir,' he said. 'I think we have found the problem.'

'OK . . . fire!'

Corporal McCarthy went through the drill once more. 'Firing now!' he shouted and pulled the trigger. There was a huge explosion, a massive cloud of smoke and dust, the tank was thrown back on its suspension and the round fired from the barrel absolutely normally. The relief was palpable.

After the tank run there was the inevitable press call and hundreds of pictures to be taken. I was keener than ever to get through this for as soon as the Prince had left I was on a sort of holiday.

Before the casualty saga I had agreed with General de la Billière that I would take a couple of days off and go to Bahrain. In fact he had written to me early in November giving me advice on this subject:

> Once you have completed your work-up training and settled into your new positions you will find there is more time to look round and take stock. I want to impress upon you, yet again, the importance of ensuring that your senior commanders and yourself, in particular, remain fresh and ready for battle when and if the moment should come. You must not be ashamed or have a conscience if you see the opportunity to take two or three days away from it all.

From the day the corps commander had telephoned me in Soltau to tell me that we were going to the Gulf I had worked seven days a week without a break. But even so it was not without a sense of guilt that I set off in a Land Cruiser with Mark and Corporal Dye for the four-hour drive south. It was a journey with little to recommend it: mile after mile of rolling sand and oilfields. The tiresome monotony was broken only by the frequent Saudi road blocks.

At one point as we neared Damman we passed the site of the first oil strike in Saudi Arabia, Oil Well No 7. I looked at it as we sped past and thought about human rights and the international order. But oil was equally to blame for our presence. Not that there was anything wrong in that. To allow Saddam Hussein control of the West's oil was to allow him to put a gun to our heads and would have appalling consequences for us all, including the third-world countries.

And then we arrived at the crossing. Bahrain is an island state off the Saudi Arabian coast. The two are linked by a fourteen-mile-long bridge, with military checkpoints at either end. After much stamping of passports and desultory inspections we were allowed to cross.

Bahrain was greener than Saudi. Palm and date trees were everywhere, luxuriant and verdant. But the architecture was much like Riyadh's – opulent, modern and impressive. We made our way to our hotel, the Diplomat, a five-star complex on the sea front.

Once again it was a wall of conditioned air that hit you as you passed through the over-elaborate doors and into the heavily marbled and gilt entrance. As in Riyadh the lobby was a mass of humanity. Traditionally dressed Arab men in long white robes and elegant *ghotras* mingled with business-suited Westerners.

It was, though, the members of the RAF who stood out. Some were dressed in their tropical uniform – a pale blue shirt, with the blue rings of rank on epaulettes and embroidered wings on the fronts. But it was those in civilian dress who jarred on us. Wearing T-shirts, shorts and flip-flops, they looked very out of place.

'And these buggers get twelve quid a day to slum it here,' muttered Corporal Dye.

In the interests of inter-service relations I said nothing, but he was right. Our twelve thousand soldiers were almost all living in the desert and received not a penny extra in allowances. The RAF had lodged their pilots and ground crews into just about every four- or five-star hotel in the Middle East, and got extra ration allowances as well. It was a source of constant irritation to the soldiers. Privately, I was pleased the pilots were getting a good night's sleep, but now that I could see the reality I was amazed that the ground crew had not been issued with slacks and decent shirts. Their discomfort was all too obvious and I felt for them – a little.

My room, or rather suite, was the like of which I shall probably never see again. There was a vast drawing room furnished with luxurious deep sofas and chairs. Off it was a dining room where twelve Arab-rococo chairs were placed around a heavily French-polished table. Then you passed into the main bedroom, about the size of the ground floor of our London home. A huge four-poster bed occupied one wall. Off that was a dressing room, and off that an enormous marble and gilt bathroom that looked rather like the lobby.

Mark and I met for supper. To be out of uniform, not eating compo rations, was a holiday indeed. The only decision to make was whether twelve pounds was too much to pay for an indifferent Muscadet, alcohol being permitted in Bahrain.

Sunday morning was spent in glorious relaxation by the swimming pool and the afternoon exploring the souks and markets. Monday too began gloriously. I woke early with the sun streaming through a gap in the curtains; I pushed a button on the vast array of controls beside my bed, the electrically operated curtains parted and I soaked it in. Thoughts of my tank, the headquarters and the ghastliness of the looming war were far from my mind.

Over a leisurely coffee in my room I read the Arab morning papers. More good news. Tariq Aziz, the Iraqi Foreign Minister, and James Baker, the American Secretary of State, had agreed to talks. Perhaps they would find a way out of this mess, I thought. There was no way I, or any thinking man in the brigade, would have wished for any other solution but a negotiated one. There was no vainglory amongst us, no lust for war. Feeling in excellent spirits I sauntered down to the lobby, to meet Mark for breakfast.

'I have found some British papers, Brigadier,' he said, clutching the previous day's *Sunday Times* and *Mail on Sunday* and Saturday's *Daily Telegraph*. 'Thought you might like to read them.'

Feeling slightly on edge I picked up the *Mail*. Glancing through I could find nothing about casualties. That is a relief, I thought. If the Sundays were not bothering about the story then it was likely that the matter was all over. I was just about to put the paper down as I came to John Junor's page when two words caught my eye – my name. I read on:

The Commander of the Desert Rats, Brigadier General Patrick Cordingley, puts the fear of God into us all, including, I suspect, the men under his command, by painting a horrific picture of what would happen if we go to war with Saddam Hussein. He talks of heavy casualties and the awful consequences which would follow Saddam's use of chemical and biological warheads. Is it really the function of a commander in the field to talk like this – especially when his own boss, Britain's Gulf Commander-in-Chief, Lieutenant General Sir Peter de la Billière said only a few days ago that he believed any war would be swift and casualties 'not necessarily high'? If I had my way Brigadier Patrick Cordingley would be on the next plane home.

As I read, all the pressures and trauma of the last few days came back again. 'Blast,' I said.

'Mark, let's have a look at *The Times*.' I grimaced as I read the leader, entitled 'A War and a Slump'. My comments filled the first paragraph. Although I still considered them to have been innocuous I felt consumed with embarrassment. Maybe I had made the most appalling mistake. Mark could see I was in the blackest of moods and to his credit tried just about everything to lift my spirits. Later he spent most of lunch desperately talking about anything at all to take my mind off the subject. He is a real-tennis player and went into the finest details of the court, scoring, the history, anything he could think of to distract me.

He just about succeeded and I was beginning to feel that perhaps I was over-reacting when, as we went back to the hotel after lunch, the manager came rushing up to me waving two pieces of paper.

'General Cordingley, sir, I have two most important messages for you. I was told you must get them as soon as possible.' And he handed the two yellow slips to me.

The first message read, 'Phone General de la Billière,' and the second, 'British Embassy Riyadh called. Ambassador wants to speak to you.' Back in my room I tried to contact them both but neither was immediately available. When I eventually spoke to General de la Billière he was surprised I had been contacted. He had just mentioned to his staff that he would be visiting the brigade again before too long.

The ambassador called again later. It was an invitation to stay over the Christmas period if time permitted. At that moment the only place I wanted to be was with my soldiers.

*　　*　　*

By late Tuesday evening I was back in the desert, where there were two problems waiting for me. The first was a sealed envelope stamped TOP SECRET. It had arrived only a few hours before. Daily we received 'Secret' messages, but only very occasionally 'Top Secret'. I tore it open and started to read and then smiled.

'Euan, read this,' I said handing the telex form over to the chief of staff, who was sitting beside me outside my tent. It was in Arabic, from the Saudi Defence Ministry, but came with an English translation:

> In reference to the letter of King Abdul Aziz Naval Base dated 28 November, stating that a female American football match was held on 25 November at the sports stadium between the marines and staff of the temporary naval hospital, the game was televised live on CNN.
>
> We would like to inform you that televising such matters on a international television broadcast has negative results which might be utilised by the enemy to accomplish opposing propaganda against the Kingdom of Saudi Arabia. Therefore I would suggest in future all coordination in all matters pertaining to providing information to the American media is carried out with our specialised information systems through the Saudi Arabian Liaison Officers in your units . . .

And so it went on. We had been so careful not to give offence to our hosts; I was just glad it was not our error.

The second item was a document headed OP GRANBY – Directive 1/90. It was the Commander's Directive for British soldiers in Saudi Arabia, except it was not written by me. It was the first official statement from General Smith.

Written in an analytical style, the directive was a coherent and thoughtful document laying down quite clearly what was expected of us. It was aimed more at those troops still in Germany than at my brigade but it had something to say about leadership and discipline. One section struck me as particularly apposite. 'Leaders who have the capacity to discipline themselves and their commands while still thinking and taking appropriate action are those who triumph in war,' it read. 'During this time of preparation you are to watch, and to insist that your subordinates do likewise, all our leaders so we can weed out those who do not have this capacity. Those leaders in my experience who failed in war were those who required all their moral and physical resources to maintain themselves in the line and had no capacity to discipline and lead their commands which were, in turn, mediocre.'

It was not my style but it seemed straightforward and effective and the author would be with us in under a week.

The casualty saga had died down, but the legacy of the defence correspondents' visit lived on. My comments about feeling unloved by the British public, which I had slipped in over dinner, had clearly hit home. I was back in Camp 4 one afternoon when Martin White came to my office to see me.

'I'm glad to have caught you in,' he said. 'I've come to complain.' A complaint from the head of the logistics operation was clearly serious.

'What is it, Martin?' I said, getting up from the desk and coming round, gesturing for him to sit in the one comfortable chair in my makeshift office. 'What have we done?'

'Not "we", you. Your comments about not being loved. You should see the mail now. We had well over a thousand bags yesterday.'

'I thought you were being serious,' I laughed. Martin told me how the mail had increased by almost a half again. Thousands of letters and now Christmas parcels were pouring in.

The size of my own mail bag also increased dramatically. I spent one day answering over fifty letters sent to me by strangers. It quickly became our policy that every letter we received in the brigade would be answered by someone. I later had to recruit teams of staff officers to while away the small hours on radio watch writing replies to people who had been kind enough to write to us.

But it was not only letters and parcels that were heading

our way. With Christmas not far off, the *Sun* newspaper had contacted the Ministry of Defence and was about to fly out 16,000 Christmas puddings, more than one per man. Not to be outdone, two days later the *Star* also chipped in, offering 25,000. I hoped the men liked pudding.

The *Sun* also gave us 16,000 telephone cards for the fifteen new telephones Mercury had installed in Camp 4. This was probably the best morale boost the soldiers had had for a long time. Rather than have to spend ages getting the right change together and then shovel it in as he tried to talk, a telephone card meant every soldier would be able to call home for free over the Christmas period when he spent a few days out of sand and in the training and fitness centre.

The *Daily Telegraph* had also taken my plea to heart and had set up a Christmas appeal for their readers. It was to raise well over £100,000. The problem we had was how to spend it. My plan was to use the money on the soldiers to buy them the most basic items that the army did not provide, such as toothpaste, soap or shampoo. My reason for this harked back to my visit to Bahrain. The airmen roughing it in five-star luxury – soap, toothpaste and shampoo provided – were getting extra allowances for living there. My soldiers, living in sandy holes in the ground, got nothing. The least we could do was pay for their washing.

The mail explosion also coincided with reaction to my casualty comments. The support was embarrassing but very welcome. It ranged from 'Patrick, trust your instincts and don't let the buggers get you down' (Sue Limb of *Dulcie Domum* and *Up the Garden Path* fame and a real friend) to a particular amusing letter from two of my friends in the Ministry of Defence, Paul Belcher and Philip Bambury.

Returning early from lunch yesterday, it must have been nearer three than four, Colonel Bambury was tripped up by a rising pavement. Toppling into the bus lane the wretched fellow grazed his nose on the back of a passing 48B which, typical of our age, failed to stop. Staunching the blood for him with a discarded *Evening Standard* I suddenly saw your face on the front page. To be honest, and I find I am always a little tired after lunch, I couldn't put a name to you at first. Bambury said he knew a fellow with a dog just like that; then we had you in a trice.

The press, as well, were now looking favourably on my reported comments, presumably as a vehicle to find fault with government policy. Rowena Webster went a little over the top with her leader in the *Sunday Express* entitled 'Churchill didn't hide the truth'. Once again I was consumed with embarrassment but relieved.

In the final week before the division's arrival I received a quite remarkable confidential American military discussion document based on discussions with employees of oil service companies working in Kuwait. It had long been known that Iraq had rigged the Kuwaiti oil wells with explosives with the intention of blowing them up if necessary. What this document suggested was that it could be advantageous under certain circumstances if we, the Coalition, were to beat them to it. The document, read as follows:

It is recommended that oil fields be ignited before troops enter them. This means blowing up well heads and also oil tank batteries.

Why should we blow them?

a.   Resulting explosions and fire will kill enemy;

b.   Fires will burn off any of the toxic hydrogen sulphide gas;

c.   Fires will clearly mark danger areas that will be automatically avoided;

d.   Fires will consume spilt oil so that it should not form a gooey quagmire;

e.   Fire will consume oil that may enter pipelines. They should therefore be mostly empty and so can be crossed and crushed with safety;

f.   Fire will consume all oil in the area denying the enemy its use for fire trenches or other uses;

g.   If blown early enough and allowed to burn off, there will be few fire obstacles but only rather hot machinery and rather blackened soil. This may take several days. What may be left will be individual well heads which can easily be bypassed.

There is no compelling reason not to blow the oil fields. Oil companies routinely detonate and ignite well heads. It is the only way to control the hydrogen sulphide. It is not considered an unusual event. The amount of oil wasted and the damage to the oil well infrastructure is irrelevant in the long term.

The Kuwaitis are assuming that all the fields will be blown and they are contracting with major oil fire and repair contractors to clean up the mess after the war. It may take years but there is no alternative since it is assumed the enemy has prepared most of the oil heads to be blown anyway.

The Wafra oil field is the least dangerous because there is little pressure in the field.

The Burqan oil field is under pressure so the burning oil heads would have a large flame jet three hundred feet in the air, requiring a larger stand-off distance.

The Ahmadi oil field is on local high ground which slopes down to the industrial city and port of Ahmadi. When this field is blown it will result in a catastrophic flow of burning oil moving eastwards towards the town like a lava flow. Given the size of the oil tank batteries at Ahmadi this may be sufficient to burn long enough to destroy the city and port and any enemy in the area.

The Gudair oil field is also under pressure, but like Burqan is fairly flat and should not flow. The Minagish oil field is also under high pressure, the highest concentration of hydrogen sulphide. This is considered the most dangerous.

Igniting several well heads that are close to each other may result in a great deal of smoke, but it will not be a sky darkening phenomenon.

I looked at my map. If they could blow the oil wells ahead of the advance then it might help the marines; they were likely to advance through some of the heaviest concentrations of well heads. If the Iraqis blew them as the marines entered then they could be a major obstacle. If we blew them early enough there was a chance that, as the paper said, the worst would be over by the time they attacked.

I doubted if anything would come of the discussion paper. The environmental damage would be enormous and I somehow could not see President Bush, or John Major, sanctioning that sort of action.

The morning of Rupert Smith's arrival, 12th December, was a cool one. The sun that had been beating down almost without a break seemed subdued and calmed. I spent the previous night in Camp 4 and went for an early-morning run around the perimeter with squads of identically clad Staffords on their morning PT session, during a three-day break from the sand.

After a shower and breakfast I went to the office to deal with the mail. I had another forty letters and Christmas cards.

'Have a look at this, sir,' said Mr McCluskey, my superintendent clerk. 'It's a card from June Brown.'

'How kind of her,' I replied, not really understanding why I should look at that particular card .

'Don't you know who she is, sir? That's Dot from *EastEnders*.'

I tried to answer as many letters as I could before going to Al Jubayl's southern airport with John Reith.

'Before we meet the general, I have to drop in and see someone. It's almost on the way,' I said picking up my beret, gun and gas mask. Half an hour later I was in Admiral Badar's office sitting on his white leather chair and drinking his aromatic, highly spiced coffee and chatting away. Since moving into the desert I had seen little of him. But he had been a good friend to the brigade and had helped sort out numerous small problems.

'So you understand,' I went on, 'that I will no longer be the senior British officer in this area?'

'Well, Patrick, I have very much enjoyed working with you and your brigade. I am sure that when General Smith arrives we will get on just as well.'

'I'm sure you will, Admiral. I have something of a small present for you. A gift from 7 Brigade for all you have done for us.' I handed him a silk Desert Rat tie.

'What a fine tie. I will wear it, I can assure you. I too have a small gift for you.' He nodded at one of the captains present, who handed the admiral a large box. Opening it, he gave me an enormous, lavish plaque of the Abdul Aziz Naval Base.

'And this is from me,' he said, handing me a much smaller box. Inside was a beautiful crystal paperweight. It gleamed and glinted, shafts of sunlight refracting off the cut surfaces. Inside the glass was his personal crest, so arranged that when you laid the paperweight down you could see it reflected hundreds of times inside.

'What a beautiful thing. Thank you very much indeed, Admiral. I will keep it on my desk, I promise.'

'We must go now,' he replied. 'I wish to meet your new general.'

Chapter 8

Saturday 15th December 1990 to Tuesday 1st January 1991

Three days after Rupert Smith's arrival the two of us confronted General Boomer with our future plans. It was a depressing meeting charged with a sense of betrayal.

The bond of friendship that had grown between us all, based on mutual understanding and confidence, was very strong. At almost every level we had mingled. We had marine liaison officers in our headquarters, and Mike Myatt had British officers in his. The three battlegroups each had a US marine ANGLICO (Air Naval Gunfire Liaison Co-ordination) team with them so that we could call upon their impressive airpower. We had developed common procedures, particularly over the breaching of minefields and then the exploitation phase afterwards.

The meeting was in the new marine headquarters building. They had moved from the port to a position further out of Al Jubayl. The concrete anti-terrorist chicane had come with them, as had the same smartly dressed and always polite marine guards. General Boomer's office was much as before. A bare, spartan room, stripped of everything but a desk, a few chairs and his camp bed and personal webbing stacked neatly in a corner.

General Boomer and Rupert Smith had already met, so we wasted little time in pleasantries. 'Before we say anything,' began Boomer, leaning forward on his desk to look at us both, 'General Schwarzkopf has told me that the British government does not want you to fight alongside us and I can't say it makes me very happy. I know you are going to be moving west come January, if there's no war before then.'

'Yes that is so,' said Rupert.

'What you, Rupert, will perhaps not be aware of, but I'm sure Pat here will explain, is the problems that causes us. But that is my problem and not yours. However, at least someone has at last made a decision and so now we can get on and make a plan.'

General Boomer was clearly smarting from the decision. I hoped he knew the fight we had put up to block the move. He went on: 'Although I'd much rather have the Desert Rats, when you do leave us General Schwarzkopf has promised me one of his brigades in your place. So, gentlemen, although you may not be with us much longer, let's get down to business and talk plans. What have you got for me?'

For the next eight hours we joined in with a select Marine Corps planning team to discuss the attack option for their two divisions. They had produced a number of scenarios and responses. For our own part we had not been idle. A few weeks earlier I had set Euan and John Moore-Bick the job of writing a study (we called it an appreciation) for an attack by the US marine divisions with an attached British armoured brigade into Kuwait. We favoured a reasonably short approach to the elbow of Kuwait, mainly for sustainability factors, and then the 2nd Marine Division breaching the minefield helped by our armoured engineers. After that the 1st Marine Division would break out into the open country behind the obstacles and advance towards Kuwait City, destroying the Iraqi reserve forces on the way. Much of this General Boomer liked, but other options were also discussed at length. There was a preoccupation with assault landings which worried the British present and also a feeling that each division might be better served making its own minefield breach. By the time we had finished, rather inconclusively, the sun was beginning to set and the lights of Al Jubayl were slowly coming on.

The daily life of the brigade changed little with the arrival of the remainder of 1st Armoured Division. On 19th December we conducted a joint exercise with the 1st Marine Division to test their engineers in obstacle crossing, with our brigade poised to exploit through as soon as a path was clear.

I went down to the crossing site with Euan. There I found Mike Myatt, also wanting a grandstand view, and with him another marine general I did not recognise.

'Patrick,' said Mike, 'this is General Krulak. He is the Force Service Support Group commander for the 2nd Division.'

'How do you do?' I said, shaking his offered hand. I was transfixed by his extraordinary sun-glasses. They were like something from Star Wars, silvery green and wrapped around his face. I had to ask if they were something special.

'These, Pat, are laser-damage goggles,' he replied, taking them from his face to show me. 'Not only do they protect you from the sun, but they will shield your eyes from a laser beam.'

'You haven't got a pair to spare have you? The soldiers, not to mention my daughters, would think I was incredibly smart if I turned up with a pair of those.'

'I dunno,' he mused. 'What can you swop for them? These cost two thousand dollars each.'

I was rather disheartened. 'I'm not sure I have anything worth that much. What do you want?'

'Well, since I've been here I've noticed the excellent boots you Brits all have. I'd like a pair of them, size eight and a half.'

'You're on.' I laughed. 'I'll have them sent over.'

Later that day, as we were heading back to my headquarters, Euan turned to me. 'Don't you think that was a bit rash, Brigadier, offering him a pair of desert boots like that? I mean if he had asked for a spare Challenger, well that probably wouldn't be too much of a problem – but desert boots! There just aren't any about.'

'The same thought crossed my mind. But I thought I would

133

try Rod Trevaskus. The RAF are always well organised. Anyway I was really only joking.'

Even so I did ask Rod, our Brigade Air Liaison officer. It was normally his job as a member of the brigade staff to liaise with the RAF to co-ordinate close air support or anything else we needed from them. Whether that stretched to spare kit I did not know. I found him hard at work in his command vehicle. I put it to him. There was much sucking of teeth. 'Well,' he said pensively, 'what can you swop them for?'

'Not you as well? What do you want?'

'I'll tell you exactly what I want, Brigadier. You get me one of those nice new Toyota Land Cruisers and I'll get you your boots.'

We had recently been offered about a dozen or so Toyotas by the Japanese for extra and much-needed transport. What Rod did not know was that I had already earmarked one for him. I gave him his Land Cruiser, he gave me the boots, I gave them to the marine general and he gave me what was by now probably the most expensive pair of sun-glasses in the world. I was not convinced I had set a very good example.

As Christmas approached the staff and commanding officers worked hard to make the season as joyful as possible for the soldiers. We were helped enormously by two visits. The first was that of Sir Harry Secombe on 17th December. The day before I discovered when talking to the divisional headquarters that no-one had been scheduled to act as an escort, so I volunteered. It would give me an ideal way of visiting all the units in the brigade in a day without causing anyone any extra effort. Also I was an admirer of Harry Secombe, so to spend an entire day in his company would be something of a treat.

Our first call was to open the new British Forces Broadcasting Station in Camp 4. Until then we had had a choice between the BBC World Service, indispensable if a little dry, the American Forces Network and the Voice of Baghdad, a wonderful attempt at Iraqi propaganda. Like the Germans in the Second World War, the Iraqis were trying to frighten or manipulate the soldiers with a variety of outrageous claims and the most blatant propaganda. The soldiers found the service at times almost hysterically funny and, as the music was to their liking, they became ardent fans of the station. However the BFBS was a link with home. Through the stations in Germany requests could be played and messages read; all of us were glad to have it.

Sir Harry spent the rest of the day helicoptering around the brigade, chatting to soldiers, having his picture taken, shaking hands and telling hundreds of jokes. He never flagged. Just watching him in action was a tonic, but also exhausting.

But the highlight of the never-ending visit programme, the all-too-brief visit by the Prince of Wales three days before Christmas, almost never happened at all.

The day before he was due to arrive I was in Camp 4 sorting out administration when, leaving my office, I passed Peter McGuigan, who was having a rather animated telephone conversation. As I walked by I heard him say, 'So what you're saying is that if that happens he won't come at all?' There was a pause for the answer, and then Peter replied, 'Well, I don't think the Brigadier will like that.'

I waited until he finished. 'What won't the Brigadier like?' I asked.

'That was division, Brigadier. They were saying that if the sand's blowing the Prince won't be coming out to us.'

'What do you mean?' I demanded.

'Well if there's a sandstorm or the weather's a bit off, then the Prince will stay in the port for the whole visit.'

I was furious, and presumed the Prince would be as well, if the soldiers in the sand, some of whom had been there for nearly three months, were denied his visit. I let my feelings be known in the most forceful way. To this day I am still surprised that some divisional staff officers felt I was being unreasonable.

In the event the weather the next day was not a problem; it was a sunny but cool day when the Prince's helicopter touched down. As he climbed out, with the rotors still turning slowly overhead, I saw he was dressed in the tropical service dress of the Colonel-in-Chief of the 5th Royal Inniskilling Dragoon Guards. I was touched.

The visit was a great morale boost. He met as many soldiers as we could possibly get him to, he was photographed hundreds of times, and fielded the press with the light touch of an expert.

As Christmas Day approached we did feel enormously grateful to the British public. For several weeks we had been inundated with cards and presents. We even had one from the Kray brothers. Everywhere people had strung up their cards and tried to make a little corner like home, even if was only in the back of an M109 gun.

However, sometimes I did think we were fighting the Foreign Office. About a week before Christmas a policy document arrived, classified 'restricted'. It began with the astute observation: '1. Christmas is a joyous occasion in which all ranks will wish to participate.' The whole question of religious celebrations in Saudi Arabia was one of some difficulty. The official line was that we did not have chaplains, but morale officers, and officially they had to remove their crosses from their combat jackets. However not many did. It was also policy that we did not hold services in sight of the press, but I could certainly remember seeing several journalists in the congregations. So we muddled through.

The serious aspect to all this was that we did not want to offend the Saudis, their country being the home of the two holiest sites in Islam. But at the same time we were in great danger of upsetting our soldiers who may not have been the most godly of people, but, as one American Army chaplain in World War Two put it, 'there are no atheists in foxholes'.

Riyadh, acting it must be said on advice from the Foreign Office, had banned the public display of Christmas cards. We could have them, but they had to be hidden away where Saudi nationals could not see them. What no-one seemed to have told the Foreign Office was that you could buy any number of Christmas cards in the shops in Al Jubayl.

What was also rather irritating was that the other allies did not have anything like the same restrictions placed upon them. Christmas trees for example, of which the Americans had literally hundreds, were, according to Riyadh's instruction, to be placed 'so they were unrecognisable. They are to be put up in discreet areas where local nationals do not have access.' When decorating them, we were told, 'a minimum of tree decorations is desirable and they are to be put up along the same lines as [the trees]'. In the desert this was not a problem, but for those in Camp 4 it was slightly trickier. The brigade office I reckoned was a 'UK-controlled area' so we put up every Christmas card we could. The cookhouses unfortunately could not be decorated. In fact the instruction had specifically ruled them out and it would have been difficult to get round that one.

We did all the traditional pre-Christmas things. There were the revues, memorably a side-splittingly funny one produced by 33 Field Hospital which I went to twice, despite being soaked three times, kissed by an unpleasant-looking man and shaved by the barber-shop quartet. On the second night I took Mike Myatt, not least to deflect some of the attention. There was a Christmas cake competition in which somehow the one I picked as the winner only came second, and there were the carol services. One of the most moving was a special *Songs of Praise* broadcast simultaneously from Bahrain, Fallingbostel and Aldershot. Some two hundred and eighty of our soldiers went to Bahrain. The BBC had fixed up an enormous television screen so they could see their wives and families in the small garrison church in Fallingbostel, Germany. For some it was almost too moving.

On Christmas Eve and after dark we held a carol service of our own at the headquarters. We sang the familiar tunes and carols under a beautiful clear sky. The stars shimmered and we were bathed in a clear wash of moonlight. We were not all that far from Bethlehem, certainly the closest I had been. You could not help thinking of all that had been and was yet to come. It was clear we would go to war, and it would not be that long into the New Year. It was also true that there are no atheists in foxholes.

After the service we gathered in the cookhouse tent, where we had a television and videorecorder rigged up. We sat around and watched a video of the Soltau primary school's nativity play.

'Oh look, it's Jamie.' 'There's Sarah.' 'That's our Anna.' The running chorus of proud fathers from all over the tent was an emotional experience. Thankfully the film quality was appalling. Had it been any better I do not think many of us would have been able to sit through it.

At midnight I made a quick tour of the headquarters to wish those on duty a Happy Christmas. The back of every vehicle was covered in cards and tinsel. I signed off a signal to be sent to the divisional headquarters: '7th Armoured Brigade would like to take this opportunity to wish all members of 1st Armoured Division a very happy and safe Christmas. It's good to have you alongside.'

Christmas Day began early. The officers, warrant officers and sergeants met in the mess tent for breakfast before waking the soldiers with the traditional 'gunfire', normally tea laced with rum. This year, because we were in alcohol-free Saudi Arabia, it was gunfire sadly minus the rum. After stand-to the brigade officers took over sentry duties, manning radios, and burning off the latrines for the next twenty-four hours to give the soldiers a well-deserved break.

I had an hour to myself before I had to put my private thoughts away and don my public face. My stepfather had died two days before and I felt deeply for my mother, alone after many years of happy marriage. As I opened presents from home I thought of the family in Soltau, indeed all the families in Germany without their husbands. A letter a few days earlier from Melissa had told me how they were coping:

It seems important to have goals and Christmas has become one of them. In the run-up there have been some stupendous parties. A surprisingly large number of wives are staying out here many thanks to the kindness of the Ministry of Defence. They have given each wife two free return flights to England to use as they will; many have used them to get their parents out to Germany.

It does one's heart good to see so many Mums and Dads out and about in a camp that is normally so dreadfully quiet. The girls and their parents are fantastic and I know that they will make Christmas as happy a time as possible under the circumstances.

I do, however, secretly worry about January, which can be an anticlimax at the best of times, let alone with the start of a war imminent.

It all made me wish I was elsewhere. However the press were filming the arrival of Father Christmas at my headquarters. I would, of course, have to meet him in a suitably festive mood for the cameras.

There were times, more of them since the casualty saga, when I really could have done without the press and this was one of them. Christmas is the most personal of occasions, the more so if one is apart from one's family. I did not want to share the moment with the media, but I had no choice. Wiping the remains of a marzipan sugar-coated bear from my lips I went out of my tent just as they arrived.

'Hello, you chaps, Happy Christmas. It's very good to see you,' I lied.

Father Christmas came and went. The press got their pictures and I got a parcel. Father Christmas was distributing parcels put together by the British Legion and the *Daily Telegraph*. Mine contained a number of useful items, including a torch, some talc and a voucher to exchange for a pint of beer when I got back to England. There was a parcel for every man in the brigade.

I spent the rest of the day with the soldiers. I had tried to get to every unit but it was not possible. I served lunch to the Scots Dragoon Guards. It amazed me how the Catering Corps managed to get the rations, but they had produced a traditional Christmas lunch with turkey, Christmas pudding, the lot. I did not investigate the brandy butter too closely, but was assured by the master chef that it was made with alcohol-free brandy, whatever that might be. The regiment was in fine form. If I had to be apart from my own family, there were few better places to spend it than with a regiment like the Scots Dragoon Guards. There was an infectious camaraderie.

I made it back to the headquarters for the afternoon church

service and the revue. For weeks little huddles had formed at odd times and I could hear them rehearsing or frantically trying to come up with new jokes. It was a wonderful show.

Training resumed on 26th December. Rupert Smith had organised a series of six map exercises to go over procedures and doctrine to help us all understand how he wanted us to fight the war. It was the first time that we had had a chance to work alongside 4 Brigade. They were keen once the first exercise was over to draw up brigade-level drills. We were not so sure. Drills do have their place and our battlegroups had honed theirs to perfection. It gave them the ability to swing into action very quickly with the certain knowledge that everyone else would be operating in the same way, with minimum interference from brigade headquarters. But I hesitated at having brigade-level drills. What one needed was not a series of predetermined actions, but the flexibility and confidence to be able to adapt quickly to any circumstance.

I made the most of a lull in these exercises to visit Hamish Macdonald and A Squadron of the Queen's Dragoon Guards, our reconnaissance troops. They had been training ever since our arrival with the marines' reconnaissance battalion in an area well to the north, called Manifah Bay. With the arrival of the division we were shortly to lose them, as they were to come under command of the 16th/5th Lancers.

Hamish told me a wonderful story about Kate Adie and her attempt to film his soldiers just before Christmas. She had heard that, being Welsh, his squadron had something of a reputation as singers and obviously thought it would make a good piece for the Christmas carol service. She wanted them sitting around a campfire singing 'Silent Night'. My permission had been given and a date for the filming fixed.

Hamish broke off. 'Do you remember that you ordered me to give the squadron a two-day break?'

'Yes, you were working them too hard, although I admit the results you were getting were quite excellent.'

'That's right, Brigadier, but it was you that nearly caused the disaster,' he continued. 'During the break we decided to have a barbecue.'

I was intrigued as the story unfolded. A few days before the barbecue date Hamish was carrying out a routine inspection with his sergeant major when he noticed a group of untidy cans and pipes. These he was told would be cleared away. He thought no more of it. The day of the party dawned and by about three in the afternoon it was going extremely well. Half-an-hour later Hamish's smile was removed from his face as his sergeant major came to him, admitting there was a problem. The untidy cans had been used as a distillery for the party.

'Sergeant Major, I am prepared to overlook this now, but never again.'

'That's not really the problem, sir. Tonight is the night Kate Adie is coming to film the boys singing "Silent Night", and I don't think they will be able to do it.'

The black coffee came out but after a further half hour it was clear it would not have the desired effect in time. So a plot was hatched. The youngest and most recently joined second lieutenant was summoned to Hamish's tent. He was told to meet Miss Adie and her crew and to guide them back. He was given the grid reference of the rendezvous.

Out in the desert the young officer sat at grid 864952 and waited. He waited and waited. Two hours after the agreed meeting he gave up.

All the while Kate Adie and her crew sat at grid reference 846952. The two Land Rovers were a mile apart but never met. The BBC did get their recording, but a few days later.

The New Year was seen in with a sense of foreboding. It was almost certain that in just over a fortnight we would be at war with Iraq. But we prayed that, somehow, someone would find a formula for peace.

It also brought the first fatality to the 7th Armoured Brigade Group. Corporal Bolam of 7 Tank Transporter Regiment was crushed to death loading a Warrior on to a transporter. It was an immensely sad way to see in the New Year and one that had a profound effect on the whole brigade. His death crystallised our thoughts about the war;

no-one relished the thought of the inevitable loss of life. Perhaps more than anything else Corporal Bolam's death brought home the reality of the situation.

Work on the new range complex finished just into the New Year. It was a huge range, the largest live-firing range area the British Army had constructed outside of Suffield in Canada. There was some dispute over what to name it. The marines, who had helped us, wanted to call it Devil Dog Range, after their unofficial nickname. We had chosen the rather less bellicose Dragoon Range. Some aspiring diplomat suggested it be called both, and thus the Devil Dog Dragoon Range (or D3 as it became known) was born. On it we could manoeuvre an entire brigade. One hundred tanks could fire at once with artillery firing over their heads. But most importantly we could fire and manoeuvre at night, something that in peacetime is well-nigh impossible due to safety restrictions.

This was to be the final live-firing training. A steely determination gripped the brigade; every minute was to be used to the full. After the problems of Al Fadili we had built this range near the coast so that the danger area extended out to sea. Also the desert was free of bushes so we did not have to waste half the day chasing away camels, nor was it in anyone's flight path, so we could fire when we liked. This was vital since we planned to carry out the most realistic and dangerous training the brigade had ever done. And once it was over there would be no more training. The next time a gun was fired, it would be in war.

Chapter 9

Wednesday 2nd to
Thursday 17th January 1991

There was something of a lull in our lives as we waited to fire on the new range, and it was about this time that food seemed to assume a disproportionate importance. We survived on the basic army compo rations supplemented by bread (we had made sure that the brigade order of battle included an Ordnance Corps field bakery which could produce 14,000 rolls or 2,000 loaves a day), eggs, UHT milk and cereal. We had the occasional supply of fresh fruit and the even more occasional fresh meat. But for most of the time it was a question of ringing the very few changes of compo. A day's supply came in tins boxed up for either one, four, or ten men and was designed to be eaten hot or cold.

A typical day's rations would start with a breakfast of tinned sausages or a lurid pink processed-meat dish called bacon grill with baked beans, all washed down with army tea. Lunch was never more than sandwiches made with tinned jam or tinned cheese (labelled 'cheese processed' but known by all as cheese possessed) and perhaps a bar of chocolate. All with more tea.

The main meal was either chicken or beef in some variety

of stew. There was beef with spices which made it goulash, with onion to form beef and onion stew, with kidneys in thick gravy surrounded by a suet coat to make it steak and kidney pudding, known as 'babies' heads'. The chicken came in an equally varied repertoire, in a brown sauce, or in a curried one. For pudding there was either tinned fruit or a heavy fruit pudding like Christmas pudding. And then there was tea. The tea bags are worth a mention; in the ten-man pack they were the size of a paperback.

In the regiments cooking was mostly done by individual crews; they enjoyed the challenge and it was time consuming. But at brigade headquarters we were more fortunate in having our own two Army Catering Corps cooks, Sergeant Long and Corporal Mercer. From a very limited range of ingredients they were able to produce an amazing range of meals. However, despite their best efforts, it became difficult to persuade soldiers to eat the same food day after day. Food parcels from home assumed an enormous importance. Even a Pot Noodle was a gourmet meal.

We ate together twice a day, between eight and ten in the morning and four and six in the evening. The mess tent became a focus for the headquarters and gave us a chance to chat together. Breakfast, my favourite meal, was always the same. A bowl of cornflakes with UHT milk and sugar from a compo tin was followed by a dietician's nightmare of a full fry-up with sausages, eggs and beans. The whole calorie and cholesterol explosion was washed down with sweet army tea. Supper was whatever combination of compo the chefs could devise, and they never stopped surprising us.

Washing-up was a problem. Swill attracted flies, so we sent the local procurement team out to buy several thousand plastic knives, forks, spoons and paper plates. These could then be burnt, not buried.

Sanitation and washing was a major issue. On exercise in Germany or Britain answering a call of nature was usually a question of either disappearing round the back of a bush or of setting off with a shovel and a roll of loo paper to find a quiet spot where you hoped you were not going to be spotted or disturbed. However, the flies precluded such ad hoc arrangements in the desert. For urination simple 'pee posts' were made, just angled pipes with funnels on the end stuck deep into the ground. The field latrines were made of wood and had four sitting places. If we were stopping in a place for any length of time we would erect hessian screens around them. Instead of digging pits we had tins made for the waste. Once a day these were pulled out from underneath the wooden boxes and burnt out. This unsavoury job fell to the pioneers who were paid 'dirty duty money' of £1.50 a day for their efforts. They deserved it.

Sometimes I found the lack of privacy quite difficult to live with. One morning when I was seated on the wooden box and minding my own business a lance corporal sitting next to me turned and said, 'How's it going, Brigadier?' I was never quite certain what he meant.

The day-to-day wash was a question of stripping off your top and washing in a bowl of water, which you would then use to shave in. When we were static it was not too difficult to get hot water, but on the move, in the tank or Warrior, you were lucky if you had a mess tin full of lukewarm water. The water was heavily chlorinated, which meant tea tasted like a swimming pool, and if you washed your hair you smelt of bleach for days. At the start of the campaign the brigade was using three quarters of a million litres a day. One of our major successes was to get hold of bottled water for drinking, a bottle per man per meal in the hot weather. Of course the water was never cold, and for the whole campaign warm water never got any nicer.

Field showers were a welcome relief. We devised our own system, built on the back of a four-ton truck. The truck had a water bowser on the back into which was put a Benghazi burner, a clever heating device invented by the World War Two Desert Rats. Coming off the top of the bowser was a beam with four nozzles. Using it was something of an art. We usually showered after dark. You would strip off and leave your clothes, gun, webbing and respirator in a place where you would be able to find them again quickly and then pick your way bare-foot across the sand to the truck. Standing under the nozzle it was water on, water off, then soap yourself all over, then rinse off. There were, however, two main problems. The first was what did you do with the soap? You had to try and place it back in your soap dish, in the dark, and then make sure you did not kick it over. If you dropped it in the sand you were in trouble. It was like washing with sandpaper.

The second problem was what to do about your feet. As soon as you stepped off the duckboards they would get covered in sand, importing half a pound into your towel as you dried. After several different ploys I hit upon the successful trick of simply not worrying. If you left your feet wet and walked back to your clothes, by the time you were there they would be dry and you could brush the sand off. Once again I found the lack of privacy difficult, not through embarrassment but because soldiers would make a point of pumping me for information in the shower, and standing naked next to them I found myself vulnerable. There is nowhere to hang your rank when you are naked.

Having washed, it was back into uniform. When we first arrived in Saudi all of us were wearing jungle combats, lightweight variants of the usual green and brown camouflage. These were woefully inadequate, not only because of their inappropriate colour scheme but also because the material, being man-made, was liable to give people crotch rot, a painful condition made none the better for the sand that got everywhere. The new desert combats, of which we were each given three sets, were a great improvement, being cotton and wonderfully cool. But they were not without their own problems. They shrank when washed and the first batch started to fall to bits extremely quickly. We were also each issued with a *shermargh*, the large Palestinian-style headscarf, and it proved invaluable for keeping out the sun and sand. When the weather started to close in in January and February we wore parkas and pretty well anything else we could find.

Headgear was equally varied. When not in my Kevlar helmet I wore a beret most of the time. Initially this was an Armoured Corps dark blue one with a staff officer's badge on it. But security advised it was too distinctive so I adopted a brown infantry beret, which seemed to keep them happy. The soldiers preferred the floppy hat issued with the desert combats.The Irish Hussars' officers wore their unique 'tent caps', rather fine green and gold peakless affairs. We all wore 7 Brigade's red jerboa arm badge.

A late addition to our wardrobe was Kevlar body armour. It was a touch bulky, but light. One soon got used to it and it was a tremendous psychological boost knowing that there was more than a layer of cotton between you and a bullet. It was also warm in the cooler weather.

Although each day was different, all shared a basic framework. Reveille was just before first light and was followed by an immediate stand-to . Everyone not manning a radio would head for their stand-to station. For drivers that meant into the driving seat, ready to move immediately if needed. For everyone else it was into a trench with gas mask, full webbing and a loaded gun. For half-an-hour, as the sun grew from a reddy-pink glow over the horizon to a ball of glowing yellow, we sat and waited.

Once stand-to was over the brigade would swing into its routine. The first hours, when the day was still relatively cool, were a chance for PT. Exercise was essential as our compo calorific intake was over three thousand five hundred calories a day. An average person taking little exercise only needs two thousand eight hundred. Every day when possible there was a run, probably only for two miles. If a run was not possible we did something, even if it was only sit-ups and press-ups. There were times, especially when there was a considerable amount of work, when it took an enormous effort to drag ourselves out for a few minutes of physical torture, but we knew that if we tried to miss it we would lose fitness very quickly.

Then the day's work would begin, be it an exercise, a briefing, meetings with the marines, or whatever else had to be done. We made no distinction between weekday or weekend, the only exception being field services on Sunday.

At seven each evening we would hold a Ptarmigan conference. 'Ptarmigan' is a communications system, half radio, half telephone – the military equivalent of the cellular telephone. Its great advantage is that it has a built-in scrambler so that if anyone does intercept the call it is impossible to understand what is being said. One very useful facility was the ability to make these conference calls. The signallers would punch in a special code and one by one the commanding officers, Euan, Robbie, Martin White and a whole list of people would be linked up. It was a most efficient way of passing information. Since we had sets in the headquarters, in my tank and Land Rover and in Camp 4, I was able to join the evening conference no matter where I was.

After the first bout of live firing, and when we had met our operational deadline, it was impossible to keep up the same intensity of training, and we had to let everyone ease up slightly. Training had to continue, to keep us prepared, but at a lower level, with the emphasis first on revising personal skills and then working up through small squadron, company or battery exercises. It was also vital to keep everyone occupied. Long periods with little activity were a great threat to morale. Soldiers would become bored and with that homesick. It was a recipe for a discipline breakdown.

One potential problem was nipped quickly in the bud. When not on exercise the regiments were getting up and going to bed with the sun and there were twelve hours of darkness each day. Although there were guard duties and radio watches to be done, most soldiers had no option but to go to bed and, since no lights were allowed, there was nothing for them to do but lie in their sleeping bags and try to sleep or think. Morale started to dip.

We hit upon the idea of putting up tents with blacked-out windows but with a generator to run lights inside. These became enormously popular. The soldiers could listen to the World Service, read, play cards or write letters. Or simply talk. Over time these tents became more sophisticated and we were eventually to get hold of videos.

But the greatest morale booster was the 'bluey', the forces aerogramme. These were free and we all made the most of them. Each day the brigade would send out thousands of letters, and would in turn receive just as many. By the middle of November a quarter of a million blueys had been issued to the soldiers in the brigade. The sheer weight of numbers leaving the sheds in the docks caused me an unusual problem. One day I was incensed to hear that a tabloid newspaper was allegedly offering soldiers £300 for every letter published – and it was looking for more than a 'weather fine, it's very sandy' offering. Basically it wanted, for some reason, the soldiers to grumble. The head of the postal service was asked to check where letters were being sent, but not to read them – we did not have that authority. Censorship of any sort is only allowed when war has been declared; until then there was nothing we could do. I pressed him to take note of mail going to non-residential addresses. He found that the most frequent destination was football clubs, presumably asking for signed team pictures. The bribery campaign soon fizzled out.

To ease my own correspondence burden my daily diary entry was sent to Gerardine in Germany. She, once it was typed up, would forward copies to the immediate family. But I was inundated with letters from hundreds of ordinary citizens simply writing to cheer us up and to offer support. We had letters from old soldiers who had served with the Desert Rats in World War Two, some of whom wished to impart tactical tips. From these I was amazed to find how much had stayed the same. Mr Guy Wheeler wrote to me very early on with a cautionary tale of desert dust and how it clogged machine guns. I had his letter photocopied and sent round the regiments. Another letter ended with the warning, 'If you are attacked by Messerschmitts when in your tanks, don't forget to zigzag'.

I struck up a delightful correspondence with Mrs Joyce Miller, a grandmother from Killingworth, Connecticut, who throughout the war sent me letters, cards, videos, food parcels and a chess set. I still write to her. Another regular was Angela from the credit-control branch of East Midlands Electricity in Derby.

But perhaps the most touching of all the goodwill wishes was a letter from a Mr John Tucker, aged ninety-six:

About twice a year a Dunkirk veteran delivers an envelope containing £10.50 from the local Royal British Legion. This week I received an envelope. However with so many of our lads and lasses in the Gulf War, I feel, in the present circumstances, my need must be much less than the needs of someone associated directly or indirectly with the war.

So I've put the 50p piece in my electric meter and enclose the £10.00 for you to apply it at your discretion.

But it was not all support. Some felt strongly that we should not be in the desert about to fight and wrote forcefully to tell us so. Some, too, felt we were being pampered; one lady remarked, 'I do not know why the troops want things so badly. Surely they have supplies and they have not been there so long.' And she had a point; the respect we had for our Desert Rat forebears was colossal.

Telephoning was another matter. As soldiers passed through Camp 4 they were able to use the Mercury-sponsored booths. But sometimes the potential morale boost backfired if the wife, parent or girlfriend was not at home – or, worse still, there was no answer.

Camp 4 had assumed a vital role in our lives. It had been transit accommodation when the brigade was moving into Saudi. When we moved out of Al Jubayl, I left it in John Milne's and Lieutenant Colonel Marti Graham's hands to set it up as a fitness and training centre. Troops were rotated through during a fifteen-day training cycle – ten days in the field, three days in Camp 4 and a day each way in travelling. John had instructors to teach NBC, first aid, vehicle recognition and basic low-level skills and to supervise PT. But the camp was more than just classrooms. Its real importance was to get the soldiers out of the desert, to get them a hot shower, a loo that flushed, a bed with a mattress and food that hopefully did not come out of a tin. There were also basic amenities – a small shop that sold chocolate bars and so on, as well as a barber who as far as I could tell spoke no known language. As a result it was futile trying to explain what you wanted; he could only do one cut, extremely short. In the six months I was in the Gulf I only had to have my hair cut twice.

Sport and games were very popular in Camp 4. We had been given fifty-five 'Welfare Packs' each containing ten packs of cards, two dartboards, six sets of darts, two chess sets, eight draughts sets, eight domino sets, two Trivial Pursuits, two volleyball nets, two badminton sets, a softball set, two basketballs, three footballs and one radio. With this John organised all sorts of competitions. We also involved the Americans, who were operating out of the next-door camp where there was a derelict swimming pool. Between our engineers and theirs we repaired the damage and although it was unheated, it was probably the single most popular place in Al Jubayl in the heat of November.

With all this effort we kept healthy in body and mind – which was just as well as biological warfare loomed large early in the New Year, starting with the inoculation programme. We knew on deployment of the Iraqis' biological capability but it was not until the New Year that we had worked out the response, a series of inoculations, in batches, against the various threats. Although it was an entirely voluntary programme few avoided it. It was a long programme as well. The initial injection of the first batch was followed seven days later by a booster, then another at seven weeks. Rather pessimistically there was a final jab one year later. I did not intend to be around for that one. The next batch, of a further three, started for me on the same day as the second jab of the first batch.

These injections could have dented morale significantly, first because they made some feel ill for about twenty-four hours, and secondly because there was a distinct feeling, although I told the soldiers that it was not true, that in making them voluntary some faceless mandarin somewhere was covering his back.

After the first jab I received a salutary biological-agent briefing outlining the likely threats we faced.

It was believed there were three main agents, starting with anthrax. This, I was told, is a very stable micro-organism capable of surviving in sunlight over prolonged periods. The disease has an incubation period of three to six days; once contracted it is almost always fatal.

The second was botulinum toxin. This is a stable compound though bright sunshine may degrade it. The toxin is

151

at least six orders of magnitude more potent than cyanide or the nerve gas sarin. Without medical care eighty per cent of victims die. With good care that may fall to twenty-five per cent. Fatal symptoms develop within six to twelve hours.

The third was the plague and most likely pneumonic plague, not that it made too much difference to us. This is caused by *Bacillus pestis*, a relatively delicate organism that is very sensitive to sunlight. It is therefore only likely to be used at night. The usual form is bubonic, which responds to antibiotics and where the mortality rate is low. The pneumonic form is uniformly fatal if untreated.

Having read this grim assessment I was glad of the injections on offer, irrespective of the problem of how to deal with the voluntary aspect. We discussed this together and despite heightening all our awareness of the threat we were thankful for the efforts being made on our behalf. Interestingly, we all were very firmly of the belief that if the Iraqis used weapons of mass destruction, and this included chemical and biological weapons, then the allies should respond with massive retaliation, even going as far as using selective tactical nuclear strikes. On my first reconnaissance to the US Marine Corps, when I asked about retaliation a colonel who could not look me in the eye said they had 'no such capability'. I knew they did. And he knew I knew. It was just that neither of us could admit it.

I was pleased when we could focus once again on the range. The first few days of firing were used to brush up old skills and check the equipment. The Al Fadili range had been too small to allow a brigade exercise. Now we could test both myself and the rest of the staff in how to handle a fast-moving offensive armoured attack. We devised, as a warm-up, all manner of exercises for each arm. For days we pounded the ranges with hundreds of tank shells, artillery rounds, mortar bombs and rockets from all manner of aircraft. By 9th January we were ready for the main series of exercises, three brigade attacks with one of the three battlegroups being the focus each time.

On the second day we invited the press to join us. Euan

and I met them as they poured off the buses. We pressed sandwiches and coffee on them as Chris Sexton briefed them. 'Gentlemen, what you are going to see today will be unlike anything any one of you has ever experienced. The next time you see this will be at war,' he began.

'For the next few hours the brigade will undertake a number of attacks and manoeuvres that will tie in every weapon at our disposal. You will see artillery, air strikes, mine-clearing weapons. You will see anti-tank missiles, anti-aircraft missiles and mortars. And you will see the most effective weapon we have – the soldier.

'Gentlemen, I need hardly warn you that this is a live-firing exercise. Safety margins are tight and we may take casualties. Please make sure you are not among them.' They were as likely to get hit as any soldier. There would be cameramen and photographers on the ground among the troops. It was a risk, especially when night fell, but one we felt worth taking. We had to show the Iraqis, who we knew would be watching the Western television news bulletins, that we could and would fight at night, something we knew they were not capable of doing.

The day unfolded as planned and as darkness began to fall we were poised for the Staffords' battlegroup night attack. Controlling tanks at night when you have outstanding night-vision equipment is not that hard. Even if you then add a score or more of Warriors it is still relatively easy. An individual tank or Warrior may go astray but it is quite simple with a series of very rigid control measures to keep things straight, get everyone pointing in the right direction and to attack with safety.

As soon as you order soldiers to leave their Warriors to assault the enemy trenches on foot it becomes a totally different operation. Anyone who has walked down an unlit country lane at night knows how hard it can be just to keep on the path. Then try to run down that path. Then try to run down that path carrying fifty pounds of equipment. Then try to run down that path, carrying fifty pounds of equipment, and shooting at a target while all around you move enormous tracked monsters that cannot see you. And all the time the air is full of explosions and flying shrapnel. You can hear the staccato burst of a machine gun, but is it firing towards you or away from you? Someone nearby shouts, 'Grenade!' How near are they? Were they in front of you or behind you? If you want to take cover, where do you do it? Where are your mates?

The night attack was really the most perfect piece of theatre. At one moment we were static, waiting. I knew what was happening but Brian Barron and the BBC team on my tank had no idea. Suddenly from seemingly nowhere came a roar and what seemed like an enormous rocket shot up into the air, trailing a huge path of red sparks and flame. It was the Giant Viper mine clearer. We watched as it snaked through the blackness of the sky and slowly arced to the ground. A second later we were blinded by the explosion as a one-hundred-and-fifty-yard-long hose full of high explosive detonated in an instant. Once again we were on the move. I could hear the whine from the engine as the automatic gearbox shifted through the gears. In no time we were grinding along through the thick sand and black night. It was moonless. Without the thermal sights you could not even see the ground from the top of the tank, but through my viewer it was as bright as day. I could make out the individual strands of the minefield fence as we passed through the charred gap the Giant Viper had blasted in the dummy defences.

I stopped where I knew we were safe and allowed the cameraman to open the loader's hatch on the tank so he could get out to film. We were on some high ground. He could see nothing. The air was filled with noise, the roar of engines as tanks and Warriors hustled in the blackness, the crack of the tank guns. Suddenly there was the distinctive crump as far to our rear an artillery battery opened up. But instead of the roar of shells exploding there was an almost inaudible pop as the parachute flares burst from the illumination shells bathing the area in an orange-pink light.

'Bloody Hell,' exclaimed the cameraman under his breath. There in front of us was the entire attack in progress. Soldiers were rushing down trenches firing weapons, throwing grenades, the adrenalin clearly rushing through them. From a flank a tank opened up, the machine-gun fire cutting through the night like a laser, its tracer burning red.

What stunned the press, and I was fairly amazed by it as well, was that this entire armoured force had moved in total darkness unseen by all of us. Only at the very last minute when the illumination was called for, did they reveal themselves. And by then it was too late for the mythical enemy to retreat.

After driving back the ten miles in the dark we deposited our BBC camera team into the safe care of the public-information minders for them to return to Dhahran. I could hear their excited talk and I felt confident the right message would be conveyed to the watching world.

Once more we repeated the exercise, offering as many as possible the opportunity of watching us. We managed to concuss Gerry Boxall, the Chief Executive of Vickers Defence Systems and a passenger on my tank, when we inadvertently nose-dived into an enemy trench; that fortunately was the worst accident to happen. With our training complete we felt confident, but not so confident as to lose the ever-pervading sense of anxiety.

On 9th January the talks between James Baker and Tariq Aziz failed. The Coalition forces now had everything they needed. UN resolution 678 gave them the authority they required. The Americans had tried to go that 'extra mile for peace', but to no avail. War, that right from September had looked likely, was now inevitable. And it would possibly start in six days' time. The question in our minds was: was a ground war inevitable? My feelings mirrored those of my senior commanders and was summed up beautifully in a letter sent by an ex-regimental friend, Alasdair Campbell: 'I am torn between praying that the bloodshed will not happen and longing to know whether all that slogging over Soltau, Hohne and Salisbury Plain training areas actually works.'

Planning to come under command of VII US Corps, itself part of 3 US Army, was now complete. As we vacated the ranges, and most of the camp in Al Jubayl, 4 Brigade would take over the facilities and we would move two hundred miles to the Wadi Al Batin. 4 Brigade would then complete their only range-firing period in country before joining us in our new base only fifty miles south of the Iraqi border.

Our move west should have been straightforward to plan. There was only one road, the tap-line road, or Route Dodge as it was known. The problem was that not only was 7 Brigade and the rest of the British division moving down this road, but so too was the bulk of the American Army. In all over fifty thousand wheeled vehicles, eleven thousand tracked vehicles and two hundred and fifty thousand soldiers would have to make the journey. This was the equivalent of moving every man, woman, child and vehicle in York to London down one lane of the M1.

The plan flew in the face of military logic. Because we were to fight so far from the port we would have to pre-dump huge amounts of supplies in a logistics base. But that base, Log Base Alpha as it came to be known, would have to be in place before we moved. We were sending our weakest and most vulnerable troops in first. It also meant that, until 4 Brigade had completed its training, the British division would be a division in name only; its two halves would be two hundred miles apart.

On 11th January we received the warning order for our move west to a concentration area we named Keyes. Lieutenant Colonel Geoffrey Keyes was awarded a posthumous VC for leading the action on Rommel's headquarters at Sidi Rafa in Libya in 1941; he was only twenty-four years old. There was to be no moving before 14th January, except for a reconnaissance party. Martin White took Robbie Burns and several of the brigade logistics staff to survey the land. They had to have thirty days' supplies in place before the war could start. It was to be a monumental task.

The next day more orders arrived. We were to move between 17th and 21st January. Once there our mission was to act as a defensive shield for the vulnerable logistics depot. The plan depended on the timing of a possible Iraqi attack. If they attacked when few of us were in place then we would fight a delaying battle to defend Log Base Alpha in

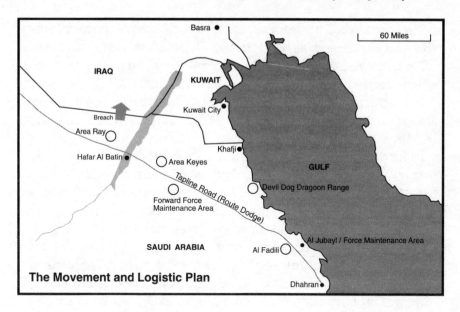

The Movement and Logistic Plan

the hope of buying enough time to get key supplies evacuated and remaining stocks destroyed. If the Iraqis attacked once we were in some force it would trigger a massive counter-attack and the ground war would be under way. In either case, because of a lack of preparation in the new position, we could expect to suffer significant casualties. It was likely to be an anxious time.

As the 15th January deadline neared, tension mounted. The intelligence staff became jittery as rumours spread about imminent Iraqi attacks. We had 'definite' confirmation of an attack on the logistics base on the night of 13th/14th. As we were miles away there was little we could do about it but hope it was wrong. At that time the only complete force in the west was the 2nd Armoured Cavalry Regiment, a formation roughly the size of a British armoured division with one hundred and twenty-nine tanks, forty-two artillery guns and about thirty attack helicopters. We would be the next force to join them with our one hundred and seventeen tanks and twenty-four guns. It was not that impressive.

We were amused by one brief that suggested Iraqi fifth

columnists were at work in our lines. We were warned they would be dressed as Bedouin and possibly riding camels. Therefore any suspicious Saudi Arabian riding a camel who spoke with an Iraqi accent was to be arrested.

To add to the portentous atmosphere there was a heavy storm on the night of the 14th. After months in the heat my tent had sprung a hundred leaks. I moved all my kit further and further into the middle until everything was piled on top of me, and still it rained. In the early dawn the desert was transformed. What had been sand was now a thick gluey paste that made even walking difficult. Land Rovers slipped and spun their wheels as they slid from what had once been tracks into the water-laden sand.

I spent a large amount of the 15th with the Irish Hussars, who were holding another updating day. Their intelligence officer, Captain Tom Beckett, gave an excellent brief on the state of forces on the eve of battle. There were thought to be roughly five hundred and forty thousand Iraqi soldiers in the Kuwaiti Theatre of Operations, organised into five corps with eight Republican Guard divisions and thirty-five other divisions of varying quality. This force was estimated to possess over four thousand tanks, two thousand eight hundred armoured personnel carriers and three thousand two hundred artillery pieces. They could draw on roughly thirty days' supplies pre-positioned in Kuwait. In addition each unit carried some three days' supplies with them. The Iraqi air force consisted of over six hundred combat aircraft of extremely variable quality. They had three squadrons of MiG29s, which were most formidable aircraft, but the bulk of their air force was made up of MiG21s (or Chinese copies), very inferior aircraft armed with near-obsolete air-to-air missiles.

Ranged against them were the allied forces of six hundred thousand men from thirty-one countries including nine US divisions, one British division, four Arab/Islamic divisions and one French light division – a force of over three thousand four hundred tanks and one thousand six hundred artillery pieces. Allied air forces consisted of one thousand seven hundred and thirty-six combat aircraft and another seven hundred and fifty support aircraft.

The enemy in our area consisted of seven divisions – the 20th, 21st and 25th Infantry Divisions, 6th, 12th and 17th Armoured Divisions, and one division of Republican Guard. They had about one hundred and fifty to two hundred artillery pieces.

After Tom Beckett's briefing an SAS captain talked about battlefield survival and what to do if you were captured. 'Appear to be thick,' was his best advice, 'and a malingerer. Act knackered the whole time, drag your feet and play up even the most minor injury. Be a pain in the arse for them. The best time to escape is as soon as you are captured. The longer you are in their hands the worse your chances become and the farther you will have to travel. They are likely to beat you up and likely to steal everything you own, especially your boots.' He went on to give a fascinating talk on how to escape, how to move in the desert and how to navigate at night. None of it was new, but coming from this rather anonymous captain in his SAS beret it carried great authority.

The tension was electric on 15th January itself. None of us knew what was going to happen. I spent the day in routine paperwork and yet more checking of details for the move. The headquarters was to travel on the 17th.

The evening conference call was full of pregnant expectancy. Despite telling everyone that I knew no more about the future plans than they, I felt they thought I was bluffing and would reveal all later that night. In much the same way I was half expecting a call from General de la Billière, or Rupert Smith, or anyone for that matter, but it never came. At nine o'clock that evening the UN mandate for the removal of Iraqi forces from Kuwait expired. Not one Iraqi soldier moved. At midnight Operation Desert Shield ended and Operation Desert Storm began.

In the early hours of 17th January eight US Apache helicopters of the 101st Air Assault Division, armed with Hellfire missiles, and escorted by four MH-53 Pave Low special-operations helicopters of the US air force crossed the Iraqi border. Their target, the generators of two air-defence radars. The Hellfire missiles, guided by the unjammable laser-guidance system, struck their targets, briefly lighting up the Iraqi sky and blackening out a radar corridor in the air-defence network. The war had begun.

Chapter 10

Thursday 17th to
Thursday 31st January 1991

At just after two thirty in the morning of the 17th one of the duty signallers came rushing to my tent.

'Sir, wake up, sir, wake up,' he shouted, shining a torch into my face.

'What is it?'

'Sir, the duty watchkeeper told me to tell you that the Americans have just launched one hundred Cruise missiles at Iraq.'

I thought for a minute. What could I do to help them on their way?

'Thank you very much. Don't wake anyone except Major Loudon,' I said and believe it or not went back to sleep. It was not for long. At half past four another signaller came running over.

'Sir, sorry to wake you, sir.'

'That's all right. What now?'

'Duty watchkeeper told me to tell you that air strikes are going in against Baghdad and we are to go to NBC State One.'

We had all recently been issued new NBC suits, some in

desert-camouflage colours. Made of a cotton outer shell with a thick inside layer of chemically treated charcoal woven into a fabric mesh, the suit was both hot and cumbersome. But in the freezing cold of the early dawn its warmth was welcome. I put on the trousers, before donning the smock. I made sure my respirator was close at hand.

I then debated what to do next and came to a quick conclusion that actually nothing was required of me. Our mission remained unchanged. We had already taken the precaution of doubling the guard and posting both air and NBC sentries. I lay on top of my camp bed and tried to doze. Within minutes I was thrown back into the real world. I heard the one alarm we feared most of all – 'Gas, gas, gas.'

It happened too quickly to be frightening. The drill, practised and practised hundreds of times, took over. Without thinking I shut my eyes, stopped breathing and grabbed my respirator case. I tore open the lid, found the respirator inside and quickly stuffed my face into the mask, snapping the straps over the back of my head in one fast move, exhaling hard and shouting, 'Gas, gas, gas' as I did so. Only when the mask was on and I was sure it was safely in position did I open my eyes and start to think. A gas attack now was unlikely, but we could not take the chance. I was inside a tent so there would be no chemical drops on me but there could be fumes around so I had better get fully protected.

I pulled the hood of the suit over my head and tightened the toggle, ensuring that suit and mask formed a good seal. Next I put on the large rubber overboots that protected your feet. If there were splashes of chemical on the ground they would be quickly absorbed by ordinary boots. Finally I found my gloves. First I put on the light cotton liners and then the thick black rubber outers, like very heavy washing-up gloves. When I was certain I was fully masked and protected I picked up my webbing, hooked up my belt with the pistol hanging on it and went over to the command post.

The atmosphere was one of complete calm. Despite the fact that we had just gone to war there was very little actually happening. I went over to the watchkeeper's vehicle to listen to the nets, but there was no radio traffic. I picked up the log and read the last entry, which had been penned in red ink: '0200 hours. War declared. Multinational forces ranged against Iraq launched an air strike of aircraft and missiles. Active service and war accounting declared at 0201 hours 17th January 1991. Rules of engagement altered. Attacks on positively identified Iraqi formations now permitted.'

After that there were some routine administrative messages that had been sent over the Ptarmigan, but otherwise nothing. I was not sure what I was expecting, but whatever it was it was not there.

Everyone was dressed in full NBC clothing so talking was three times more difficult than normal despite the respirator having a special valve that was supposed to make it easy. The operators had been busy: headphones needed to be re-adjusted to fit over the hood of their suits, special microphones had to be fitted to the respirator and then plugged in. Writing up the log was an effort in the thick insensitive gloves. I found Euan in the plans vehicle. 'Morning, Euan,' I shouted. 'What's up? Why the fancy dress?'

'Morning, Brigadier,' came his muffled reply. It sounded as if he was talking through a pillow. 'NBC alert from division. I have no idea why or where the attack was based. Probably a false alarm.'

'What news of the air strikes?'

'Officially nothing, but the World Service is full of it. Have a listen.'

Despite the war being only a few hours old, the BBC was pouring out information. Most of it seemed speculative. Apparently there had been a massive Cruise-missile strike on downtown Baghdad. It seemed that all sorts of targets had been attacked, including Saddam Hussein's palace, bridges and command centres. There were also reports that the Republican Guard were being bombed and had taken very heavy casualties. Since we had no way of verifying these reports we took them as true. And the 'experts' were already pontificating. I was surprised by one who said the Iraqi army would be slaughtered in the desert because it had nowhere to hide. The point he seemed to miss is that in the desert you are extremely difficult to hit because you are so spread out. I listened for a few minutes more before giving Euan his radio back.

'Doesn't seem much for us to do. Any NBC reports from the regiments?'

'None. All the sensors are clear.'

'Right, I think we will start unmasking drills.' I was keen to get everyone out of their respirators as soon as possible. The fear of going to war would be compounded by the masks, which had the effect of making you feel isolated and alone. By stand-to we were out of the respirators, but kept the suits on. It was a good way to reinforce the new reality.

Scud alerts, with their accompanying dressing-up quickly, became a way of life. But the first such launch caused every one of us real concern. At around three in the morning on Friday the 18th the alert sounded again and we dived into our respirators. Again another signaller came running over to my tent to warn me but this time he had more news.

'Sir, Major Loudon is in plans and says it's important.' I made my way, with some difficulty in the dark, to the headquarters complex.

'Sorry to get you out of bed,' said Euan as I clambered into the back of the vehicle, 'but I thought you ought to look at this.' He handed me the log. It told me seven Scuds had been launched from western Iraq into Israel.

'Blast,' I said, 'this is not good news. I wonder what the hell will happen next.'

As I walked back to my tent I thought of the significance of the attack. Saddam Hussein had threatened to consume half of Israel with chemical weapons. Had he just done that? Even if he had not, it was inconceivable that the Israelis would just sit back and let him shell them. They would want to attack, but if they did it would split the Coalition. There would be no way the Arab forces could fight on the same side as the Israelis against their brother Arabs.

I was glad that I was only a field commander. Back in Riyadh, and particularly in Washington, they would be agonising over how to keep the Israelis out of the war.

* * *

We moved two days late to Keyes, on the 19th. We set off in the early morning. My headquarters vehicles were loaded on to transporters and I made the two-hundred-mile journey with Corporal Mac by Land Rover – and what a remarkable journey it was. Those who travelled Route Dodge and survived, and tragically some did not, will never forget it. At times barely more than one lane wide, it was nose-to-tail with military traffic. Almost every nation in the Coalition seemed to be using it, along with every lorry in the Saudi kingdom. There were seemingly endless American heavy equipment transporters (HETs), each one groaning under the weight of an Abrams tank or a Bradley. Then there were the rag-tag transporters carrying Egyptian and Syrian tanks, or French logistic vehicles. More than once we passed the wreck of a burnt-out vehicle lying at the side of the road.

What was once a fine road was now in places hardly better than a tank track. The relentless traffic had etched deep ruts through the cracking tarmac. And the terrain was mind-numbing. If we had complained about Al Fadili and the Devil Dog Dragoon ranges, they were as nothing compared with the moonscape we were crossing. Mile upon mile upon mile of void. It was as if someone had simply rubbed out the landscape. There were no features, no trees, no dunes, nothing, nothing but empty sand as far as you could see, and of course stretching out into that void was Route Dodge in all its terrifying danger.

After an interminable drive and with some relief we were guided off Dodge and on to the route up to the divisional alternate headquarters where I was to be briefed on the deployment of other troops in the area and any change to our future intentions. Divisional alternate was an exact duplicate of the divisional headquarters. Every formation, from an army-level headquarters right down to a battlegroup had the ability to divide itself into several parts. The logistics element formed what was known as 'rear'. The command element would normally split into two parts, identically equipped with identical capabilities and identical information, the only difference between them was in their manning. Whichever one the commander was in was 'main' and the other automatically became 'alternate'. This allowed the headquarters to move without the commander ever being out of touch. Typically alternate would move and then spend some time setting up, testing communications and digging defences. When they were ready the commander and other key staff would drive or fly by helicopter to the new site. As soon as they arrived it would become main, and the now alternate would be able to pack up and move.

In combat it is probably necessary for headquarters to move several times a day. As each headquarters broadcasts on numerous radios they are not difficult to locate. Once one is identified it becomes a priority target for any enemy.

The alternate headquarters was seemingly in the middle of a vast empty desolate plain. The sand had given way to something more like gravel. The rains from the east had also just arrived. It was cold and foggy and very damp. Although the desert around Al Jubayl was not exactly inviting it seemed like home compared to this place. And the possibility of a night or two in Camp 4 for the soldiers was over, so were the telephone calls home once a fortnight, something the veterans of World War Two would have scoffed at but our soldiers had come to expect.

Division, manned very much by the second team as the rest were with 4 Brigade, were well co-ordinated and able to brief me exactly on where the brigade was to go. However, they were not quite so knowledgeable as to who was around us. They reiterated that our first priority after getting all our men and equipment in place was to conduct reconnaissances for the counter-surprise plan.

That night my headquarters vehicles arrived and were set up with the now customary slickness. My tank, under the command of Richard Kemp – the Royal Anglian officer whose turn it was to act as my personal staff officer – also arrived. The driver, too, had changed and was Corporal Stevely from the Scots Dragoon Guards. During the night and for the next few days the remainder of the brigade assembled. But on that first night we felt very alone. We were only some forty miles from the Iraqi border, outside artillery range but well within rocket range. I had few forces at my command and we were being protected by a very thin line of American troops right on the border. My sleep was disturbed at one in the morning by a thunder clap which I felt through the ground first. I looked out and on the horizon could see the unmistakable blasts of bombs falling on Iraqi positions. I actually felt sorry for them. Miles as we were from the explosions, it was frightening. To be under it would be terrifying.

On 24th January the first Kuwaiti ground was liberated. The small island of Qaruh, twenty-two miles off the Kuwaiti coast, was retaken. It was thought it was being used as an Iraqi observation post.

Once the brigade was fully operational and while waiting for the rest of the division, the commanding officers and I spent some time tackling the thorny issue of how to defeat an Iraqi brigade in a well-dug-in position. Conventional wisdom has it that you need at least a three-to-one superiority against a dug-in force, so, in theory, it takes a division made up of three brigades to destroy a brigade of, perhaps, five thousand men and one hundred tanks.

'What does an Iraqi brigade dug in look like?' asked Charles Rogers on one of the many debates we had. 'We've all seen the aerial shots and we all know what his tanks look like, but how do they actually do it? What we need to know is how much of a target a dug-in T-55 or BMP presents. Will we be able to hit them, as we plan, at three thousand metres range?'

'I have an idea,' said Euan, who as usual was taking copious notes on our discussions. 'This is where we go,' he said, pointing at an area on the map about ten miles due east of us, 'the Egyptians.'

Our neighbours to the east, who had arrived over the last few days, were an Egyptian infantry division. They had dug in all their tanks and would no doubt be very familiar with Iraqi tactics, having also been taught by the Russians.

We sent over a liaison officer who later told us the nearest Egyptian brigade would be delighted to show us around the next day. So we landed at the grid reference given and were met by the brigade commander. We walked over to what was obviously the command centre, which was mostly lorry-borne but with huge Bedouin-like tents dotted around the place. The men seemed remarkably relaxed.

The commander, a serious man who clearly took great pride in his brigade, showed us into his tent. It was a marvellous place with the sides hung with gaily coloured drapes and the floor covered in wonderful carpets. There was even a bowl of fruit on a small table.

'Sit down, please. Some tea?' he said in a deep, heavily accented voice.

He shouted loudly and a soldier in clean olive-green fatigues appeared with an enormous samovar-like urn and started to pour out the inevitable sweet-scented tea.

We talked for about an hour. The brigadier said he had no intention of taking on a dug-in armoured force. And nor could one blame him. However, he was very familiar with Iraqi tactics and was able to offer us much advice.

'You have many anti-tank missiles, yes?' he asked.

'We have the Milan.'

'Ah yes, the Milan. Well, be careful. A typical trick is to put up anti-missile screens in front of every vehicle. Very fine wires. You won't see them, but they will stop your missiles. And the Iraqis are very well practised in *maskirovka*, you know, deception.'

'We have been listening to the radio reports about the great American bombing successes. Sure they are doing well, but not as well as they think they are. A lot of what they are hitting will be decoys and dummies.'

'But I've heard pilots are reporting strikes,' said John Sharples.

'We did the same against the Israelis. They are looking for strikes, give them strikes. A few barrels of petrol inside your decoy and it makes a very nice explosion.'

After yet more tea we set off in some waiting jeeps to see the dug-in tanks. Like the Iraqis, the Egyptians had anti-missile screens and had constructed several decoy positions, something we had yet to do. After a good inspection of the tank scrapes and the general layout we drove some three thousand yards out and looked back. The turret was still quite visible.

Relieved, we returned to our troops. The trip had been well worthwhile.

The first intelligence summary of 28th January made interesting reading. It told us that the 16th, 20th, 21st and 25th Iraqi Infantry Divisions had been identified close to the border due north of us and that behind them was a first line of reserves. These reserves were made up by the 26th and 36th Infantry Divisions, the 12th and 17th Armoured Divisions and the Tawalkana Infantry Division of the Republican Guard. Apparently the majority of the front-line infantry divisions did not have berms or overhead cover and were therefore very vulnerable to air attack.

It went on to say that mines for these units were in short supply and as a result some were being lifted from south-east Kuwait and transferred to the west.

As far as the air war was concerned, thirty-one Iraqi aircraft had been shot down and twenty plus were reported flying to Iran; the significance of this move was not known.

But perhaps of most interest to us was the final paragraph: 'Enemy morale: very low. General Officer Commanding 18th Division sacked and thought to have been executed. Estimated Iraq getting less than ten per cent of essential combat supplies through to front-line troops.'

We received two such intelligence summaries each day; they were eagerly awaited.

On 29th January, which started as a cold, almost frosty morning, we were given the final plan for VII Corps' attack into Iraq. Divisional headquarters had moved on the 24th. They had dug in some forty minutes' drive away and the four of us, Rory Clayton, Euan, Robbie and myself, set off in our Land Rovers.

Their headquarters was organised in a typical layout – the command vehicles were arranged in groups called 'diamonds', their canvas penthouses – the tunnel-like tents fixed to the back of each vehicle – joined to form an enclosed area in which numerous staff officers busied themselves. It

169

was much the same as my own headquarters, simply larger and with a lot more people.

An open area, away from the command vehicles, had been laid out for the briefing. There were chairs or benches for everybody. 'Everybody' consisted of the commanding officers of the regiments and battalions and the principal staff officers in the division and brigades; a fairly sizeable affair. In front of us was a sort of rostrum for the speaker and behind it were various maps, overlays and drawings pinned up on boards. The word SECRET, written in red, hung on a board on the rostrum. The sun soon begun to heat the place up a little, and as we sat down I could feel it on the back of my neck.

Rupert Smith, wearing a green pullover over his desert combats, was sitting facing us on a small canvas chair at the front, studying his notes. He remained there as we all filed in and then, with no preamble or introduction, began the most important set of orders of his life.

'The ground phase of Operation Desert Storm, which will be known as Desert Sabre, will take place in two phases. On G-day the Marine Expeditionary Force and the Arab Joint Force Command will attack into Kuwait through the most heavily defended sector of the Iraqi defences, here.' He indicated several points along the Saudi/Kuwait border.

He then went on to tell us that at the same time in the west the French division and the American XVIII Airborne Corps would launch an attack into Iraq to provide flank protection for the entire operation.

On the second day, G+1, VII Corps would punch north into Iraq through a breach in the Iraqi defensive belt and then swing east towards Kuwait. The corps' mission was to destroy the Republican Guard.

So, as expected the marines and the Joint Force Command East were going to have a very hard fight on their hands. They were going to break through the most heavily defended and best-prepared sector of the Iraqi defences. The French and XVIII Corps were going to have to cover a massive distance, several hundred miles, at great speed. VII Corps was going right into the heart of the Republican Guard.

Rupert Smith then went into greater detail on our particular

task. The 1st US Infantry Division would breach the obstacle belt and push into Iraq to secure a bridgehead twenty-five miles deep. The British division was to go through this breach first and swing east almost immediately after leaving the bridgehead, fighting our way to the Iraqi–Kuwaiti border and acting as right flank guard for the corps; once at the border we were to take up a blocking position facing north-east. Our mission was 'to attack through 1st US Infantry Division to defeat the enemy's tactical reserves in order to protect the right flank of VII US Corps.' The remainder of the corps was to move to the north of us and then swing east and attack the Republican Guard positions on the western border of Kuwait.

The division was to fight in two phases: an artillery preparation and then the attack itself. In the week prior to G-day British artillery would move forward with the American artillery, a total of some sixty batteries of eight guns each, and attack known Iraqi positions to soften them up before the assault. The barrage to be endured by the enemy in the bridgehead area and along our front would be the equivalent of seventy-five thousand Scud missiles. Rory

171

Clayton nudged me at this point with a look of pride on his face.

The question of which brigade led the British division through the breach was dependent on the enemy. If there was some space to deploy then 7 Brigade would lead. If the enemy were dug in right to the breach then 4 Brigade would go first. This uncertainty was caused by the different structure of the two brigades. 7 Brigade, with two tank regiments and one infantry battalion, was suitable for fast-moving open operations. But if the Iraqis were close to the breach it would need infantry to clear the area and 4 Brigade, having two infantry battalions and one tank regiment, would be better suited for this dangerous task.

'It is my intention to fight the division one fist at a time,' Rupert Smith continued. 'This does necessarily mean one brigade at a time, only that if a proportion of the division gets stuck in a hole it is important to make sure that the rest of the division is in a position to be of some help. We must constantly outflank the enemy, cut him off and attack in a series of well-defined and limited objectives, objectives that will be the enemy, as in the desert ground is of no tactical significance. Each objective must be isolated, attacked with maximum force, taken and then we must move swiftly on to the next, by-passing any and all enemy forces of no consequence.'

He told us that the artillery, the 16th/5th Lancers, our reconnaissance regiment, and the helicopters of the Army Air Corps would be grouped together to form what he called the reconnaissance-strike complex. This brigade-sized group could attack targets in depth before we, the two armoured brigades, arrived. Although they would not be able to destroy the enemy they would cause casualties and stop them moving west to help those we were fighting.

He finished by reminding us to bear in mind we were attacking a large force deployed over a big area and that the battle was likely to last for some time. 'We must expect to be exposed to chemical and biological weapons with the ensuing morale and logistics problems that that will entail. You all know the significance of what you have to do. The staff will give you a copy of the warning order when you leave. Do not yet discuss details of anything you have heard today with the media.'

The timing of this briefing was excellent. Up till then we felt slightly cut off from the rest of the war. We knew the air campaign was continuing to pound the Iraqis because all day we saw the vapour trails of aircraft above us, and at night we saw and heard the relentless explosions. But we did not really feel a part of it. It was as if it was someone else's war – an almost antiseptic affair being waged elsewhere. But now we could start our own detailed planning despite not knowing which brigade would lead or quite what we would be expected to attack. However as we drove back to the headquarters I put these thoughts aside because I wanted to discuss with Euan, Rupert Smith's order about the media. It was not as straightforward as it should have been.

Not long before we had been joined by a Media Reporting Team. This consisted of journalists whom we had agreed to look after in every respect until the war ended. They wore uniform, dug trenches, ate and slept with us. In return they let us see their copy before it was transmitted. They called this censorship; we simply wished to correct factual errors and stop security breaches. We could not have been more fortunate in those assigned to us. Philip Jacobson of *The Times* had covered many wars, as had Martin Bell of the BBC – in fact they had seen more action than any of us. John Fullerton of Reuters, who afterwards wrote that he was richer for the experience, was an expert on the Middle East. Colin Wills of the *Sunday Mirror* wanted the human story rather than complex plans. Joe Paley, the energetic BBC radio reporter, and Nigel Bateson, Martin Bell's cameraman, completed the team. But although they worked in such close proximity to us and in spite of the trust that existed, there was still a problem over when to give them the information they needed to write or tell sensible news. Give them the classified information too soon and you inhibited their reporting; delay too long and it could cause irritation.

'Euan, we have got to let them hear the briefings so that they can understand what's happening.'

'Yes, Brigadier,' he said in a firm voice, clearly understanding my dilemma.

Training with VII Corps started on 30th January and with it came the first real feeling we had of the task we were about to undertake. The 1st US Infantry Division, nicknamed the Big Red One after their distinctive arm flash, had constructed a replica of the minefield breach and crossing lanes in total detail. Where the Iraqis had wire, they had it, where the Iraqis had tank ditches, they had them. The commanders of every vehicle in the brigade, from the tanks and Warriors down to lorries, were loaded on to open-topped eight-ton trucks to be shown the spectacle and to be briefed by the Americans.

Here in front of us, in the emptiness of the desert, was a mock-up of an operation for an entire corps. Everywhere you looked there were soldiers. There were eighteen prepared lanes through the minefield, each marked with an enormous eight-foot-high red letter board. There were military police in Humvees at the gaping mouths of each one, guiding and controlling traffic, bright orange boards with 'Follow Me' fixed to their roofs. Engineers in a whole array of vehicles stood on stand-by to repair routes, drag broken-down vehicles out of the way, or deal with uncleared mines. There were infantry dug in defending the area. In the distance I could see M1s hidden in tank scrapes, their turrets slowly scanning the horizon. And in the middle of all of this was Major General Thomas Rhame, the rather larger than life cigar-smoking commander of the 1st US Infantry Division.

We then rehearsed the plan, which called for the brigade to move to four staging areas, one battlegroup to each, plus one for the brigade headquarters. Each staging area had four lanes leading through the breach, two for tracks and two for wheels. The Americans insisted on accompanying every vehicle through the breach and an exercise that should have taken a few hours stretched into the afternoon and evening. I went through at the front of my column as I would on the day and then drove back to the headquarters. Euan met me as I drove up. I could instantly tell that all was not well.

'Brigadier, we have a problem. The Iraqis are up to something. Things are confused but division suspects they may be planning to mount some sort of an attack of perhaps brigade, or even as much as divisional, strength, down the Wadi Al Batin towards Log Base Alpha.'

I went in through the canvas flap into the dimly lit headquarters complex. The whole place was buzzing. We were still on radio silence but I could hear the crackle of static of speakers turned up louder. Groups of officers huddled around finely detailed maps in the back of command vehicles trying to second guess the Iraqis.

As part of the counter-surprise plan we had dug a complete brigade defensive position with infantry trenches and tank scrapes. I thought we were ready for every eventuality. Every eventuality, that is, bar one.

Every one of the brigade's vehicle commanders and drivers was, at that very moment, sitting in the back of some lorry being driven down a sandy track through a pretend minefield several miles away. I had no troops with which to fight.

To our front there was one American brigade straddled across the exit to the Wadi Al Batin, and the Egyptian infantry were nearby. If the Iraqis managed to get between the Americans and the Egyptians then we had a problem. Log Base Alpha stood at the end of the wadi and a determined and strong enemy force could destroy it.

I could hear a watchkeeper talking to divisional head-quarters on Ptarmigan. 'Sir,' he shouted to me, 'the Americans see no activity in the sector to our north, but just in case they have A-10s on stand-by.'

Alone and unguarded we sat and waited.

Chapter 11

Friday 1st to
Saturday 23rd February 1991

The wadi attack never materialised, our suspicion being that it was simply reserves being moved around. Log Base Alpha was safe. Eventually we were a full brigade again and all efforts were put towards planning, now that we had been given the preliminary orders for the division and corps battle. It was now up to me how I would fight the brigade. I called in all the commanding officers on 1st February.

The conference was held in a briefing tent with the minimum of staff: Euan, Robbie and myself, the three battlegroup commanders, Rory Clayton and John Moore-Bick.

'My proposition is to split the three battlegroups into two forces,' I began. 'First a hard-hitting, fast-moving, pure tank force of at least three tank squadrons, to lead the brigade. They are not to get bogged down in assaults but will, if necessary, provide fire support for any brigade attack.

'The second force will be made up of two assault battlegroups. These troops will attack enemy positions and actually clear them of Iraqis. I do not envisage much hand-to-hand trench fighting. Get into his trenches and we will be soaked up like a sponge taking up water, so we want to try and persuade him to surrender as quickly as possible. This will mean considerable force being used initially.'

'I think we should form the tank force,' immediately volunteered Arthur.

'John?' I looked to John Sharples, a man whose calmness and thoughtful advice had helped so much in the preceding months.

'That makes sense,' he replied. 'We've worked alongside the Staffords for longer than the Irish Hussars and probably know them better.' I had already decided on such a split but was happier that it seemed to come from the three commanders by agreement, rather than by my fiat.

Arthur Denaro would take three of his own tank squadrons to form the tank force. This left us with five squadrons and three companies to split up. After some discussion it was decided that Charles should take one Scots Dragoon Guards squadron and the one remaining Irish Hussar squadron to add to two of his own companies. He would give one company to John.

'This is how I want to play it,' I said. 'The point battlegroup, yours Arthur, should make the initial contact with the enemy. You should attempt to destroy them by direct fire and artillery but if that is not possible keep the enemy pinned down while John and Charles move round to assault, preferably from the back.

'Charles and John, I don't want your infantry to dismount unless entirely necessary. I am hoping there will not be too much resistance from the Iraqis once they understand how much firepower we have.'

Logistics were a major concern. In the typical NATO battle plan, with which we were so familiar, each battlegroup had immediate supplies on hand held in the first-line echelons. These were replenished from second-echelon supplies held in the brigade administrative area. This was fine for the defensive and relatively slow-moving battle foreseen in Europe. It would not work in the vast open spaces of Iraq. We would be operating so far in advance of our supply line that our main supply route would be in danger of being over-stretched and prone to counter-attack. Therefore we decided that the brigade administrative area would travel just behind us and would close right up to us if and when we stopped. Then the brigade would go into a triangular formation with the headquarters and bridge administrative area in the centre.

We spent about another half hour discussing the engineers and the merits of holding them centrally or dividing them among the three battlegroups. In the end I went along with John Moore-Bick, who thought it best to keep them in two separate groups that could be switched quickly to wherever they were needed.

We touched again on morale. There was no doubt it was holding up well despite the uncertainty of the situation. We were all spending hours with our soldiers discussing fear. Our common line was we expected people to be anxious; it was completely understandable. And as Charles put it so succinctly, 'I am more worried about those who show no fear.' It was their ability to cope with that fear that mattered and our job to help them work this out. And of course it was not just the thought of being wounded or worse, but also the realisation they were going to be asked to kill.

That afternoon I decided to take up Martin White's long-standing invitation to meet him in the Force Forward Maintenance Area at Log Base Alpha. I wanted to check everything was all right with them and I was keen to make sure we got the support necessary when the time came. I also wanted them to know how much we needed them.

The trip there was about forty minutes by RAF Puma. Although the Coalition had declared air supremacy, flying was still a risky affair and for safety the Pumas flew as low and as fast as they could. As we left Keyes I could see the camouflage nets of my headquarters being swallowed by the desert. In the far distance I could just make out the nets of one of the battlegroups. Even viewed from this low height, the size of the area that opened in front of us was overwhelming.

Flying south we crossed Route Dodge, still solid with traffic. Huge sand-coloured lorries stacked with ammunition, supplies or fuel pulled their way along the black tarmac road. As we flew on, this road, too, was sucked up by the desert sands. We were still some distance from our objective but to the south-east I could just make out marks in the sand, dark patches in an empty expanse.

As we flew nearer these dark patches began to take shape. It was Log Base Alpha – at least twenty-five miles across, and the perimeter berm and barbed-wire fence could not have been less than one hundred miles. Everywhere you looked there were containers, grouped in threes or fours, a high sand berm built around them. There were boxes and boxes of ammunition, containing thousands upon thousands of artillery and tank shells, rockets and mortars. It was an arsenal for sixty days of the most high-intensity warfare the world had ever contemplated.

In other areas I could see whole acres of plastic water bottles. Some, like germinating seed pods, had spilt from their cardboard boxes and lay scattered on the desert floor. In another neatly compartmentalised area there was a huge pile of black tyres, the recent rain making them shine like jet. It was only when you saw the whole thing laid out in front of you like this that you really realised how big the war effort was.

It took us a long time to find Martin's headquarters among all the American stores, but eventually we spotted a Union Flag. His entire headquarters was dug in underground. Since the base was not going to move, there was no need for mobility. We discussed life in general before I told him of our plans; we parted on the best of terms, I being certain that the visit had been completely worthwhile. It was very easy to get too bound up with one's own immediate logistical problems and to forget those further back. In a war, you really learnt the true worth of these people and realised just what an absolutely pivotal role they play. There is no glamour in it, there were no gallantry awards to be won in Log Base Alpha, but we were dependent upon them.

I waited a week before briefing all the commanders, down to and including the rank of major, on the plan and the countdown to war. We now had a date – 21st February.

Maurice Gibson prepared an extremely elaborate model

about twenty feet wide and forty feet long to illustrate the talk. He put chairs down two sides so that people could look in comfort at the masterpiece. Just before midday they started to arrive. It was the first time since arriving in Keyes that many of them had seen each other. It was good to see genuine friendship among them. Even before we started I could feel a unity of purpose, a very strong sense of togetherness.

Maurice's model dominated the briefing area. He had spent days collecting pieces of wire, cans and just about anything he could find to make this most fabulous representation of our area. Unfortunately it was an unusually windy day and officers kept having to be dispatched to rescue the 23rd Iraqi Infantry Division or C Company, the Staffords, as a gust blew them under a Land Rover.

I spoke first about the operation in general terms. 'The soldiers are well aware that orders have been given for the attack and that it is now a waiting game. I know intelligence on what is immediately in front of us is not good but I can assure you all that a considerable amount of damage is being done to the enemy and in particular to the Republican Guard. Last night I listened to a report of their radio nets after a B-52 strike. It was swamped with calls for ambulances and repair teams, commanders repeatedly asking for permission to move.

'Their main supply routes have gone and they are desperately short of spares and food. There are no bridges intact to the north of the Republican Guard and they are having to route convoys round long and tortuous detours. The longer they are on the road the easier it is to find and destroy them. Some units are down to only twenty-five per cent combat effectiveness. Priority targets at the moment are artillery positions.'

The briefing went on, but still missing were the two key facts – which brigade was going through the breach in the minefield first and what was to be attacked after breaking out of the bridgehead. The frustration of not knowing this was considerable. Nevertheless, there was more than enough to speak about and everyone got their chance to have a say. The gunners told them about the artillery plan, the engineers about theirs. By mid-afternoon it was my time to talk again.

'You will have heard a lot of talk in these last few hours about how we are going to fight. There is nothing new in what we are going to do. The Desert Rats have been through all this before, so I thought I would tell you about some of the things I have been sent from their previous battles.'

I held up a small, yellow book, on its front was embossed a gold crown. 'This arrived last week from Rome. It was sent to me by a retired Italian general. It is Saint John's Gospel as issued to our troops in 1939. He found it in the desert in 1941 and believes it belonged to a soldier in the 7th Armoured Division. In his letter he said he knew it was a Desert Rat's prayer book because "we were often engaged in combat with mutual respect, I believe".'

I then held up the pennant that had been flown by successive generals commanding the 7th Armoured Division from 1942 until 1953. It had been sent to the Gulf and to Major Tim Browne by his uncle, a retired major, Harry Gauntlet. He had asked Tim, a Veterinary Corps officer serving with us as water-purification expert, to pass it on to me. Harry had come by it in a rather unusual manner. In Hamburg in 1953 the 7th Armoured Division took part in a Coronation Parade; the finale was to be a drive-past of their three-hundred-and-fifty tanks led by their commander, General 'Splosh' Jones, in a tank of the Scots Greys. This broke down just before the general arrived and Harry's tank was hurriedly called to the front and the general's pennant handed to him to fly from an antenna. All this I quickly explained before reading from Harry's letter to Tim.

I was told the pennant was a very special relic and that I was responsible for its safe custody and warned not to lose it. As you can see, I never did.

I have already told you that I got my tank to the head of the column but not that no-one had really briefed me. I did have the wit to ask a staff officer the route to the parade ground, but he gave me such a withering look, and told me so convincingly that it would be controlled by the Military

Police that I believed him. I was naive in those days but ever afterwards I have never trusted staff officers.

Within minutes of arriving at the head of the column the general appeared and clambered abroad. Almost immediately we got the signal to start and for a few moments I fell into a euphoria of great power. Behind me was about sixteen thousand tons of armoured might and we were driving through one of the greatest cities in Europe, Hamburg. Everything depended on me, it was very heady stuff for a twenty-one-year-old. All went well until we got to the first crossroads. There was nobody there. I gave the general a confident look and ordered the driver to go straight on. Followed, of course, by three hundred and forty-eight other tanks.

We passed several other crossroads all unmanned and no sign of the Military Police. My confidence began to wane, and only finally collapsed when I began to recognise certain features of an area, commonly known as the Rieperbahn. Even I realised that this was an unlikely venue for the saluting base.

Now, you will realise why the general left my tank without taking the pennant with him. A military policeman eventually arrived and we got past the saluting base roughly on time, but the manner in which we did it obviously did not please him. He never even thanked me for the lift.

This story was much enjoyed and I was grateful not only for the precious gift but also for the excuse to lighten the proceedings.

I continued my address on a risky, though heartfelt note. I read to them three of the verses of Kipling's 'If'. People listened, people smiled, people thought. It was not an over-dramatic, cloying moment but one that seemed strangely appropriate.

And so I finished: 'You must go away from here and explain again to your soldiers what is needed of them when they go to war in a few days' time. It is not a thing that any of us would want to do, nor indeed chose to do, but we must do it unless by some miracle it can yet be averted.

'We are very lucky in the 7th Armoured Brigade. We have

had two years together and have assembled a team of truly exceptional commanders at all levels. Since our arrival in Saudi Arabia we have become as one unit. I know we will tackle whatever is asked of us and we will be successful. There is still some divisional training to do; the details we have not got yet. But this is probably the last time we will all be together like this. I don't quite know when the ground war will start but I wish you all the very best of luck.'

The division had two forty-eight-hour exercises planned in the run-up to the ground war. These were designed in part to occupy the soldiers but also to test yet again our procedures for passing through the American division and the minefield.

The first of these exercises was called Dibdibah Drive, – *dibdibah* being the Arabic name for sandflat. It had a near-tragic start; an M109 gun from 40 Field Regiment blew up and the M548 ammunition limber that went with it was destroyed. The largest piece of wreckage was the driver's seat. An electrical fire in the turret had apparently ignited the ammunition. Amazingly, no-one was hurt.

The exercise was hampered by a restriction on the distance we could travel due to the spares availability, and there was also a real-estate problem as we were now sandwiched between Syrian and Egyptian divisions. The compromise solution was to exercise in a big circle around the concentration area and end up roughly where we started.

Driving towards the staging areas to the lanes leading to the minefield I came across a queue of vehicles clearly well short of their objective. Moving to the front I found a lone lance corporal with a red armband standing in the middle of the track stopping every vehicle that approached.

'Wait here,' I said to Richard Kemp, who was standing in the turret next to me. I clambered off *Bazoft* and walked over to him.

'What on earth are you doing?'

It took him a few moments to realise who I was, as my NBC suit covered my brigadier's insignia.

'Guiding vehicles into their correct lanes, sir,' he replied

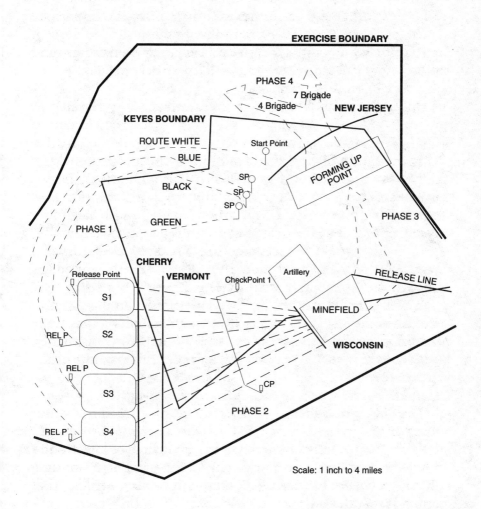

Exercise Dibdibah Drive

in the voice of one who knew that he was doing something wrong but was not at all certain what.

'Well, bloody well stop it. There are some four hundred vehicles in the column you have just stopped. If you continue to do this it'll take us until next Christmas to get through.'

'I'm sorry, sir, but I was told—'

'It's not your fault. Don't fuss. But each vehicle should know where it is going. All you need to do is help if someone isn't sure. You don't need to stop each one.'

'But I am supposed to tell my control as each vehicle passes.'

'Oh, for heaven's sake.'

I then made a big mistake. I started to direct traffic myself, flailing my arms around in a Patton-like manner. I should have been sitting back worrying about much more important things. This put me in a foul mood, something I had told myself time and again I must avoid at this critical stage.

To make matters worse, when I rejoined my headquarters I was told of a fatal accident in one of the engineer field squadrons. Sapper Richard Royle had been working in the back of a lorry when he dropped his submachine gun and a round went off, going straight through his neck. This was shattering news. He was the second soldier from 7 Brigade to be killed. It cast a very sad and unpleasant pall over the entire exercise.

All exercises, whether they are in the run-up to a war, or in the middle of Salisbury Plain, are compromises between what you set out to do and what actually happens. The night move through the minefield, which we had discussed and planned and rehearsed many times, did not go smoothly. There was chaos at the crossing sites with columns of vehicles getting lost and criss-crossing with other columns. It was not helped by the American guides getting lost themselves and taking packets of 4 Brigade through our crossing points. My own tank was being directed the wrong way when Richard stepped in and took us away from the guides. He had had the foresight to check the route in daylight and therefore got us to the right place.

We went straight from the crossing into our forward

assembly areas, again exactly as we planned to do for real, and then prepared to launch into the first assault against enemy positions. But there we stopped.

It was not perhaps an auspicious exercise. It did nothing to dent our own morale and confidence in ourselves, but, perhaps not surprisingly, we wondered if we would get the crossing right for real with the enemy artillery firing against us.

The second exercise, Dibdibah Charge, was to be combined with a move to the final assembly area, Ray. This was well to the west of the Wadi Al Batin. It was from there that we would go to the forward staging posts just behind the Iraqi minefields. Then we would be only one step away from war.

It was to start on 14th February, Valentine's day. It was planned that we would not use our radios until we broke out of the minefield. In fact our radio traffic from the previous exercise was being used as part of the deception plan to convince the Iraqis that we were still in support of the marines. Our messages had been recorded and electronic-warfare specialists were playing it back near the marines by the coast. It was known from deserters that Iraq possessed sophisticated radio-monitoring equipment and was certain to be picking up our now bogus messages. Since they had no air force left they had very few other means of gathering intelligence. They would therefore rely heavily on the one good channel they did have. Unfortunately for them we were feeding them the information they wanted to hear. From intercepts of their traffic we knew they were taking the bait.

Our own intelligence at the same time was proving patchy. We had from satellite and other airborne surveillance systems a reasonable idea about Iraqi divisional locations and strengths, but we felt the assessment of battlefield damage was way over the top. Also what we wanted to know was the exact location of the units to our front which in a few days' time we would be attacking. We had at that stage little real detail.

Another concern we had was the so-called 'blue-on-blue' problem, in other words getting shot by our own side. The marines had already lost nine soldiers to an A-10 in the battle at Al Khafji. Since then we had painted every vehicle with an inverted 'V' on its side for ease of recognition, and placed orange marker panels on the top for recognition from the air. However, I was still uneasy and was determined to make sure the Americans knew the difference between a Challenger and a T62 or a Warrior and an Iraqi BMP. I decided to pay the American A-10 base at King Khaled Military City a visit.

The base appeared in constant activity as the squat and ugly airplanes took off and landed. Most were returning with empty racks. No sooner did a plane come to a halt than the canopy swung back and the pilot got straight out as ground crews scurried around it.

I watched as they reloaded one. Belts of 30mm ammunition to re-arm the eight-foot-long Gatling gun were fed in. This gun could fire seventy of these milk-bottle-sized rounds a second. Elsewhere Maverick missiles were being fitted to the empty racks. On one somebody had chalked the message, 'Up yours, Saddam', a terse rendering of popular sentiment. From landing to take-off could not have taken more than fifteen minutes.

The squadron leader, a very serious major with a Southern drawl, accompanied me and explained how it all operated, how they acquired a target, the choice of weapons, how the Maverick missile worked. We then went over to the control room, housed in a group of makeshift wooden huts on the edge of the airfield. Inside were several desks and pinned to the walls were huge briefing maps and state boards showing how many aircraft were serviceable, where they were and which pilot was on stand-by.

I was shown a brief video of some of the engagements. 'Watch here, sir,' said the major. You could see the Maverick being fired and striking a vehicle in a ball of flame. The next shot showed the vehicle being ripped to pieces and scattered.

'Notice the crew members of neighbouring vehicles.' The crews of every other vehicle in the area had abandoned their tanks and were running away. 'Standard Iraqi response to an attack. They run for it every time.' I hoped they would do the same when they met us.

From the video it was hard to tell whether a vehicle was a tank or a truck, let alone whose it was. 'How do you identify friend or foe?' I asked.

'Well, sir, we have a problem there. We have to rely on good and accurate reporting of friendly positions. At twelve thousand feet you can't see that much but your orange panels should help some.'

It did little to assuage my worries over fratricide. On my return to my headquarters I called for Rod Trevaskus. 'Rod, make sure that every one of your forward air controllers knows what's going on all the time.'

'Of course,' he said, looking concerned.

We left Keyes at midnight on the 14th. Dibdibah Charge, like the previous exercise, was a rehearsal for the real thing, starting with a simulated minefield crossing and then a breakout followed by attacks on 'Iraqi positions'.

There were irritating snarl-ups yet again. The result was that we did not get through the minefield until five o'clock the following morning. Tempers were snapping everywhere. No sooner had we built up some momentum than we were informed that our objective was full of logistic vehicles. The attack was aborted and frustration reached new heights. I was not in the mood for interruptions when a signaller stuck his head in through the hatch of my command vehicle and shouted, 'Brigadier, have you heard the news?'

'Of course I haven't heard the bloody news. We're in the middle of battle.'

Just then Richard Kemp opened the back door. 'Brigadier, you really must listen to this.'

I took off my headsets and picked up Richard's radio. The World Service announcer was repeating the headlines: 'Iraqi radio announced a few minutes ago that the Revolutionary Council was prepared to withdraw its forces from Kuwait and comply with the conditions of UN resolution 660.'

'Incredible, isn't it?'

'Wait, Richard, wait.' But we had missed the main part of the bulletin.

'God! I wonder if it's true?'

It is nearly impossible now to recollect the incredible switch of emotions that occurred. One minute crabby and snappy over stupid little exercise mistakes, the next jubilant and exulted with the thought that it could all be over. I immediately got on the radio to speak to Rupert Smith for confirmation of the news.

'Haven't heard that. I'll contact Riyadh. I am going to stop this exercise now. Push on to Ray as soon as you can.'

I went over to my tank and climbed on to the turret. The sun was now fully up and in a cloudless sky. It felt warm as I clambered out of my NBC suit. As we set off there were tears in my eyes. The feeling of relief and happiness was too great. It was fortunate that we were moving at speed and not even Richard could see this moment of private joy.

We had already sent the engineers and advance parties to the staging area so it was just a matter of driving in to the holes they had dug for us and erecting camouflage nets. The brigade was complete in our new position by five in the afternoon, just in time to have the whole day shattered and collapse about us.

Rupert Smith called on Ptarmigan. 'I have bad news, Patrick. The Iraqi agreement to withdraw was no such thing. Saddam Hussein said he would withdraw on condition that all foreign troops be withdrawn from the Middle East within a month of a cease-fire, all UN resolutions against Iraq be rescinded and the political future of Kuwait be based on the wishes of the Kuwaiti people and not the royal family.'

My emotions went into turmoil. It was abundantly clear that nothing had changed and that Saddam Hussein was merely, once again, playing for headline space.

After the evening meal I retired to my tent. The only positive aspect to all this was the thought that at least 7 Brigade would get home within six months. But we would have to fight – and at what cost in human lives?

*   *   *

I awoke the next morning still feeling depressed. If I felt that way I assumed others would as well. I needed to get out and see as many soldiers as possible as soon as I could. I planned with Euan that I should visit all the units under my command. I would give them as full a brief as I could and then spend as long as possible answering questions. It seemed to work well.

'What do you want to hear from me?' I would start. 'We are on course to attack at sometime around 25th February.'

'How's it going to go? Well, I can tell you it will be noisy, frightening, chaotic and stressful. But I believe it will be quick. We have colossal firepower, we are well provided for from the logistic point of view and morale is high. The enemy's must now be at rock bottom. He has been bombed for six weeks and any minute now we are about to bombard him with artillery.

'And then we will head for home. It has to be quick because I've got a skiing holiday with my family booked for the first week in April!

'What else do you want to ask me? Will they use gas against us? I expect so. But so what? We have the best NBC suits in the world; also just watch the American response to a chemical attack – their suits are not as good as ours.

'And never forget this is a just cause.'

I then went on to tell them about letters I had received – letters of support from home. I read them part of one from the author Fiona Kendall.

I have never before experienced a poignant moment in a supermarket queue but last Saturday, while I was buying the enclosed chocolates, a lady commented 'somebody has a sweet tooth'. I replied that I planned to send them to a good home in the Gulf, whereupon the entire queue burst into an impromptu and inspired rendering of 'there'll always be an England', finishing with three very rousing cheers for you all!

I quoted too from a letter I had received from the Prince of Wales.

My thoughts are constantly with you. The great thing is after my visit I can visualise you all and thus my thoughts and prayers for your safety are even more heartfelt. Take care of yourselves.

I told them about the prayer book and pennant. I then reminded them of the state of the brigade. 'We are the best-trained and equipped brigade in the British Army. The nucleus has been together for over two years. We have wonderful family regiments and battalions and a real brigade spirit.

'But there is a downside to this family closeness. When we take casualties they will be known to us all. The solution is to be bold as well as aggressive when we attack. If we do that we won't take casualties, only prisoners.

'And one more thing, when the press refer affectionately to us as "our boys in the Gulf" I would just remind you of Kipling's poem, "If".

If you can keep your head when all about you
Are losing theirs and blaming it on you, . . .

If you can fill the unforgiving minute
With sixty seconds' worth of distance run,
Yours is the Earth and everything that's in it,
And - which is more - you'll be a Man, my son!

'I will end by simply saying for the last five months you have done an outstanding job. We are now about to do something which will bring good to the whole world and which is honourable and just. And for the rest of our lives, just like the Desert Rats after 1945, we will be proud to be able to say we were here.'

As the visits continued my voice began to go. Eventually I had to ask Alun Price, the senior padre, if I could use some of his communion wine to keep me going – but it had run out.

Inevitably the media was not going to be left out and asked to record my talk to the Staffords. I could see no objections but I did ask the Media Reporting Team, 'Please, should I swear, as I intend to do at one point, leave it out.'

It was my younger daughter, Miranda, who had given me an opportunity for humour; I felt the Staffords would enjoy it. When talking of stress I read them the joke she had sent me: 'Stress is the confusion created when one's mind overrides the body's basic desire to choke the living shit out of some arsehole who desperately needs it'.

The Media Reporting Team respected my wish but I had forgotten that all recorded footage was to be pooled with the journalists waiting in Dhahran. Sky Television leapt on my words and out they went to the world, much to Melissa's embarrassment. The first I knew of this was when I received a letter from General de la Billière on 22nd February: 'Since I wrote my last letter I have telephoned Melissa. She asked me to say that you were seen on Sky using the word "shit". Watch your language! She said you had been too long in the desert and it was high time you came home. I could but agree.'

On the 18th the guns moved forward for artillery raids to last over the next five days. The raids had several functions: first to continue the pounding, already started by the air forces, of the Iraqi front-line positions and secondly to provoke an Iraqi response. Any guns that did fire back would swiftly be targeted by counter-battery fire.

On the 19th the clock stopped. The count was frozen at G-3 pending the latest peace proposals. We all listened to the politicians and diplomats talk, and we all prayed they would find a way out. Tariq Aziz's plan called for an immediate cease-fire and then six weeks for the Iraqis to pull out of Kuwait, and a lifting of UN sanctions. The American counter was a one-week withdrawal, not long enough for their equipment to be moved, and no lifting of sanctions. It came to nothing. The clock started again on the 21st. G-day would be 24th February. President Bush gave the Iraqis until midday on the 23rd to start their withdrawal from Kuwait or suffer the consequences. Even I accepted that the so-called 'last mile for peace' had been run.

The last day of peace was very quiet, very calm. My

headquarters was fully prepared. There was no rising tension, no nervous anticipation. We had rehearsed the difficult minefield breach time and again. All we needed now was to find out which brigade would go first and what enemy positions were to be attacked on the other side.

The midday deadline passed without incident and, much as everyone predicted, there was no move from Iraq.

I went to the Staffords in the afternoon to see Corporals Keeling and Radford. Both of their wives helped Melissa in Soltau, and Mrs Keeling had recently had a baby. We chatted about that and the pictures were passed around. It was a relaxing hour; during it I was interested to find out at this last moment what the soldier on the ground was thinking and what his worries were. They told me younger ones were nervous and a little scared about what lay ahead. The older ones were simply anxious to get it over with and get home. We had, after all, been in the desert for five months, a long time to be away from wives and family, and a long time to spend in these tedious and harsh conditions. They, like me, were worried that Saddam Hussein would pull out as soon as the ground war started and that we would be left with an uneasy peace. Because there were no plans to replace us we could be in Saudi Arabia until the problem was resolved. The best solution we knew was to fight and win quickly.

That evening the weather closed in and at about five o'clock the rains poured down. On getting back from the Staffords I joined Euan and Robbie in the back of the command vehicle. We had a few things to discuss which were quickly sorted out, and then, for the first time since we had deployed, the three of us sat back and talked.

It was a relaxing, cathartic time. There were no operation orders to get out, no commanding officers to brief. We had nothing to do but wait. We talked about our families, about what we were going to do when this was all over, about some of the funnier moments.

It is hard to believe that there was much to laugh about, but somehow we found plenty. And all the time the guns roared and the bombing continued.

Chapter 12

6am Sunday 24th to
7pm Monday 25th February 1991

The deluge continued. I awoke early, having slept badly. Area Ray was awash. I splashed my way over to the command post for a brief from Maurice Gibson. 'Division reported that at four o'clock this morning the first phase of Desert Sabre began. The French 6th Division and US 82nd Airborne Division have crossed into Iraq' he said. He continued by telling me that at five thirty our reconnaissance regiment, the 16th/5th Lancers, had begun its move forward to cover the artillery who would be firing in support of the Big Red One's minefield-breaching operation.

'What of the marines?' I asked.

'No reports from division I'm afraid, Brigadier.'

'Any casualties reported?'

'None reported.'

'NBC state?'

'We remain at medium Category One.'

Everything seemed to be going smoothly. The final divisional orders were later that morning. We were not due to move until the Monday, G+1, hitting the minefield crossing at around four in the afternoon.

After my usual unhealthy breakfast I set off for the divisional headquarters in the Land Rover with Euan and Rory. The staff there seemed almost irritatingly confident and controlled. The briefing tent was set up as usual and the maps, which had become so familiar, were pinned up on the boards. An army television team was poised to record what was clearly an historic event. The other commanders arrived, each appearing outwardly calm.

The weather was by now even worse. The rain hammered down on the tent and the wind picked up its sides and shook the canvas with an eerie rumble.

First to speak was Major Jim Sugget, the divisional intelligence officer. 'We can now confirm that our initial objectives will be from the 12th Iraqi Armoured Division. American intelligence sources suggest they are sixty-five per cent combat effective. We calculate that one hundred and fifteen tanks out of two hundred and fifty and forty artillery pieces are still in working order.

'Across the Kuwait Theatre of Operations one thousand six hundred tanks have been destroyed, twenty-seven per cent of the Iraqi total, also one thousand four hundred artillery pieces, forty-six per cent of his total.

'The 48th Infantry Division in the mouth of the breach has lost ninety-eight per cent of its artillery and its tanks.

'It is believed that the 12th and 48th Divisions will remain in place. An independent, and as yet unidentified, brigade to the north is expected to counter-attack.

'From interrogating prisoners we believe that Iraqi forces are likely to put up limited resistance at long range, but surrender as the allies approach. Be warned, one prisoner surrendering to the marines had a Claymore mine strapped to his chest. He detonated it, killing himself and a number of his captors.'

He sat down. Again I heard the Egyptian brigadier's words in my head: *maskirovka*. I found the American figures too good to be true. And of course we were going to find out how good some analyst in Washington was at his job.

Rupert Smith stood up. He was dressed as he usually was, a green jersey over his desert camouflage.

'Gentlemen. Our mission is to attack through the 1st US Infantry Division to defeat the enemy's tactical reserves in order to protect the right flank of VII US Corps.

'What I have done is to divide our area up into a series of objectives, each given the name of a metal. These have been calculated on our assessment of the current enemy situation and where the enemy might be, and then grouped into objectives I think brigades can manage on their own and where I want to go, or be, in order to develop the situation within our area.

'In effect, there are three lines of divisional objectives. The first is marked by phase line Rose and includes objective Bronze. The aim when we attack up to this preliminary line is to gain room to get the rest of the division out and away from 1st Infantry Division's bridgehead.

'The second line takes us to phase line Lavender which gives us four sets of objectives, Copper, Brass, Zinc and Steel. These get us poised so that I can start to manoeuvre the division as a division with clear air on one side of the area or the other. The third line is phase line Smash, the final divisional objective.' He finished by saying he didn't

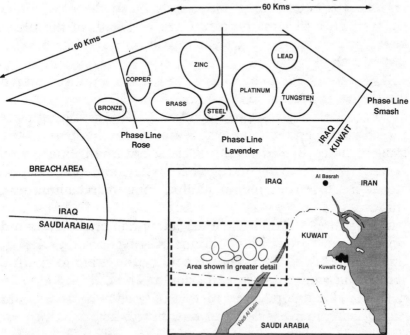

1st ARMOURED DIVISION'S OBJECTIVES

know which brigade would lead but 7 Brigade would be in the north and 4 Brigade would be in the south.

He sat down and John Reith, the divisional chief of staff, gave the detailed co-ordinating instructions. As he did so, staff officers scurried in behind him to hand Rupert Smith scraps of paper. I guessed that the battle was going better than planned and that the timings that even then we were being given, to be ready to move at first light on 25th February, were going to be altered. Nevertheless the general, unmoved, summed up.

'We have talked about this and we have thought about it for some months and now we are going to do it. About fifteen per cent of what we think we are going to do and the way we plan to do it will be proven wrong. It is our business to stop things going wrong and to put them right. We must be adaptive to the circumstances in which we find ourselves.

'Don't let the enemy dictate to you. The moment that happens we are failing to carry out our task and are co-operating with him.

'But above all remember that with very few exceptions the whole of this division has never done anything like this before. People are now getting very excited and twitchy. So take the first jump nice and steady, keep the boys under control. Don't let them go running on, or we will make a series of elementary errors which will only serve to slow us down in the long term.

'Over-confidence, over-high spirits, is in my opinion often the mark of an amateur. With it, when setbacks occur, comes depression and gloom. We, gentlemen, are professionals and our object overall is the reduction and final dispatch of our enemy with economy of effort in so doing.'

For the first time, aerial photographs were handed out. It was an interesting moment as I stared at the black and white pictures with what looked like worm trails on a mud background. It was disappointing. Having seen the mass of footage on CNN, knowing we could drop a bomb down a ventilation shaft and remembering all the modern imagery deployed, I had hoped for a picture of exactly what we would be attacking in a few days', or possibly hours', time. Instead there were only vague interpretations of possible enemy positions.

There were virtually no questions at the end, but as we were about to leave it was confirmed that we should be prepared to move earlier than expected; the timings were not yet known. I walked out of the tent and into the rain with a map about five foot long and three foot wide, a stack of papers and a sense of foreboding. I was almost certain we were going to get orders to move that night. I had assumed that we would have at least half a day to make a final plan before writing my own orders. We had been in the desert for five months building up to this moment yet the culmination of it all was going to have to be done in a couple of hours. I radioed ahead to get the commanding officers ready for confirmatory orders at one o'clock.

On arriving back at the headquarters at midday the pressure was intense. Both Euan and I needed the photograph to do our work, which made life even harder. The problem was to make a plan which would give everyone an enemy position to aim for, yet not get them bogged down in detail. I studied the aerial photograph with dismay. I had so little to go on. I decided it would be best to plan a brigade advance on a broad front with the possible enemy brigade in Zinc as the main objective. There could well be small pockets of enemy on the way, but I was hoping they would not slow us down. For instance I knew for certain there was a defended communications site in the north of Copper that we had to destroy. But there were so many other imponderables. Which brigade would advance first? Would the advance be at night? Would the 16th/5th Lancers, the medium reconnaissance regiment, be well clear of our positions? Would I have support from the American Apache helicopters?

My biggest challenge would be to get the brigade moving in an aggressive way. We could do it superbly without an enemy; would the first sight of a tank or a mine cause us to grind to a halt? I also had a totally irrational wish not to put our first attack in at night. Irrational because all the advantages were with us in the dark. We had thermal sights and satellite navigation; the enemy had neither.

As the commanding officers began to arrive Euan and I had just about finished marking up the briefing map. Our orders will not go down in military history as a textbook example of how to do it, but at least we had a plan. 'The Irish Hussars [three squadrons of tanks] will lead out of the bridgehead with the Staffords [two squadrons of tanks and two companies of infantry] left and the Scots Dragoon Guards [two squadrons of tanks and one company of infantry] right. 40 Field Regiment will be behind brigade main,' I began.

'Irish Hussars, you are to approach objective Zinc' – I pointed it out on the map – 'from the west avoiding the enemy in Copper and conduct an aggressive reconnaissance to fix and locate enemy strengths and dispositions.

'Scots Dragoon Guards, you are to destroy the enemy communications site in Copper.

'Staffords and Scots Dragoon Guards, you are subsequently to manoeuvre north and then east to position yourselves to attack Zinc from the rear. I will co-ordinate all

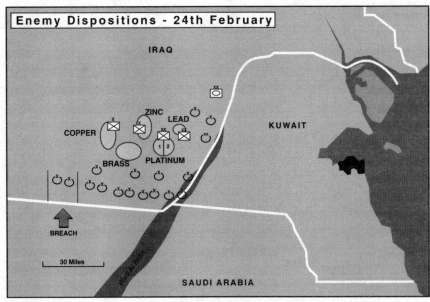

moves.' And then in an almost direct replay of the divisional commander's orders, as first Euan and then Robbie went over the co-ordinating and logistic details, messengers started to hand me notes.

The first was a report from VII Corps on progress at the breach. The Big Red One had met almost minimal resistance and had taken a large number of prisoners. Breaching operations were well ahead of schedule. All divisions were warned off for a revised timetable.

A few minutes later came another message from division: 'All units are to come to five minutes' notice to move. Warning order for move to staging areas imminent. 7 Brigade be prepared to move by track. No move before 1530 hours.' This was a jump forward of at least sixteen hours in the timings we had been given not three hours earlier, and even tighter than I had expected it would be.

Despite my anticipation it did cause us to blink. The original plan had called for both brigades to move their tanks from Ray to the staging areas behind the minefields on tank transporters. 4 Brigade was already loading with just a few 7 Brigade tanks, mine included. There was now not enough time to shuttle both brigades by transporter. We would have to drive the remaining thirty miles to our next positions.

'Interesting news, gentlemen,' I said as Robbie finished. 'We have just been given a revised schedule. We move in two hours – by track.'

'Two hours!' exclaimed John.

'You're kidding. We're not ready,' said Arthur.

'I've still got half my Warriors being worked on,' said Charles.

'There's no use complaining. We move at three thirty. I suggest we call it a day here unless you have any questions. You need to get back to your men. I can't say it's how I would have chosen to go to war, but at least we are not going to have time to brood. But – well, good luck.'

I had wanted to make some sort of speech, but in the end there was no time. I had concerns about going to war with a thirty-mile approach march. Although engine reliability was now much better, I could still expect to lose some four or five tanks before we had even seen an Iraqi. But the rush was on and perhaps it was a blessing in disguise. The waiting would be over in a flash.

When the commanding officers had left we set about packing up. We had been in Ray for over a week and there was grounded equipment everywhere. Corporal Mac had already started clearing up my kit and organising the stowing of my tent. I doubted I was going to see that for a while. What sleep I got would either be grabbed on the back decks of my tank, or if I was very lucky in a bivouac beside it.

At two o'clock I left the headquarters and made my way forward in my Land Rover to the staging areas where I could rejoin my tank. As we picked our way forward down the carefully prepared routes, for the first time I saw what it meant for a corps to go to war. We passed literally hundreds of tanks, armoured vehicles, trucks and light vehicles. It was a foul afternoon; the wind was blowing even harder and despite the earlier rain, dust and sand were being kicked up all over the place.

I arrived in the staging area to find it even more poorly marked than during the rehearsal. We had made considerable criticism of poor signposting and yet our remarks, it seemed, had been totally ignored. Suppressing mounting irritation I set about trying to find my tank.

It was dusk before we located it but without the rest of the headquarters there was little I could do. Fortunately Rory Clayton had arrived in his command Warrior and I sat in the back, dressed in my NBC suit, listening to the guns firing in the distance. The chess board came out and Richard and I played two rather ineffectual games. He won both.

For some hours we waited, until out of the darkness came the familiar rumble of tracks and engines.

'They're here,' said Richard as he went forward to guide the vehicles into place. A few minutes later I was extremely glad to see Euan's smiling face peer round the back door of Rory's Warrior.

'That was a bloody awful drive,' he said, wiping the dust from his face. 'What happened to the route markers?'

'Quite. Anyway we're all here now so no point in worrying.'

'Not quite all, I'm afraid. Your command vehicle has broken down about ten miles back.'

'Who's with it?'

'Mark was commanding it. The fitters were there when I passed so it should be all right.'

It gave me some concern. Although I intended to command the battle from a tank, the FV436, which was the normal command vehicle for a brigade commander, was a useful back-up and had excellent communications.

At twenty-three minutes past nine we received the latest intelligence update.

'The 25th and 48th Iraqi Infantry Divisions to our front are not presenting a challenge. Large numbers of prisoners have been taken. The unidentified independent tank brigade presents a threat to us and is reported moving south. The Republican Guard Divisions, Hamurabi and Tawakalna, are reported to be removing sandbags and preparing to move.'

By eleven o'clock, seven and a half hours after we had been given the order to move, I reported to division that all of 7 Brigade's vehicles were fit and in the staging areas. We were ready. Then, as it seemed we were going to be in the waiting areas for some time, I lay down beside the tank, under a groundsheet to keep off the rain. I was not there very long.

'Sir, General Smith is calling you.'

I looked at my watch; eleven thirty.

'All stations orders. Order of march: 7 Brigade, Artillery Group, 4 Brigade. 7 Brigade is to take 2 Field Regiment, Royal Artillery, under command. Helicopter reconnaissance is at priority call. 7 Brigade is to advance to objectives Copper and Zinc and cut enemy routes east to west. No move before 0800 hours 25 February. Limit of exploitation, phase line Lavender.'

I smiled. We were going through the breach first. Although I had tried not to make an issue of it I felt it was our due. We had been here for five months; the soldiers wanted to go first. Inter-brigade rivalries apart, it also meant that the Americans had cleared the bridgehead, which was very good news. A quick back-of-the-envelope calculation and I reckoned we would hit Zinc around midnight on the 25th. Our first attack on an unknown position would be done in the pitch black, almost certainly in the rain, against an enemy about which we knew very little. It was a daunting prospect.

I called my commanders on the secure radio. 'We are leading the division. Confirmatory orders at this headquarters at 0630 hours tomorrow morning. Priority now is replenishment and rest. No move before 0800 hours. We are to be at thirty minutes' notice to move from 0730 hours. I suggest you and all commanders get a good night's sleep. It may be your last chance for a bit.'

I tried once more to sleep and tossed restlessly into Monday 25th February.

The rain was relentless and at five in the morning I had had enough of tossing and turning. As I did not want to wake the crew by starting the tank engine there was no hot water, so I washed with cold and had a miserable breakfast of cold sausages and baked beans out of a tin.

Orders got under way twenty minutes late. John Sharples, whose battlegroup was some twelve miles away, got lost when the GPS satellite navigation system ceased to work. First thing in the morning, and then just after dark, the satellites that provided the signals would go out of range. As a result every morning and evening for about fifteen minutes we would get lost.

Orders were brief and perfunctory.

'Situation: enemy no change.

'Friendly forces: 3 US Brigade of the 1st Infantry Division will move forward from phase line Colorado to New Jersey by 1200 hours.

'Concept of operations: confirmed.

'Mission: confirmed.

'Execution, general outline: the main objective remains Zinc, but there is still the known enemy position in Copper to deal with. That is to be a Scots Dragoon Guard battlegroup task.

'No move before 0800 hours.

'So that's it. I just wanted to get you all together to see all is well, check on your vehicle state and that nothing is worrying you. Otherwise, I will see you in Iraq.'

As they departed I went over to my tank. Climbing into the turret I looked around the area and the men of the headquarters. Not for the first time a momentary feeling of concern gripped me. What if . . . ? I had no idea when I would next get out of my tank, nor what I would find when I did. That we would win was certain, but at what cost? More than anything else I wanted to bring back every man in the brigade alive. But I knew that was a forlorn hope. And then the fear of battle. How worried were the soldiers? Were we about to drive into the first modern chemical war? How would we cope with the claustrophobia of a respirator worn for hour after hour?

And then what of the enemy? How much had they suffered already and to what effect? Did they understand what we were capable of, the deluge of destruction that was about to be meted out on them? And all of this for the sake of one totally evil man.

'Ready to move, Brigadier.' A voice in my headphones. It shook me back into the real world.

'What was that?'

'Ready to move, sir.' It was Corporal Stevely, the driver. I looked over to Richard. He nodded. I gently tapped Corporal McCarthy on the shoulder with my boot. He half turned giving me the thumbs up sign.

'Right then. Let's go.'

We drove the short distance to the staging area, where we waited again. The brigade was assembled in four such areas. The route from each was colour coded. The headquarters would move down the White route to the border, which was codenamed phase line Vermont. There we would be met by guides and taken through the border and then into the breach. As in the rehearsal there were sixteen tracks through the breach, lettered A to P. The White route split into four separate tracks through the breach, E to H, two for wheels, two for tracks. We were to take route G. The mouth of the breach was codenamed phase line Iowa, the exit from the breach was phase line Wisconsin. Once we crossed Wisconsin we would say goodbye to the American guides and pick up British ones who, in turn, would take us along the remainder of route White to the forming-up points in Iraq.

It was the same for the entire brigade. To our left the Staffords would travel down route Green, and to my immediate right the Irish Hussars would take route Blue. Out on the far right, on route Yellow, was John Sharples' Scots Dragoon Guards battlegroup.

I could hear on the divisional net that there was a monumental jam ahead of us. The 16th/5th Lancers could not get past an American brigade. This was the stuff of war.

Then suddenly, at half past eight, the brigade net burst into life. 'We need a helicopter fast. A rifleman has been shot. Gunshot wound to chest.' It was Charles Rogers on the radio net.

Private Shaun Taylor, a member of Captain Tim Sandiford's Milan platoon, had been hit in the chest when a SA80 rifle was accidentally fired. For what seemed an eternity I could hear the radio traffic as Charles directed a helicopter to take the lad to a hospital. It was incredibly worrying. With nothing else to do or to listen to, their problems seemed to be monumental. I was immensely relieved when an American Blackhawk helicopter arrived and lifted Private Taylor away.

At ten o'clock we were told to move from the staging areas to phase line Vermont, the border. Once again there was the inevitable stop-start as traffic jams farther up the routes entangled those of us behind.

At seven minutes past twelve we crossed into Iraq.

More sand, more gravel, more rocks. It was depressingly anticlimactic. The border was marked with a sand berm, about eight feet tall. This had mostly been smashed down by American bulldozers. To one side stood a large board. On it was painted, 'Welcome to Iraq. Courtesy of the Big Red One.'

At the mouth of the lane leading into the minefield breach there was a huge letter G; we followed behind a military

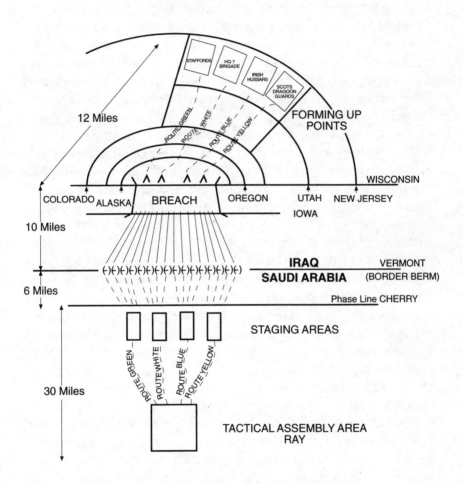

The Minefield Breach   24th - 25th February

police Humvee. Our guides took us on a most circuitous route through the obstacle belt.

'Are you sure we're still going north?' I asked Richard after one turn that seemed to point us due west.

He shrugged his shoulders and eventually we emerged. Our guide saluted us and sped off back through the crossing to pick up his next customers. We looked for the British guides who were meant to meet us and take us to the forming-up points, but the plain was empty. Richard and I looked at the map and plotted a route that would take us straight there.

'Go for it,' I told Corporal Stevely.

The reality of war touched us as we saw evidence of earlier artillery and air attacks. In one area was the remains of a gun line. Instead of a well laid out artillery position, there was carnage. Shards of barrels lay scattered in the sand, trenches and bunkers were burst apart. We drove past the grim tableau in silence.

At twelve twenty further radio orders came through from division. 'Only few enemy expected in the area of Bronze. In Copper their prepared position has only fourteen tanks in it. Destroy the enemy in Copper and Zinc in sector, then set up a blocking position on Lavender to stop the enemy moving west.'

A quick look at the map. No real change. The orders for the action on Lavender were new, but Lavender was some way off and I could worry about that later.

By half past one the first tanks from D Squadron of the Irish Hussars, commanded by Toby Maddison, entered the forming-up points. By twenty past two brigade headquarters was in position. I got on the radio to Rupert Smith to report.

'We should all be firm within the hour. It is my intention to refuel the tanks and Warriors. There is a slight problem with one of my engineer squadrons who seem to have been left behind, and the Staffords are being held up by the 16th/5th Lancers. Otherwise all is well.'

Happily, apart from a few minor problems, all of the tanks were running and fully fit. It bode well.

At three fifteen in the afternoon on 25th February I gave the order to advance. The signal to the headquarters was by hand. Richard Kemp checked we were being followed!

The Staffords' battlegroup attack into Objective Platinum on the afternoon of 26th February. The detail is taken from a painting by Michael Turner. The original now hangs in the Officers' Mess of the 1st Battalion, The Staffordshire Regiment.

Our first attack of the ground war. The Royal Scots Dragoon Guards' battlegroup assault a well-defended Iraqi communications centre. Once the tanks opened fire and the Iraqi T55s began to burn there was sufficient light for the infantry to dismount to assault the trenches. We then put up illumination and gathered in the large number of prisoners. News of this success spread quickly round the remaining parts of the brigade and was a great boost to morale and steadier of nerves.

The moment we crossed the border from Iraq into Kuwait we stopped to have a cup of tea. It seemed a typically British way of celebrating.

27th February and in Objective Varsity. It was the first time I had seen my commanders for two and a half days. The strain is evident.

Michael Turner's impression of my tank, *Bazoft's Revenge*, leading the headquarters towards the Kuwait City to Basra highway at seven o'clock in the morning on 28th February 1991. Smoke from the burning oil wells dominates the morning sky.

Terence Cuneo's impression of the headquarters of the Queen's Royal Irish Hussars after they had arrived ten minutes before the cease-fire at the Basra highway just north of the Muttla Pass. The scene of devastation is not over-dramatised.

Shortly after the cease-fire had been announced we were tasked to clear a route through the devastation at the Muttla Pass.

There were not thousands of Iraqi soldiers to be buried but certainly hundreds; it brought home to us the true horror of warfare.

In early March the preparations to return home started and some of them were personal. On the left I try to remove the sand from my hair; on the right my crew burn our portable loo.

The Prime Minister, John Major, visited us on 6th March and delivered the welcome message that we would return home within a few weeks. Here he greets two soldiers of 40th Field Regiment dressed in British and Iraqi NBC suits. Behind them is a captured Frog missile.

The press kindly provided champagne for the wives in Fallingbostel to celebrate the news of our extraordinary victory. Melissa shares a bottle with Fee Sharples, Maggie Denaro and Gay Rogers. To be honest, they were more stunned with relief than euphoric.

'It is great to be back'. I am greeted at Hanover Airport by Major General Jeremy Mackenzie, commander of the 4th British Armoured Division and Major General Hartmut Behrendt, the commander of the 1st German Panzer Division.

At an investiture held at Buckingham Palace on 5th November 1991 with Melissa and our two daughters, Miranda (left) and Antonia. Forty-one members of the brigade group received honours and awards from the Queen that day. Eleven of the awards were for gallantry.

Major General Mike Myatt, commander of the 1st US Marine Division during the Gulf War and for four months my boss, takes the Royal Salute in York on the occasion of Her Majesty The Queen's Birthday in June 1995.

'Well done,' Rupert Smith replied. 'When will you be ready to move?'

'When do you want me to move?'

'That's up to you.'

It came as something of a shock to hear him say that. It was almost as if neither of us wished to take the final step.

'Shall we say 1500 hours?' I said

'1500 hours it is, then. Best of luck. Out.'

It all seemed so casual. In a war where everything had been timed to perfection – the co-ordinated missile and bomber attacks, the intricate co-ordination of the ships and bomber forces – but when it came to our bit it just fell between the two of us to pick a time to start Britain's largest armoured action since the Second World War.

By ten to three, with ten minutes to go, it was clear we were not going to be ready. There were problems with refuelling and I did not want to start with tanks low on fuel. The errant engineers, due to follow the Irish Hussars, had still not made it to the front. I pushed the deadline back fifteen minutes.

Just after three o'clock Charles Rogers came on the air.

'We're not going to make a three fifteen H-hour. We are still waiting for fuel. I am not prepared to launch with half empty tanks.'

'Roger, I agree.' I called Arthur and John. 'What's the state of refuelling and where's that missing engineer squadron?'

'Ignore them,' replied Arthur. 'I'll go without them. They can catch us up. I'll be ready by three fifteen.'

'We won't make 1515 hours,' said John. 'But I could make 1530 hours.'

'OK.' I said. 'This is the plan. Irish Hussars will cross New Jersey at 1515 hours, followed by Staffords and Scots Dragoon Guards at 1530 hours.

'You are all to make best possible speed to phase line Rose. You should bypass small pockets of enemy if possible. We must be clear of Rose as soon as possible to allow the remainder of the division to get out of the bridgehead behind us.'

I looked at my watch and waited for the minute hand to drag itself around the face. On the brigade net there was almost no talk, just the occasional update on administrative matters. On the divisional net I could hear the 16th/5th Lancers reporting their moves. I wanted them well to our front when we advanced. I did not intend to shoot them.

As the few remaining moments passed, that feeling of concern returned to my stomach. Was all our hard training enough? What if we had got it wrong? Even if it was right hundreds, possibly thousands, of people were going to die; not my soldiers, but people nonetheless.

Fourteen minutes past three; a minute to go. Do I say anything? Would it be better just to let people get on with it?

John Sharples did it for me. When training, because of the scarcity of old tank hulls or steel plates to fire at, as at Al Fadili, most targets are wooden screens. Exceptionally, and only when permission is given, can you fire at the hulks, or hards, as they are known.

Fifteen minutes past three. Sharples: 'We are ready. Permission to take on hards?'

Bless him.

The second hand moved more cheerfully round the watch face as I stood up on my seat. I could neither hear nor see the Irish Hussars, but we had crossed the start line. I felt relieved.

It was time for me and my small group of tank, command FV436 and Rory's Warrior to move as well. This group, 'Tac', allowed me to command in this fast-moving situation. I had the necessary communications in the tank and the command vehicle; I needed Rory for artillery advice. For all the other assets we might need – engineers, close air support, air defence, supply – I would have to contact the brigade headquarters. 'Main' would travel just a short distance behind us and would join us when I expected to stop for more than an hour.

So from the front I raised my hand to give the signal to move. The tank lurched forward into Iraq.

Arthur pressed his regiment hard and they made excellent speed, despite having little idea what lay in front of them. I stayed as close to them as was sensible. I needed to be prepared to move to any trouble spot. The weather closed in again and even the thermal sights started to give a very blurred picture. It was only because of the satellite navigation that we could move at all. The Irish Hussars also had a Gazelle helicopter reconnaissance section under command. Under normal peacetime rules they would not have been allowed to fly in the murky conditions.

At four thirty Arthur shouted over the radio: 'Contact, dug-in infantry, wait out.'

A few seconds later came the full report. 'Contact at 1628 hours, grid PT075655, enemy trench system. My tanks have engaged. Wait out.'

I heard Euan relay the report on the divisional net. There was a simple acknowledgement.

The grid reference put the enemy about four miles in front of the first objective in Copper. Out on the ground a young trooper in one of the lead tanks of Toby Maddison's squadron peered into the small television screen to the right of his laser sight. He was looking not at a visual picture of what lay ahead, but a thermal one. Normally, and all through our training, it had worked wonderfully. Now, in the driving rain, it was intermittent.

As they pushed forward he suddenly saw a white spot in a sea of grey clutter on the screen. Too small for any detail, but it was certainly a thermal contact. 'Hot spot,' he shouted into the intercom.

The commander dropped into his seat and swung the small television monitor on his left, just beside the firing handle of the commander's 7.62mm machine gun, to a locked position and peered in to it. He too could make out a single white dot. On the radio he called his troop leader and relayed the information – a call that Toby Maddison, in his own tank, heard.

He ordered the other troops to move round to get more information on the enemy, and to engage if needed.

It soon became clear it was a small position and need not delay them. A burst of machine-gun fire from the 7.62mm machine gun, mounted alongside the main 120mm gun, was put into the enemy trenches. There was no return fire, and as they watched the position white flags began to appear.

'My lead tanks have engaged with machine guns and it appears the enemy are trying to surrender. They report white flags flying. I am moving forward to investigate,' Arthur said.

Then, just minutes after that: 'I can confirm the position is surrendering. From the look of things, it is platoon sized, probably a reconnaissance screen. The soldiers are in a pretty shabby state, with little food and water. Ambulances have been dispatched.'

'Well done. I hope this is a taste of things to come. Press on as fast as you can.'

The Irish Hussars barely had time to sort them themselves out before the next engagement. Simultaneously from the helicopter flying with them and from the Irish Hussars headquarters, we heard, 'We're under fire, wait out.'

The Gazelle had drawn the attention of the enemy and from another position, some few hundred metres south of the first objective, small-arms fire was spitting out at it. It was now past five in the afternoon and the Irish Hussars were clearly hitting a sizeable pocket of enemy. But the first real battle of the war was over before I could even get in a position to see.

As light began to fade Arthur came on the net: 'My part of Copper is clear. We have taken several prisoners, including a captain, and destroyed two tanks.'

'Well done. You are to push on to Zinc at best speed. Be careful, the 16th/5th Lancers are not that far ahead. I do not want you to engage them.'

With the upper half of Copper clear I could now bring up the Scots Dragoon Guards to clear the middle part. It was here we believed there to be a communications centre for the Iraqi 12th Armoured Division. If we destroyed that they would be unable to talk to anyone.

I was worried about the approach. By pushing too far south we would be in danger of exposing our southern flank, which might allow the Iraqis to hit us in the side. Nevertheless my orders were quite clear and I had to risk this to press on quickly.

Irritatingly, and predictably, at exactly seven o'clock we lost the GPS navigation system. I was reluctant then to move too fast. If we were not careful there was a possibility that somewhere we could score an own goal. I held the Irish Hussars and Staffords for fifteen minutes until the satellites were in range again. I was keen to let the Scots Dragoon Guards move on since they had a target to aim for, the communications site. My orders to John were clear. Destroy it.

Chapter 13

7.30pm Monday 25th to 7.30pm
Tuesday 26th February 1991

The Scots Dragoon Guard battlegroup, three squadrons of Challengers and A Company of the Staffords, moved out with D squadron, under Major Jacko Page, the attached Parachute Regiment officer, in the south, A Squadron under Mark Ravnkilde in the centre and John Biron's C Squadron in the north. The Staffords' company, commanded by Simon Knapper, travelled behind.

Just after seven thirty, and by now in pitch darkness and driving rain, John Sharples came up on the air with a thermal contact. The communications site.

His battlegroup was well deployed. Jacko Page's squadron made the first contact, a camouflaged vehicle and some soldiers in trenches.

'Do you need anything from us?' I asked John Sharples as he reported his progress

'Just get me some artillery. We'll need high explosive and illumination.' I immediately discussed it with Rory.

'We can do it, Brigadier, but I don't think we should,' he said.

'Why on earth not? It's our first attack.'

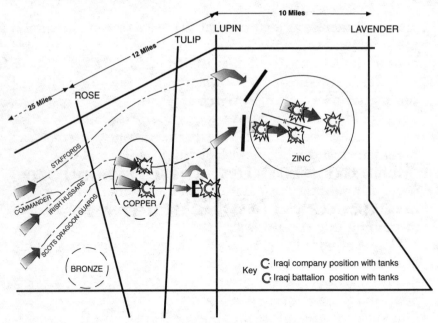

The Breakout - 25th February

'It's not that big and do we really want to unmask the guns for some illumination? It's not advisable. We still don't know what his counter-battery capability is like.'

I got back to John. 'I'm sorry to say you are on your own. And you'll have to use your own illumination.' John's reconnaissance troop was equipped with the Scorpion, which had a 76mm gun. It had a very good illumination round, in many ways better than the artillery round and certainly easier to control.

Meanwhile Jacko Page was attacking. With little time available he swung a tank troop, under command of the recently joined Second Lieutenant Richard Telfer, into position to lead the infantry into the heart of the enemy trenches.

In the driving rain the tanks and Warriors moved around into position. Telfer's troop of three tanks was in the centre with all the Warriors lined up behind him. Either side, but some distance off, was a troop of tanks and off to the north again the squadron's fourth troop was waiting to give covering fire. Unfortunately for Telfer, one of his tanks broke down. Even more unfortunate, just as the attack was about to be launched there was a worry that there was enemy lurking in the south and the other tank was told to watch for a possible counter-attack, leaving Telfer on his own.

Nevertheless he led the infantry on, knowing that his thermal sights were greatly superior to any sights the Warriors had. For forty-five minutes he sat exposed in the middle of the Iraqi trenches, bullets clattering off the armour, as he directed the infantry and machine-gunned the trenches.

In the backs of the Warriors the men of A Company sat nervously waiting for action. Over the intercom they could hear the battle raging. And then, like so many times before in training, the countdown.

'Three hundred metres . . . Two hundred metres . . . One hundred metres . . . debus, debus, debus.'

The Warriors braked hard and slewed. The rear doors flew open and the men were swallowed up by the darkness. They ran forward and threw themselves to the ground, quickly scanning ahead to find the target. A burst of machine-gun fire from a Warrior pointed them in the right direction and they were off.

Simon Knapper ordered one platoon to clear the area around the mast. Another was ordered into the trenches to the left of the mast near the now burning vehicles, destroyed by devastatingly accurate fire from the Challengers. The third platoon was sent to clear the bunkers to the right.

As they continued the attack, another position, unseen before, was found. One of the platoons was ordered to remount their Warriors, drive forward and destroy it. They did.

Suddenly another report of a further depth position. More fighting.

And so it went on for an hour and a half. Incredibly they only took five casualties and no fatalities. Here on our first attack, at night, in the rain, it had all worked. Our painstaking rehearsals and drills had been correct and the message flew round the brigade.

Meanwhile A and C Squadrons investigated the depth site some four miles east. They swung north round the battle to approach what was believed to be a supply point from

217

the north-west. John Biron was the first to make contact. Picking up a weak and confusing thermal contact, he halted his squadron. What he found was a straggle of bewildered Iraqi soldiers. They surrendered. The advance continued.

At fourteen minutes past eleven came the first significant contact. One of Mark Ravnkilde's tank commanders, a corporal in 1st Troop, spotted dug-in infantry and several vehicles. With a spectacular shot, one of the armoured personnel carriers was consumed in a fireball that sent the infantry running for cover. But it was also a guide for the Iraqi counter-attack. Ten minutes later, as John Biron's squadron cleared a small crest they were confronted by a line of tanks and armoured personnel carriers.

With little time for thought John shouted over the net, 'Fire!'

All fourteen tanks fired at once at the enemy some eight hundred yards to their front. In one volley the Iraqi counter-attack was devastated.

'We have at least five T55s confirmed destroyed and six armoured personnel carriers. I couldn't tell you how many trucks we've taken out. We have around fifty prisoners and about as many enemy dead. No friendly casualties,' said John Sharples on the air.

'I do not want to continue the assault, as I believe there is an Iraqi hospital in the middle of the logistic complex we are looking at. Is that all right? We will seal off the area, deal with the prisoners and wounded and continue at first light or when we can see better.'

'Well done,' I replied. 'Hold off the assault until first light. I am sending you our American psychological-warfare team. Tell them to get the remaining Iraqis to surrender by using their loud hailers.'

While the Scots Dragoon Guards were fighting around the supply point, I had changed the Staffords' orders and pushed them just to the north of the Irish Hussars, telling both to halt and observe the enemy in Zinc. But I had done this and agreed to John's pause without fully assessing the consequences for the division and 4 Brigade. I now realised that slowing down could affect 4 Brigade's ability to manoeuvre behind us. But if I did not wait until daylight and the return of the Scots Dragoon Guards I would have only two battlegroups for my attack into Zinc. My knowledge of what waited for us there was far from complete. It was possibly an Iraqi brigade position with up to a hundred tanks. Also the weather was atrocious. It seemed sensible to stall but I knew I had to think of something else.

I spoke on the brigade net to Arthur and Charles. I explained the problem.

'What do you reckon? My plan is to split the position north and south and put the Irish Hussars through the north and the Staffords through the south, advancing west to east.'

'Will we have artillery?' asked Charles.

'You'll have every gun I can get my hands on,' I replied.

'In which case I can't see a problem,' said Charles.

'Me neither,' said Arthur. 'When do you want us to go?'

'Give me a few minutes and I'll get back to you,' I replied.

I ordered the tank to stop. As it rolled to a halt I heard the familiar ratcheting noise as Corporal Stevely pulled on the handbrake. I reached above me to release two steel clamps and then with some effort pushed open the heavy hatch, my only exit to the outside world. I crouched at first on my seat then slowly straightened. I closed my eyes as my head left the dingily lit interior of the turret so they would become accustomed to the night outside as quickly as possible.

A minute or so later I opened them. Nothing. It was pitch black; and rain was falling gently. After a while I could just make out the tail lights of Rory Clayton's Warrior about twenty yards to my left.

I lowered myself once more on to the commander's seat. 'This is hopeless,' I said over the intercom, to no-one in particular. 'Richard, see if you can get me the general on the radio.' I saw him flick a switch on a control panel just behind his head.

'Hello Zero, this is Delta One Zero. Is your commander available to speak to mine?' The reply was an unintelligible crackle. Richard looked at me and shrugged. 'Same as the last forty minutes, I'm afraid.'

'Look, keep trying. I'm just going to stretch my legs and bounce an idea off Rory. I'll be away five minutes. If you make contact, tell them that somewhere not that far to the west there are over a hundred Iraqi tanks which we are going to have to destroy. Point out that it's bloody dark, we can see little through our thermal sights and that a third of my brigade is already fighting ten miles to the south. It's not that I'm anxious, but I wouldn't mind discussing the problem with the boss.'

As I stood up again I pulled off my helmet; the relief was instant. It was the first time I had allowed myself that luxury since leaving Saudi Arabia. For the last sixteen hours I had listened to the constant crackle and fizz of the radio, a radio that every five seconds gave out a warning peep to remind you it was secure; the continual pressure of the headsets had given me a headache. The noise of the radio was replaced by the thud of tank guns. To the north the Americans' battle was under way.

Cautiously I climbed on to the wet turret roof and gingerly made my way past the smoke-grenade dischargers, steadying myself with one hand on the 120mm gun. From there I slithered a little way down the glacis plate before jumping the remaining three feet to the desert floor. 'You all right, Brigadier?' Corporal Stevely was leaning out of the open driver's compartment.

'Fine, but the next phase is the real problem. You're not too tired, having to strain to see anything through your sights, are you?'

'I'm all right but I can't see anything at all it's so dark, Brigadier. I'm relying entirely on your directions.'

Moments later I clambered into the back of Rory's vehicle. He looked grey but was as enthusiastic as ever. 'What artillery is supporting us at the moment?' I asked.

He told me we had all five British regiments of artillery, including the MLRS regiment, as well as a complete American artillery brigade. He added, in case I was in any doubt about the firepower available to us, that we had more artillery, in terms of the amount of high explosive that could be fired at one time, than General Montgomery had at the battle of El Alamein.

'Well let's use it to make up for the absent Scots Dragoon Guards,' I said. 'Give me a fireplan that will devastate each known enemy position one after the other, starting at the front and lifting to the eastern positions as we advance.'

He looked concerned. 'We can do it, but the British army won't have fired anything like that since World War Two.'

'We're going to win this battle quickly, Rory. See if you can have it ready for one o'clock.'

When I returned to the tank I found Richard had made contact with the division; I asked to be put through to Rupert Smith. It was the first time I had spoken to him for several hours. I explained my particular problem and then said, 'What would you say if I asked to wait until daylight before attacking Zinc?'

There was a pause before he replied in a calm voice. 'That would be disappointing.'

It was all the encouragement I needed. At eleven thirty I gave radio orders.

'Zinc will be cleared from west to east. Staffords right, Irish Hussars left. H-hour not before 0130 hours. Artillery fireplan will commence at 0100 hours and will last thirty minutes.'

Shortly afterwards Euan and the rest of the headquarters caught up with us. I walked back to my command vehicle, where I found him working, as ever. This time it was the co-ordinating instructions for the attack into Zinc.

'Any news?' I asked.

'Taylor died. Private Kelly and Corporal Heaven took serious injuries in the assault on the communications site. Doctors reckon they both should make it.'

That was the first I heard of the news of Taylor. It was extremely upsetting – the first 7 Brigade soldier to die in the ground war.

'What's going on elsewhere?' I asked, pulling myself together.

'It's incredible. The 101st are somewhere up around Highway 8 and the Euphrates, or at least if they are not there yet, it won't be much longer. The rest of VII Corps is winging round in a huge arc. You can hear their battle from here.'

'What of the marines?'

'Apparently they smashed through the minefield and other obstacles and are half way to Kuwait City already.'

I let Euan get on with his work.

We waited for the artillery barrage, not knowing quite what to expect. I was concerned. We had no real idea what was in Zinc and I was sending in just two battlegroups to clear what could be a very large brigade position. The Iraqis were not yet a total walkover. John Sharples had had quite a battle. So far we had only one fatality, it was inconceivable we would get to Kuwait without any more.

Just before one o'clock the command net crackled into life warning us that the shells were in the air; the guns had fired.

Then, on the dot of one, the ground to our front erupted. The high-explosive shells burst with a blinding flash and a deadly plume of bright yellow and orange fire.

But it was the Multiple Launch Rocket System that was the most fearsome. The rockets streaked across the darkness and, over the target, with a bright flash, burst apart showering their lethal contents to the earth. There was a noise almost like a machine-gun and the ground boiled with fire as the hundreds of tiny bomblets exploded. Again and again came salvoes of these rockets. Each rocket contained over six hundred bomblets.

Twenty-six minutes later Rory Clayton came on the air. 'Rounds complete, end of mission.' It was over.

'Roger,' I replied in acknowledgement. 'All stations prepare to move.'

It was a cautious move forwards which seemed to go on for ever.

At half past three Arthur called me. 'Multiple contacts across my front. At least fourteen hot spots, no, wait . . . more. D squadron are engaging.'

'Do you need assistance?' I asked.

'No, not yet. I think we can deal with it. Have we still got the guns?'

'I'll make sure you have if you need them.'

Toby Maddison's squadron had come up the back of a slope and just over the rim had picked up the thermal contacts. They took them on immediately, firing at almost maximum range. As Toby's squadron battled on, more and more Iraqi vehicles appeared. It was almost certainly a counter-attack.

For ninety minutes Toby commanded his squadron outstandingly. The Iraqis, without night vision, were at a terrible disadvantage. The only thing they could fire back at was the flash of a muzzle, but they were out of range. As fast as they could pour vehicles in, Toby's squadron destroyed them. The lucky few withdrew.

My own plan had been quite clear. We were to be on phase line Lavender, only some three miles east of us, by dawn. But I felt it was hazardous to keep moving. We had been counter-attacked once and fought it off. It was possible that, having tried and failed once, they would try again. If by first light we were able to cover Lavender, if not actually physically be on it, I argued with myself that we were complying with our mission. I gave orders to the battlegroups to slow up, consolidate and wait for dawn. The division's main effort then switched to 4 Brigade, giving us a chance to replenish and re-arm.

As 4 Brigade went into the south of Copper, Christopher Hammerbeck gave me an urgent call. 'A company of T-55s has broken clear and are heading north into your area. I am unable to stop them.'

I looked at the position they were last reported at and the direction they were travelling in.

'Bloody hell,' I said to Euan, sitting next to me in the command vehicle, 'they're heading straight for us.'

I shouted at one of the signallers to get Richard Kemp as quickly as possible. Within moments he came running over.

'Get the tank out as fast as you can. We have a company of T-55s heading towards us from the south. You are the only defence we have.' I gave him the grid of their last known position and he sprinted off. A few seconds later my tank roared off into the darkness. I heard Rory give the same orders to his Warrior crew. Meanwhile Robbie Burns had shouted 'Stand to' and Maurice Gibson was trying to organise a hasty defence. Every man in the headquarters was heading for a trench armed with whatever anti-tank weapon he could find. Drivers rushed to their vehicles and clambered into their cabs, ready to leave at a moment's notice.

I found Mark Shelford in the back of a command vehicle with a torch in his mouth trying to read the instructions on a 66mm anti-tank rocket launcher.

'I've not fired one of these since I left Sandhurst,' he muttered, taking an armful of them and running out to his trench.

Despite the threat I had to concentrate on the battle. There were still sporadic contacts from both the Irish Hussars in Zinc, and the Scots Dragoon Guards back at the supply point. It was an interesting few hours.

Dawn broke on another filthy day.

With daybreak we sorted ourselves out. The threatened T-55 attack never materialised. Either 4 Brigade were wrong or the enemy took a different route. To our front Lavender was clear of live enemy.

I called John Sharples.

'We've been taking prisoners all night,' he said. 'About one hundred and thirty at the last count. We've destroyed ten tanks and nine armoured personnel carriers.'

'Excellent,' I replied. 'How much longer before you could be clear of the area?'

'About another couple of hours and we'll have it sewn up.'

'Too long. Make it an hour.'

I then checked with Robbie that we could cope with all these prisoners and he assured me that the battlegroups had it in hand, grouping them centrally with their echelons and guarding them there until they were collected by the specially established Prisoner Guard Force which was following a short way behind.

I relayed the current information to division.

'Sitrep as at 0600 hours. We are firm on Lavender with

two battlegroups up. Scots Dragoon Guards continue at the command centre and logistic site, but should be clear in one and a half hours' time. Remainder are ready to move.'

'Excellent,' came Rupert Smith's reply and he went straight in to the next set of orders. 'The divisional point of main effort remains 4 Brigade. Once the enemy have been broken and the medium artillery regiment has moved to support 7 Brigade then 7 Brigade will be the point of main effort to destroy the enemy in Platinum, then Lead and then to deploy to phase line Smash.'

Platinum was thought to be the main force of the 12th Armoured Division. Originally it was a divisional objective. Now the general had given it to us. It was a huge area, over twelve miles long and ten miles wide. Once again we had only the haziest idea of what it contained, getting precious little new information from American surveillance systems.

Euan and I pored over the map.

'We'll split it west to east,' I said. The western half we called Platinum I. From our meagre intelligence we believed it to be the less heavily defended.

'Platinum II may contain up to a brigade, possibly even more,' said Euan reading the latest intelligence summary.

'Right, we'll need to do this in phases then.'

We planned a three-phase attack.

The Irish Hussars would move due south of their present position to a start line to the north-west of Platinum I. They were then to sweep through the objective heading first south, and then east until they reached the boundary with Platinum II. There they would be in a position to give support for the second phase, as Staffords swept through the other half of the position.

'The force ratios are out of the window,' said Euan.

'I don't think that matters now,' I replied.

Meanwhile the Scots Dragoon Guards were to pass behind the two battlegroups and attack into Lead. Lead I was told would have been neutralised by the reconnaissance/strike complex of the 16th/5th Lancers, artillery and, in this instance, American A-10s while we were attacking into Platinum.

I realised that I would have to move a company of infantry from the Staffords to the Irish Hussars to make the first part of the operation feasible. Regrouping, as it is known, from one battlegroup to another is a complex operation that needs time.

At seven fifteen I gave orders.

'Mission: to destroy the enemy in Platinum I and II and Lead.

'Concept of operations: Scots Dragoon Guards battlegroup – brigade reserve for Platinum I and II. You are to attack Lead on orders. Irish Hussars – you are to take C Company, the Staffords, under command and to attack Platinum I. You are then to provide fire support for the Staffords' attack on Platinum II. Staffords, attack Platinum II on orders.

'H-hour: not before 1200 hours.'

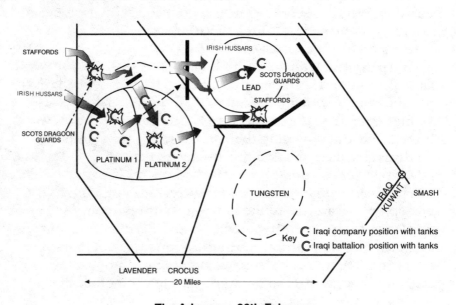

The Advance - 26th February

As 4 Brigade continued their advance to our south we refuelled and had a moment to wash and shave. Richard knocked up some cheese and jam sandwiches which, despite tasting of diesel and sand, were more than welcome. It was the first meal we had had since the war started some twenty-two hours previously.

As the battlegroups readjusted their position in daylight to sit astride Lavender, Arthur called up on the net.

'We've seen another enemy position.'

'Any details?' I asked.

'Too early to say at the moment. There appears to be a large number of dead and wounded.'

David Swann's B Squadron, in moving to Lavender, had found a depth position in Zinc. It had been devastated by the artillery barrage and the area was covered in unexploded MLRS bomblets. After a few warning shots the Iraqis began to surrender. It was then that B Squadron discovered the appalling injuries these men had taken. Dispatching both their ambulances and anyone else they could spare they quickly cleared the area of wounded.

Pushing on, it became clear they had hit a much larger position. There were numerous vehicles scattered around, some apparently intact. The enemy were neither fighting nor surrendering, but B squadron took no chances and destroyed the tanks.

'I think this is a bit of a problem,' Arthur said about twenty minutes later after a full brief by David Swann.

'OK,' I said. 'You and Charles will need to sort that one out. I suggest the two of you meet and make a plan. I'm too far away to see for myself.'

About twenty minutes later Charles was back on the radio. 'We'll clear the area. I'm sending in my Irish Hussar squadron with B company. H-hour not before 0910 hours.'

At just after nine fifteen, in a sandstorm that cut visibility to less than six hundred yards, the Staffords attacked with C Squadron of the Irish Hussars, under Nigel Beer, leading. The enemy was dug in along a sand berm. Chris Joynson's B Company and the tanks attacked from the north, taking the enemy, who were facing south, totally by surprise.

The tanks broke through the enemy defences, leading the Warriors into the heart of the position. The infantry stopped on the far side, debussed and began to clear the trenches. An Iraqi truck went tearing across the position. A Milan missile streaked across and smashed through its cab. At the same time, machine-gun fire spat from the

Warriors and cut through the canvas-sided vehicle. It crashed to a halt.

By eleven o'clock the position was cleared. The Iraqi wounded were evacuated and their equipment destroyed. The large number of prisoners was once again a problem. The reports of helping the wounded were interesting. Captain Tony Hood, of the 5th Royal Inniskilling Dragoon Guards, and attached to the Irish Hussars, dealt personally with one trench area. To get the ambulance as near as possible to the wounded, Tony, with only a shovel, cleared a path through the hundreds of unexploded MLRS bomblets, each one a lethal mine that could have killed or maimed him.

The attack on Platinum I was scheduled for midday. Just before then I called the three commanding officers for an assessment of the Iraqis' morale.

'They're a broken force,' said Charles. 'B Company were just rounding them up.'

'Well, I'm not so certain,' said John. 'We had quite a fight on our hands.'

'But you didn't have artillery,' replied Charles. 'They can't take the guns.'

'We'll play it like this,' I interrupted. 'Where tactically possible you are to fire warning shots before assaulting positions. Give them a chance to surrender. Artillery will be used, but in moderation only. A small barrage should be enough to persuade most to give up.

'But you are to take no chances. All enemy tanks are to be treated as hostile and destroyed on sight. Likewise artillery and anti-aircraft guns. Get the word out to the boys to be careful. I can see problems if half of a position wants to surrender, but the other half doesn't.'

As we moved forward once more the wind, which momentarily had subsided, picked up again. Visibility was cut to under five hundred yards as we launched the attack on Platinum I.

Artillery rained down, but we held back with the MLRS.

The Staffords company dismounted only once, but found the position abandoned. The only real threat came from a battery of artillery defended by a platoon of three T-55s.

At twelve thirty I called Arthur, asking him for a progress report.

'We are almost firm. There is limited resistance only. Most of them are waiting to surrender. We have destroyed six T-55s and several infantry-carrying vehicles.'

'How many prisoners?'

'Too early to count them. B Squadron say two surrendered on a camel.'

A few minutes later Arthur was on the air again.

'Platinum I secure. There's an English speaker here who says the men want to surrender and the local commander has ordered them to do so. I doubt Charles will need to use any artillery.' I thought about it for a minute.

'Artillery will be used on Platinum II but only for the initial assault.' I could take no chances. It could be a ruse, although I doubted it.

At exactly twelve forty-five the second attack started. It wasn't long before we realised there was no fight left in the enemy.

'This is the most extraordinary sight,' said Charles. 'I can see hundreds of Iraqis quite literally moping around in the centre of this position. They are not fighting, they're not doing anything but walking around smoking fags. When we engage the armour behind them they scatter, but a few minutes later they all drift back again.'

'Armour remains a threat and must be engaged,' I said. 'But minimise enemy casualties.'

Meanwhile I decided the time was right to order the Scots Dragoon Guards to move to the north of Platinum to Lead.

At nineteen minutes past two a very irate Charles Rogers came up on the command net shouting at John Sharples.

'One of your tanks has just engaged my alternate headquarters. For God's sake stop him firing again.'

Immediately I got on the Ptarmigan to Charles to find out what was going on.

'Some bastard in a tank has shot at my alternate headquarters vehicle. I have an officer wounded with two broken legs.'

'Where was he? What happened?'

'I left my alternate headquarters on the start line to co-ordinate prisoner handling. He was in a dip in the ground when they get attacked firstly by machine-gun fire, and then by a HESH round.'

'Are we sure it's us?'

'Yes, damn sure.'

I spoke to a very shaken John Sharples. 'I have no idea how this happened. I knew they were there, I heard it on the command net. I've sent Mark Auchinleck to the scene to see what we can do.'

'Don't let it throw you, John. You've got a job to do. We'll take over from here.'

I called Euan and ordered him to co-ordinate the rescue. I heard the traffic as he called up the helicopter and got a fuller picture of what had happened. The injured officer was Captain Toby Tennant, a Green Jacket attached to the Staffords.

Manoeuvre warfare is a very risky business. To move one battlegroup across the back of another is a calculated risk. The modern battlefield does not have neat front lines and so soldiers are ready to find the enemy almost anywhere.

I felt sorry for the commander of the tank. I never wanted to know who it was. There was a sandstorm blowing. He was deep in enemy territory. He saw what he thought was an enemy vehicle so he shot it. At a time like that there is only one person who should be blamed, the man who gave the orders for the manoeuvre. Me.

I forced my concentration back to the battle. Platinum II would be cleared in a few hours and I wanted us all to be in Lead before nightfall. There was not much time. After a quick consultation with division I gave orders for the rest of the brigade to move to Lead. The Scots Dragoon Guards were to press on and attack as soon as possible. They were then to take up blocking positions on phase line Smash covering north through east.

Once Platinum II was cleared the Staffords and Irish Hussars were to join them, the Staffords taking up positions covering east through south and the Irish Hussars covering our backs from south through to north. The move was to be done as quickly as possible.

But it took until five thirty. Not because of the fighting, but because of the huge number of prisoners, including a brigadier and two full colonels, who had to be rounded up. I would have liked to have met the brigadier, but there was no time. The pathetic sight of hundreds of bedraggled men, most of them extremely hungry, was the enduring image of the war. Curiously there seemed to be none in their middle age; they were either boys or old men.

'Corporal Stevely. Let's go,' I said into my intercom and once again we were on the move.

Meanwhile Mark Ravnkilde, leading the Scots Dragoon Guards, had made excellent progress and was into the heart of Lead. After a brief firefight in which his squadron destroyed three T-55s and Jacko Page's squadron in the south brushed off a slight mortar attack, John Sharples reported the position clear.

Lead was much as every other part of the desert – flat and featureless. The charred and burnt-out hulks of Iraqi tanks and armoured vehicles bore witness to the 16th/5th Lancers' earlier battle. They had become embroiled in a major battle with an Iraqi brigade. In a lightly armoured Scimitar, which has questionable protection against a machine gun, let alone a 100mm gun, this is dangerous. Their Striker anti-tank missiles had broken an Iraqi counter-attack, but they were forced to withdraw, tragically taking two fatalities, Sergeant Dowling and Lance Corporal Evans, both of the REME, killed when their 548 tracked carrier was sprayed by machine-gun fire from a T-55.

'Over there,' I ordered Corporal Stevely as we approached what looked like a likely place to stop for the night. Looking through my sight I noticed a small single strand of wire. Not thinking anything of it we drove straight on.

'This'll do,' I said. 'Park her up here.' Corporal Stevely brought the tank to a halt and I heard the ratcheting of the handbrake coming on. I threw open the commander's hatch and had a look around. It was then the significance of the wire hit me.

'Whoops!' I said. 'We're in a minefield.'

All around us were the unmistakable shapes of mines laid just under the surface. It was a miracle that we had not hit one. I looked behind. It was still just light enough to make out our tracks. Fortunately we had come in an almost straight line.

'Corporal Stevely. Start her up again and get her in reverse.'

Richard clambered out on to the turret and hung over one side peering at the ground just ahead of the tracks. I did the same on the other side.

'Right, very slowly, let's retrace our tracks.' The tank lurched. 'I said "slowly".'

Inch by inch we crawled the fifty yards back to the wire fence. I prayed these mines were nothing clever. There are some that are designed to go off not the first time you drive over them, but the second.

'Thank heavens for that,' said Richard as we made it to the fence. 'Next time you see a wire, sir, may I suggest we drive round it?'

Reports began to come in of an enemy position to the south of Lead. John Rochelle's C Company, having been released by the Irish Hussars after Platinum, were making their way to rejoin the Staffords when they found it. Charles Rogers ordered them to clear it.

John got the company to deploy and then, before assaulting the position, fired several warning shots. This was the first the Iraqis knew of them. True to form they started to surrender. It was only then that we got the first idea of the size of the position. Far from being a weak company as was first thought it turned out to be at least a battalion in size, perhaps four hundred men.

With only three platoons it was difficult for John to cope with the huge numbers of prisoners. He sent his reserve platoon, 9 Platoon commanded by Lieutenant Andy Nye, round to the right to take the surrender of yet more enemy. While some were surrendering and flying white flags, one small section tried to resist. An Iraqi armed with an RPG7 rocket-propelled grenade stood up in his trench and fired at a Warrior. Private Carl 'Ted' Moult was struck in the chest. Hit by a round designed to destroy a tank he died instantly.

It took some two hours to sort the position out. When the shooting was finally over John's company had taken nearly three hundred prisoners, eleven of whom were severely wounded and evacuated immediately.

By seven thirty the fighting elements of the brigade were in Lead and secure. We had a reconnaissance screen out covering all around us. We had reached the immediate objective in two days. Division had planned on ten. Miraculously only two soldiers in the entire brigade had been killed. It was a monumental effort.

Chapter 14

7.30pm Tuesday 26th to 8am
Thursday 28th February 1991

The headquarters assembled itself with a well-rehearsed efficiency. Soldiers armed with machine guns ran out covering all approaches, guarding the area while the tracked command vehicles arranged themselves in two rows, back door to back door, about ten feet apart. As the last one manoeuvred into place the canvas penthouses were pulled out and erected, encasing the area between the vehicles in one long covered area.

Outside, soldiers started to put up the sand-coloured camouflage nets over the entire complex while others were busy digging trenches and erecting the myriad of antennae that were our life-line to the rest of the brigade and division. In one corner, away from the main complex, I could hear the generators that powered the whole ensemble being run up and tested. Inside, battery-powered lights soon lit the gloom.

In fifteen minutes I had a fully operational, lit, camouflaged and defended headquarters. As ever Euan was working. He looked shattered. His hair was unkempt and he was filthy. I knew I looked worse.

'What news of future intentions?' I asked.

'Nothing.'

Our rapid advance had caused problems at division and corps headquarters. The collapse of the Iraqi army was on a scale no-one had anticipated. The torrent of prisoners that had to be disarmed, fed, watered, collected, searched and then shipped back to camps was straining our logistics, as indeed was the distance to be travelled by our re-supply vehicles. In the British division we were perhaps better placed to cope with that than other formations. Rupert Smith had organised a unique engineer squad, under the command of Captain Chris Goddard, whose sole task was to construct a supply route behind the lead elements of the division as it advanced. By pooling all the division's heavy engineering plant he had formed the Route Development battlegroup. They literally cut a road through the desert behind us. It greatly speeded up the movement of supplies and the evacuation of prisoners.

Our inactivity was not to last for long. At eight thirty John Reith called on the Ptarmigan.

'Warning order.

'Mission: to exploit east to objective Varsity then be prepared, on orders, to advance north.

'Execution: concept of operations: 7 Brigade as divisional point of main effort is to exploit east as the divisional forward detachment and pass through the area currently watched by 16th/5th Lancers. Destroy the enemy in that area and thereafter advance swiftly to Varsity to destroy enemy and block routes, being prepared to attack north on orders.

'Grouping: under operational control for phase one; one medium reconnaissance squadron (A Squadron, the Queen's Dragoon Guards), MLRS artillery battery, Javelin air defence battery, engineer regiment, field ambulance.

'Timings: 7 Brigade to move at 0730 hours.'

I passed on the details to Euan and decided to grab some rest with the aim of being back in the headquarters at midnight for the detailed orders. I made my way over to the tank. The rest of the crew were already asleep.

Climbing into my sleeping bag was a luxury. That I was filthy, covered in sand, dust and oil was of no concern; I had only managed three hours' sleep in the last sixty. Just to get inside that cocoon and zip it up was enough. My eyes stung with tiredness, and my back, injured when we crashed in Al Jubayl, was hurting. My ears rang with the noise of the radios. But despite the extreme fatigue I could not sleep. To our south 4 Brigade were being particularly noisy with a repeat performance of our massive barrage of the night before, and we seemed to be in the flight path of every American Apache in the Middle East. I lay there, my mind racing with jumbled thoughts.

At midnight, after two fitful hours, I got up, found my boots and walked back to the headquarters to await the full orders. I found Euan still working in the back of the command vehicle.

'Euan, what on earth are you doing here? Get some sleep.'

'I was just roughing out the co-ordinating instructions.'

'Never mind that. Get your head down for a couple of hours. If I need you, I'll call you.'

As I sat at the map board trying to second-guess the future, Sergeant Major Lynch came up to me.

'I'm sorry to disturb you, Brigadier, but I wonder if I could have a word in private.'

'Of course, climb in. What is it?'

'Well, I'm not sure if it's any of my business,' he said, looking rather uneasy, 'but as I was walking past the prisoners' cage just now I saw some of them being . . . well, the only way I can describe it is, mistreated.'

'In what way?'

'The guards were making them lie flat on the ground and they were being handled very roughly.'

'Were they being hit?'

'No, nothing like that. But being pushed about. It just seemed really unnecessary to me.'

'Right. Leave this with me. Thank you for reporting it.'

I was incensed. Although the prisoner-handling force had a pretty thankless task (to a man they would rather have been fighting), to mistreat prisoners was utterly inexcusable and almost certainly illegal. It had been a characteristic of the war so far that we had taken great care of the hundreds of men we had captured. Almost everyone had a sense of pity, not hate, for the Iraqis left in the middle of the desert with no food or water. Already I had heard of dozens of examples of soldiers giving up their rations, cigarettes, chocolates and even their spare boots to these men.

I went storming off to find the detachment commander. 'What is it, sir?' he said on recognising me.

'Listen to me,' I growled. 'If I hear one more instance of a single Iraqi being mistreated I will have you court-martialled. Is that quite clear?'

'Er . . . yes, sir. Quite clear, sir.' For a minute he looked like he was going to salute me.

I stormed off, still livid.

At forty-three minutes past two came division's confirmatory orders. It was Rupert Smith who gave them. If he was as tired as I was he certainly gave no hint of it over the air.

'7 Brigade are to destroy the enemy in the triangle between phase line Smash and the north and south boundaries, then move to objective Varsity. You are to start your operation at 0730 hours. Centre of Varsity is grid QT 1566.'

'What news elsewhere?' I asked.

'To our north VII Corps have made excellent progress. They have not secured Collins [an area just west of the Republican Guard's dug-in defences] but have destroyed large amounts of enemy armour at very little cost.

'To the west XVIII Corps have reached the Euphrates and sealed exits along the valley west and north. The only way out for the Iraqis is now through Basra. We are pushing hard to seize the Basra–Kuwait City road. The door is swinging shut.'

'What news further east?' I asked.

'Kuwait City has been liberated.'

This war was all but over, I thought. We were on the edge of Kuwait now. It couldn't last more than a few days more.

With the orders now confirmed I was able to give out my own. I let Euan rest as I filled in the detail. Within half-an-hour I was ready to give the brigade its new task. We were going into Kuwait.

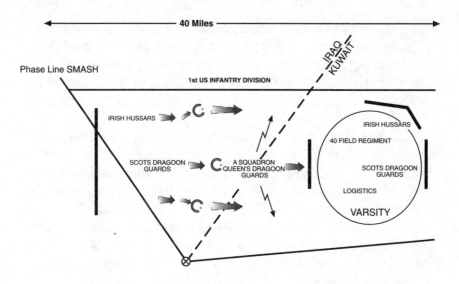

The Pursuit - 27th February

The Scots Dragoon Guards were to lead with Arthur rear left and Charles rear right in an arrow formation again. To our front, initially, would be the 16th/5th Lancers with helicopter support. They would locate and identify enemy for us and if need be call in artillery.

'Please note,' I went on, 'that, as we cross the border, to our south will be forces of the Joint Arab Command East, mainly the Egyptians. They are equipped with similar equipment to Iraqi forces. You are to exercise extreme caution.

'Likewise to our north will be 1st US Infantry Division. We have already had one own goal, I don't want any more.'

There was now nothing to do until we set off again. I tried once more to get a few hours' rest. But the noise was too much. To our north the night burned orange. There was a major battle going on. Every few minutes I felt the crump of a high-explosive round, and then, most frightening of all, saw the white streak of an MLRS rocket, followed by the muffled bang as it blew apart over the target, and then that awful machine-gun-like burst as its deadly cargo showered on the enemy.

I gave up the unequal struggle. Instead I thought a good

wash would work wonders. I rooted around in the command vehicle and found a bottle of shampoo. I gave it a good sniff before using it. One had to be careful; shampoo bottles were the principal way the soldiers smuggled alcohol into dry Saudi Arabia.

When the time came for the move the most unexpected thing happened. Unlike the previous morning, when the brigade had been chomping at the bit, there was an almost palpable lethargy. From my own headquarters right across the battlegroups there seemed to be a reluctance to face the day. I had assumed we would romp into Kuwait. After all, it was the culmination of six months' work; six months when we had endured everything from the blazing heat to a rain-sodden deluge.

Perhaps it was a feeling our luck could not hold. Perhaps also it was the inequality of the battle. We were killing a lot of Iraqis, men with little or no will to fight.

We set off and made good progress. Several times we passed groups of Iraqis seemingly wandering around the desert. They all tried to surrender, but I ordered the advance to continue. Several times there were calls for artillery, calls which I was reluctant to agree. As we were still due to meet the Republican Guard, it seemed prudent to conserve our stocks. I was particularly keen to husband MLRS ammunition.

At nine fifteen on 27th February, G+3, Major Hamish MacDonald of A Squadron, the Queen's Dragoon Guards, took his men across the Wadi Al Batin and into Kuwait. Fifteen minutes later I too crossed the border. I called a halt. It was a moment to savour. I asked the crew for a cup of tea. It seemed a quintessentially British thing to do.

I was later told by Arthur of their problems at the border. B Squadron, under David Swann, had to make frequent stops to keep in line with the Scots Dragoon Guards and Staffords. Just short of the border they had to stop again.

'Why the halt?' came the insistent voice of the adjutant, Andrew Cuthbert.

'There appears to be a problem at customs,' came the

laconic reply from David, a comment that later appeared on the BBC news.

As we entered Kuwait I ordered Arthur's battlegroup to move a little farther south to avoid any problems with the Americans running parallel with them to the north. As we pushed east Arthur called on the radio.

'We're still running damn close to the boundary. Where are the Americans? I really think we ought to have some liaison up here.'

Since setting off his staff had been badgering mine on this subject, and despite constant reassurances that the Americans to our north knew where we were, and we had a liaison officer with them, David Limb, they were not convinced. I relayed their position to division just to be certain and asked for confirmation that they had passed it on.

'Sunray, I am extremely concerned about this boundary,' Arthur repeated just a few minutes later, using my personal codename.

'You worry about the enemy, let me worry about the friendly forces. Out.' And I cut him off.

Needless to say the inevitable happened. A few minutes after eleven o'clock Arthur called again. 'The Americans to our north have just engaged my reconnaissance troop. I have reports of at least two casualties and vehicles destroyed.'

Captain Alasdair Murdoch (christened affectionately by his troop 'one-minute Murdoch' – it was how long they thought he would last in war) and his section of two Scorpions had been detached from Toby Maddison's squadron to look after prisoners. Lance Corporal Balmforth was standing in the turret of his Scorpion covering the Iraqis when there was a burst of machine-gun fire and an explosion.

A round from an M1 smashed into the second Scorpion, destroying it. Lance Corporal Lynch, who had been standing near it, also covering the Iraqis, was showered in shrapnel and fell, bleeding, to the ground. A second burst of machine-gun fire hit Lance Corporal Balmforth in the chest, ripping off his radio-gear harness.

Immediately Alasdair ran forward to grab the men and get

them to safety behind a ridge some twenty yards away. The Iraqis scattered.

Still the Americans continued to fire. Another burst of machine-gun fire hit Lance Corporal Balmforth again.

While under fire Alasdair crawled forward and retrieved the Iraqis' white flag. He started waving it furiously. The firing stopped.

A platoon of M1s came racing over to take what they thought was an Iraqi surrender. Alasdair left them in no doubt about what they had done. Fortunately both soldiers were evacuated within seven minutes of being wounded and neither was found to be seriously injured. The body armour had saved their lives.

While this was going on the divisional commander flew out to see us. I climbed out of the tank and walked over to him. I wondered who was the more tired.

He was full of praise for what had been done. He then asked what had happened with the Irish Hussars and I explained.

'People are getting tired, very tired,' he said. 'I have ordered my headquarters to issue only written orders. It's too risky to give out radio orders now. All it takes is a couple of grids to be inaccurate.'

'What next?' I asked. 'How much longer can this go on?'

'Not much longer. Saddam Hussein has ordered his troops out of Kuwait, although there is nowhere for them to go. The Republican Guard have attempted to break out north to cross the Euphrates but XVIII Corps have blocked them. You'll already know that VII Corps have destroyed the Medina and Hamurabi divisions. American intelligence tells us there are less than ten combat-effective Iraqi divisions in Kuwait. Communications between Baghdad and the front have ceased. We've taken over forty thousand prisoners.'

'What news of the Fusiliers?' I had heard on the divisional net of what appeared to be a blue-on-blue against the Royal Regiment of Fusiliers, one of Christopher's battlegroups. It appeared that two Warriors had been hit by American A-10s.

'Nine dead, several more injured, a couple seriously. It's not good,' said Rupert. 'We can't let it happen again. Get the message to your men to be very careful. A cease-fire must be soon and that is probably even more dangerous. People will slacken off and that's when mistakes happen and soldiers die.'

'You probably want to know what next,' he went on. 'The answer is, I don't know. Corps are still hammering away in the north. There is an option for you to swing north out of Varsity and push towards Basra, but I don't like it. It will put you right across the American's line of advance. Otherwise my guess is to push for Kuwait City to cut off any Iraqi movement north. That will leave them trapped around Basra.'

We talked for a little bit longer but then I had to press on. We were still heading for Varsity, where it had been thought we would find at least one Iraqi brigade, the 50th Armoured Brigade, and possibly more. I doubted they would be there.

They weren't. Varsity was empty. It bore testimony to air bombardment. There were a few Iraqis left behind, but they were the wounded or dead. It was a moonscape of craters – huge black scars gouged from the earth by the deadly cargo of the B-52 bombers. Allied propaganda leaflets were blowing around in the wind, fluttering in and out of the abandoned vehicles.

As we stopped I noticed how dark it was. At first I thought it was just another cloudy day, but it was more than that. There was a smell that had been with us throughout, a smell of cordite and explosives, but now there was a more acrid, sulphurous edge to it that caught in the throat. It was the stench of burning oil wells.

When I was certain the place was abandoned, I called in the commanding officers just after midday. It was the first time I had seen them since we had left Saudi Arabia, three countries ago.

Arthur arrived first and brought Martin Bell with him, which was welcome; they told me in detail about the incident with the Americans.

Charles and John came next and they, like all of us, were very tired indeed. The strain showed on all our faces. I told them the little I knew about future plans and then spoke about fatigue.

'Arthur is right to be worried about tiredness and the possibility of more blue-on-blue problems. Break out more flags is one answer. I don't care what they are, Union Jacks, the Red Hand of Ulster, the Cross of Saint Andrew, whatever. I don't want anyone to mistake us for the enemy. I know your men have all got them. Now's the time to fly them.'

We waited in Varsity for much of the day. It was the first chance the men had to rest and I made sure they took it. I had little idea what the future held. After my talk with Rupert Smith I drew up plans for the move east to objective Cobalt, which looked a likely task, lying astride the Kuwait–Basra road.

At half past seven the planning looked for naught. Far from pushing east, the division gave a warning order for a push south into Saudi Arabia. The plan called for 4 Brigade to clear a route along the Wadi Al Batin to open a new supply route for VII Corps. It was a disappointing task, particularly as we had to detach our engineers and a complete battlegroup to them by eight o'clock the next morning. I told Charles the news and he was less than happy.

At three in the morning the plan was thankfully abandoned and the Basra option and an attack north appeared favourite.

'Routes and timings to follow, but,' said the divisional chief of staff, 'the mission is confirmed.'

An hour and a half later that mission was abandoned and we were back to the push east. This one, division assured us, was a certainty. I waited.

Shortly after five thirty in the morning Rupert Smith called me on the Ptarmigan. 'This is on. Your mission is to attack east to cut routes from Kuwait City so as to prevent the Iraqi army from retreating north to Basra.

'The division will attack in column on light scales. You are the point of main effort. Move at first light.

'It looks like the cease-fire is to come into effect at midnight Washington time, that's eight in the morning here. I want you on that road by then.'

I glanced at the map. I guessed it was at least forty miles away. 'That's some way away,' I said.

'I know,' replied the general.

It took us five minutes to sort out the plans. I gave orders at half past five.

'It's Cobalt. We've got to be there by the cease-fire at 0800 hours,' I said. 'Be ready to move at 0630 hours.'

'We'll be ready at six,' replied Arthur.

'0600 hours it is,' I replied. 'Can the rest of you do it?'

'Not a problem,' said John.

'I'll be there,' said Charles.

The adrenalin was pumping again. I knew there was no time to give formal orders, but I knew they did not need them. Sure enough, out on the ground the battlegroups were getting into position. It was only after they started to move that they were told where they were going.

With Hamish and his reconnaissance squadron to our front we set off exactly at six o'clock. This was a cavalry charge and nothing more. Point battlegroup was the Irish Hussars with Arthur, I suspected, leading from the front.

Behind them were Charles on the left and John on the

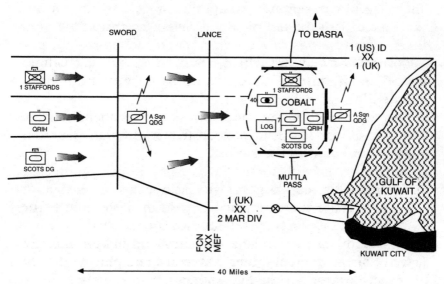

To the Cease-fire - 28th February
(This diagram is a copy of the commander's map)

right. We had two hours to make it. Unless we ran into the Republican Guard, or what was left of it, we were not stopping for anyone.

As the weak light struggled to pierce the ever-thickening clouds of burning oil, a scene of devastation opened before us. The deeper into Kuwait we went, the more we found the detritus of an army not just defeated but utterly routed.

The reports flooded over the radio net. 'Crossing the two zero easting.' 'Crossing the two five easting.' Cobalt sat astride the five zero easting.

Suddenly Corporal McCarthy shouted down the intercom from the gunner's position: 'Contact, T-55 slightly right.'

Just then I too saw it, behind a sand berm, its barrel pointing straight at us.

'Hard left,' I shouted to the driver, and then gave the fire orders to the gunner.

'Fin, tank on.' Inside the turret the crew swung into action. Corporal McCarthy pushed open the cover on his control stick and flicked the switch initiating the firing circuits. I heard the laser cooling fan kick in.

Richard meanwhile had grabbed one of the bright orange fin charges and rammed it up the breech so its cupped end mated with the tail of the depleted-uranium fin round already there.

Corporal Stevely brought the tank to a swift halt behind a sand berm, just as Richard slammed shut the breech. 'Loaded.'

Another quick look at the T-55. A moment's hesitation. Was it manned? Did I need to destroy it if it was. It looked lifeless, but could I take the risk?

'Fire.'

'Lasing,' shouted Corporal McCarthy.

There was the characteristic whine as the laser fired at the T-55. A fraction of a second later the range flashed up: 2100 metres. Another fraction later and the twenty-two-ton turret slewed hard as the computer-driven motors put the gun in the exact position for the first shot.

'Firing now!' Corporal McCarthy squeezed the red trigger. The tank was thrown back violently. Through the sight I saw a blinding white flash as the round smashed through the Iraqi tank.

'Target,' said a jubilant gunner.

'Target, stop,' I replied. It was over. I did not have time to fret too long over its occupants, if there were any. Arthur was on the net.

'I am very concerned about what lies to our front. We could be badly wrong-footed at this speed.'

'Just crack on, best speed,' I snapped back and immediately was angry with myself. We were all very tired and tempers were short. He had a fair point but Hamish was to our front and reporting that there was nothing there.

Seven o'clock and it looked as if we were not going to make it. Rupert Smith came on the air.

'Where are you?' he asked.

'Still some way off,' I answered.

'It would be good if you could be there by the cease-fire.'

'We'll be there.'

About thirty minutes later I spotted a line of pylons. I was certain that they must mark the road. We headed towards them.

Fifteen minutes to go and Hamish was speaking.

'I can see the objective.'

'Very good; kick on,' I replied.

And then just before ten to eight, with manifest pride in his voice, Arthur came up on the air.

'Time 0750 hours. We have Cobalt.'

Ten minutes later the cease-fire came into effect.

Epilogue

We had stopped some twenty miles north of Kuwait City, astride the highway leading to Basra. Black smoke from the oil wells hung over us; the scene was one of darkness and foreboding. Vehicles, bodies and other military wreckage lay strewn around in every direction. This dampened our euphoria, as did the uncertainty of a temporary cease-fire and a lack of sleep.

Orders then arrived for the sappers to clear a route through the Muttla Pass, only a few miles south of our new position, and for the rest of us to help bury the Iraqi dead. It was far from the ideal note to finish on. But we had been warned of the carnage caused when the American air force and the 2nd Marine Division had caught the retreating Iraqi army leaving Kuwait City on the road to Basra. There were not thousands of bodies, as the media had claimed, but certainly hundreds; it was a reminder to us all of the horror of war.

And then sleep.

Small problems surfaced almost immediately the next morning to catch us by surprise. Having spent months preparing the soldiers for the most unpleasant of wars, preparing them to cope with violence and death, we had not thought through the immediate effects of the cease-fire. Some were clearly still spoiling for a fight, some were disturbed by what they had seen or done, some felt cheated that they had not met the enemy; fortunately the majority were just relieved to be alive and delighted by the result. But, whatever, it was clearly going to be a time when we needed the comfort of each other's company – I as much as anybody else.

Then there was the problem of loot. The understandable desire to return from the war with a souvenir was an overwhelming one and, as we could have predicted, the soldiers were as imaginative as ever in what they hoped to smuggle home. Putting aside the legal requirements, the danger of collecting the spoils of war was immense. The area was strewn with unexploded mines and bomblets and the deserted bunkers and even some dead bodies were booby-trapped. The control measures we applied were not popular but very necessary.

The next few days were characterised by many touching messages of goodwill, agitating about our return to Germany and numerous visits. The Prime Minister, John Major, impressed by promising that it would not be long before we were once more at home. General Peter de la Billière was more realistic, which caused some consternation. But one of the most poignant incidents was totally unannounced: two Huey helicopters suddenly arrived in the middle of my headquarters and out stepped Mike Myatt. He had spent hours looking for us. I learnt later that his division had fought gallantly through Kuwait, ending up at the airport. There was something very special in the relationship that existed between his marines and my brigade.

But by 8th March, and much quicker than expected, a recovery plan was issued and morale soared. The tanks were transported to Al Jubayl and the soldiers started to fly out on the 11th. Six days later, on Sunday 17th March, St Patrick's Day, I returned to Soltau with the Irish Hussars.

This then brought to a close the brigade's involvement in an international coalition pitted against a moderately sized regional state. It now appears to have been a ridiculously unequal contest, with the Iraqi strength probably over-estimated. But we had studied their success in a different sort of war against Iran and then focused on the quantities of manpower, artillery and tanks rather than on an investigation into human qualities. We had lived in harsh conditions through a long preparatory period and expected when we went into the attack to meet all sorts of horrors which didn't materialise. And so we must be careful about the lessons we take from a war where we defeated a technologically inferior enemy on featureless terrain and met very few reverses.

However, it must be of immense value for the future that a new generation of soldiers now understand the realities of war. We won't, I hope, pretend that for us it was violent. We had, after all, complete air supremacy and almost total domination on the ground with our superior equipment and with the enemy having been bombed by the Coalition air forces for over six weeks. But we won the land war so quickly because we were aggressive and used to full advantage the staggering artillery firepower available to us. Also our outstanding tanks could pick off the enemy at three thousand yards range; our infantry was well equipped and trained; we could, and did, fight at night. We moved with remarkable speed, covering some two hundred miles in four days. We destroyed three-hundred enemy tanks and armoured personnel carriers and took eight-thousand prisoners of war. I believe that even if the enemy had been more resolute we would still have been unstoppable.

There are two aspects of the story which I have only mentioned in passing, the logistic efforts to maintain us and the situation with our families in Germany. The logistic support was herculean. Thirty-five thousand British soldiers were deployed to the Gulf with four hundred thousand tons of equipment, munitions and freight, and thirteen thousand five hundred vehicles. From Al Jubayl, when the decision to move west was taken, twenty-three thousand tons of ammunition, six hundred and fifty tons of rations and nearly two million litres of petrol were moved over two hundred miles to Log Base Alpha in only nineteen days. During the ground war the logisticians were prepared to cope with a daily consumption of one thousand tons of ammunition, half a million litres of fuel and three-quarters of a million litres of water. They also delivered to us half a million parcels and nine million letters.

This contact with home was so very important, more important to the soldiers than food. To know that our families, wherever they were, were being looked after was vital for good morale. And the situation was unusual as large numbers of our wives chose to remain in Germany and did not go home to live with their parents or relations. The responsibility this placed on commanding officers' and various volunteer wives was considerable. Melissa reported after the war:

> You must remember that the average age of an army wife is the very early twenties. Often they have not set foot outside their home towns before. Therefore, to be left alone in a foreign country, often with small children, was a formidable hurdle for many of them.
>
> The dramatic shortage of men meant it fell to the wives themselves to make a community. The lead was given by the commanding officers' wives and many others volunteered to help. They organised events of every sort and became deeply involved in the casualty-reporting chain, actually visiting the next-of-kin if the awful need arose. The latter was a horrid responsibility; after the knock on their own door, they dreaded most of all having to knock on somebody else's.
>
> The remaining army in Germany leapt to our aid. Extra welfare posts were created and information centres set up. The latter were invaluable as refuges for anyone in need of a chat or advice. It was very apparent that a problem shared was a problem halved.
>
> We blessed the efforts to keep the lines of communications open, the postal system, the Mercury telephones in Camp 4, the radio programme and even the swop of home-made videos.
>
> When the ground war began, every communication stopped. The contrast was quite dreadful and one's imagination ran riot. Then, after four hellish days, President Bush announced that the war was over; it took time to sink in. When I went to Fallingbostel that morning, I shall never forget seeing so many wives, who had constantly put on a brave face and a smile, quietly crying with sheer relief, shedding months of bottled-up anxiety.

*   *   *

Five years and some three hundred lectures later my views have changed little on what happened to us and whether we got it right. I remain convinced that the cease-fire was called at the optimum moment. From the brigade's point of view we had defeated the enemy and stopped before his destruction was complete. This seemed to us to be honourable; enough people had already died. Practically we would have had some difficulty in pushing on to Basra without at least a day's break. We were extremely tired and making mistakes, we had very little water and there was none available in the immediate area. Our field hospitals were a long way behind us.

Also by 28th February it was clear that General Schwarz-kopf's plan to annihilate the Republican Guard with a left hook through Iraq had failed. The expectation that the American marines and Arab Coalition Forces would take days to fight through the defences in Kuwait and perhaps draw in Iraqi reserves as well, never materialised. They were proud and determined – nothing was going to stop them reaching the city gates. Saddam Hussein had no time to dispatch his Republican Guard as reinforcements, even if he ever intended to. VII US Corps' target was a will-o'-the-wisp by 27th February. The majority of the Iraqi soldiers were already on their way back to Baghdad.

President Bush had another awkward problem, presented by the media's reporting of the 'turkey shoot' at the Muttla Pass. It seemed that he would almost certainly lose support from the Muslim world if he allowed another such incident to happen.

The political conundrum as to whether Saddam Hussein should have been removed from power is perhaps more difficult to comment on without the interference of hindsight, but I remember thinking at the time that no-one wanted a vacuum in the Middle East nor did the Americans want to be seen as king-makers. Militarily and politically the cease-fire called on 28th February was therefore inevitable.

I also remain firm in my view that our re-subordination from the American marines to the VII US Corps was regrettable. Politically, we would have gained most glory if we had been involved in the liberation of Kuwait City itself. Militarily, we joined what the Americans termed 'the main point of effort' and, despite being involved in some of the hardest fighting, we were seen after the war as the troops who held open the door for the American Army in its pursuit of the Republican Guard. That was not what our planners had envisaged.

I worry now, as I did then, about the effects of the media on modern warfare. I detected, during the initial settling-in period, the belief among reporters that they should encourage emotion. If an interview could be turned to probe fear or shock, this seemed to win favour at home. The intrusion, if challenged, was justified as caring and in the public interest. But don't the public, and indeed the armed forces, shape their behaviour to the media's demands? Did we not confess in the Gulf, under this examination, to being frightened? Well, of course we were – but was it not unpatriotic to ask us to say so? And then the reporting of the very clinical nature of modern weapon systems and their effects on the bunkers and buildings in Baghdad led the public, particularly the American public, to lose touch with the reality of war; a grim, ghastly and bloody affair. Such reporting also heightened the public concern over casualties. This is also a dangerous preoccupation. I wonder if commanders can now be ruthless enough, in a television age, to pursue the enemy to the limit, if the stakes are anything less than national survival.

There are, however, two matters on which my opinion has altered with hindsight. First, during January 1991, Saddam Hussein and his generals were much criticised over their tactical handling of their forces in Kuwait and Iraq. 'Their defences are similar to those used on the Western Front in 1916' was a common cry. I felt, even at the time, this was a little disingenuous. There were, after all, very few options open to them. The defensive strategy was centred on Basra and consisted of three layers or lines. The front, manned by the rag-tag conscripts, was nevertheless well prepared on the Kuwaiti–Saudi Arabian border. Behind this came the regulars and then in reserve the Republican Guard. The Iraqi engineers had built an elaborate network of interconnecting roads, allowing for easy redeployment and logistic supply.

But that was their problem. Once a single vehicle moved, the sophisticated American surveillance systems spotted it and the resultant onslaught from the air was devastating. But it was only later that I came to the conclusion that Saddam Hussein probably did not care what happened to any of his forces except the elite. His aim was all but achieved the moment his troops entered Kuwait and then refused to withdraw. He had demonstrated to the Muslim world, by standing up to the Americans, that he was their natural leader. Most of his huge conscript army was expendable. It was, after all, too large; he was having trouble feeding and paying it. The loss of one hundred thousand was but a small price to pay to achieve his misguided ambitions. The Republican Guard on the other hand was essential to his survival.

Secondly, I turn to the subject of political negotiations between the belligerents. There was hardly a single one of us in the desert who did not pray for a peaceful solution to the crisis, despite the fact that we recognised that the quickest route home lay through the defeat of the Iraqi forces. This hope was probably naive. Once the Coalition was ready to fight the temptation for the politicians to find a military solution to the problem must have been overwhelming.

Finally, an anecdote about one of the many and varied occasions I have had the privilege of taking part in since returning to England. After some discussion it was decided that on Friday 21st June 1991 the City of London would host a Welcome Home Parade. One thousand of us would march the traditional route along Finsbury Pavement, Moorgate, past the Bank into Cheapside and then to the Guildhall. The Queen would take the salute at the Mansion House, en route, and the Prince and Princess of Wales would join us for lunch. Initially we felt embarrassed about the plan; it seemed a little un-British. At midnight on the Wednesday, when the City streets were emptied for our rehearsal, we felt a trifle foolish. But nothing had prepared us for the sensations of the actual event. As we left Armoury House and turned into the City Road we were engulfed by a cloak of emotion. Thousands of Britons, standing five deep on the pavements and in the drizzle, were waiting to greet us; you could sense it was the same people, in spirit at least, who had supported and encouraged us every day during the long and tense days in the Saudi Arabian sand. We felt so proud to be representing the country, at one for once, celebrating together.

As I marched towards the City Marshal, resplendent on his grey horse, I knew I would not remember the correct words to ask his permission for the men and women of the Gulf Forces to enter the City. But for the first time in many months it probably didn't matter if I made a mistake.

Appendix I

7th Armoured Brigade Group Order of Battle on 1st November 1990

The Fighting Echelon

Headquarters

7th Armoured Brigade	Brigadier Patrick Cordingley
	Major Euan Loudon
	Major Robbie Burns
207 Signal Squadron, Royal Signals	Major Mike Dyer
640 Signal Troop (Electronic Warfare)	Captain David Macreath

Armour

A Squadron, 1st The Queen's Dragoon Guards	Major Hamish Macdonald
The Royal Scots Dragoon Guards	Lieutenant Colonel John Sharples
The Queen's Royal Irish Hussars	Lieutenant Colonel Arthur Denaro

Artillery

40th Field Regiment, Royal
Artillery

Lieutenant Colonel Rory Clayton

10 Air Defence Battery

Major Chris Nelson

Engineers

21 Engineer Regiment, Royal
Engineers

Lieutenant Colonel John
Moore-Bick

Infantry

1st Battalion,
The Staffordshire Regiment

Lieutenant Colonel Charles Rogers

Second Line Logistic Support

Transport
1 Armoured Division   Lieutenant Colonel Gavin Haig
Transport Regiment

Medical
1 Armoured Division   Lieutenant Colonel
Field Ambulance   Malcolm Braithwaite

Supply
3 Ordnance Battalion   Lieutenant Colonel Alan Taylor

Maintenance
Forward Repair Group,   Major Chris Cromack
7 Armoured Workshop

Provost
Two platoons,   Captain John Petrie
203 Provost Company

Third Line Logistic Support

Headquarters

Force Maintenance Area — Colonel Martin White
FMA Signal Squadron — Major Scott Ewing

Engineer Support

Two squadrons, 39 Engineer Regiment — Lieutenant Colonel Bob Pridham
14 Topographical Squadron — Major Nick Rigby
49 Explosive Ordnance Disposal Squadron — Major Nick Larkin
Detachment, 1 Postal and Courier Regiment — Major Rod Small
527 Specialist Team, Royal Engineers — Major Alan Kay

Transport

10 Transport Regiment — Lieutenant Colonel Philip Chaganis
50 Movement Control Squadron — Major Phil Alberry
52 Port Squadron — Major Ian Hurley
16 Tank Transporter Squadron — Captain Howell Lewis

Medical

24 Airmobile Field Ambulance — Lieutenant Colonel Paddy Magee
33 Field Hospital — Colonel Ian Creamer

Supply

6 Ordnance Battalion — Lieutenant Colonel Tim Murray
221 Explosive Ordnance Disposal Company — Major Nick Bell

Local Resources Section   Lieutenant Tom Lishman
Bakery and Laundry
  Expeditionary Forces Institute

Maintenance
Main Repair Group,   Lieutenant Colonel Rod Croucher
  7 Armoured Workshop

Provost
203 Provost Company   Major Nick Ridout

Royal Army Pay Corps
Field Records Unit   Major John Bailey

Royal Pioneer Corps
518 Company   Major Colin Code
908 Labour Supply Unit   Major Martin Wyke

Index